INSIDE THE
HERMIT
KINGDOM

INSIDE THE
HERMIT
KINGDOM

Football Stories from Stalinist Albania

Phil Harrison

First published by Pitch Publishing, 2024

Pitch Publishing
9 Donnington Park,
85 Birdham Road,
Chichester,
West Sussex,
PO20 7AJ
www.pitchpublishing.co.uk
info@pitchpublishing.co.uk

A CIP catalogue record is available for this book
from the British Library.

ISBN 978 1 80150 689 2

Typesetting and origination by Pitch Publishing
Printed and bound in India by Replika Press Pvt. Ltd

Contents

Acknowledgements

THIS BOOK was written by accident. Eighteen months ago, in my capacity as writer and co-editor for *KIT Magazine*, I approached its founder hoping to pilot four essays on Albanian football covering its inauguration, early successes, formation of Partizani and Dinamo Tirana and Albanian clubs' performances in Europe.

We both agreed that the project was probably too niche – who'd want to read about Albanian football during the communist era anyway? – but I started writing regardless, to sate my own inner need to do so more than anything. In adding texture to the essays, I reached out – via my Fussball Geekz Twitter page – hoping to find an authority on Albanian football who could help infuse detail into the text.

I put out the feelers, approaching a few sites I felt had the credentials to assist. After initial glimmers of hope, their interest and cooperation waned, leaving me short of what I needed to complete my essays. Then I ran into Irvin.

Irvin had left some positive comments on my Twitter posts regarding his beloved KF Tirana, and after his continued interest in Fussball Geekz, I cautiously broached the question, 'Can you help me?'

Literally, within a minute, he responded on DM, 'Anything I can do, I will try my best.'

Since his pledge, Irvin has provided me with a treasury of invaluable nuggets contained within these pages. Where questions loomed, Irvin answered them; where there were gaps in knowledge, Irvin plugged them; when I needed the additional glint of fine detail, Irvin shone the light. In short, he has been a diamond from start to finish; a man who embodies the endemic Albanian trait of *besa*.

With his help, the essays grew into the book you hold in your hands. Chapters two, three, ten and thirteen, in particular, could never have been written without Irvin, although his kindly influence and contribution is felt throughout the book. Thanks a million, man!

I would also like to give thanks to Paul McQuade from fanzine *The Shamrock*, who contributed his immense knowledge and fantastic photographs to the Partizani–Celtic part of *Inside the Hermit Kingdom*. You're a gentleman, sir.

Thanks also go to Edmond Xega and Tirona Fanatics; Facebook sites heathily fixated with all things KF Tirana, for the provision of photographs that embellish the stories, and to Rob Fletcher and Alex Ireland offering support when needed.

I reserve the biggest thanks for my long-suffering and thoroughly wonderful wife, Dawn, who has been forced to endure a year and a half of loneliness as I have regularly disappeared into a rabbit hole of furious research and writing. Also, to my beautiful children, Dayna and Taylor, who have given their continued support despite them constantly referring to the source material as 'a bore-fest'. You are the centre of my world.

I would also like to thank my social media followers who kept convincing me – despite my own self-doubts – that a publication on Albanian football during the Stalinist years was a 'good' idea. This book couldn't have got itself over the line without all of you. Many thanks.

Introduction

I FIRST became interested in Albania as a footballing entity in March 1989. Part of the BBC's coverage of England's World Cup qualifier in Tirana included a news item depicting life in this small, forgotten, communist outpost.

The film, short and derisory, included arcane images: a woman steering a horse-drawn cart past a concrete bunker; a man appearing from a crowded grocery shop joyously wielding a cabbage; a small boy wheeling a solitary bicycle wheel across a deserted square; visual snapshots designed – one can only surmise – to instil in the viewer a sense of Western, capitalist superiority.

I continued to watch; England players and staff dismounting a bone-shaker of a coach observed – not greeted – by a horde of dark-haired, black-eyed 'fans' each, to a man (literally – only men were present), dressed in brown polo necks and flared trousers as Paul Parker and Steve Hodge were bullied into a small entrance at Qemal Stafa Stadium by secret police wearing earpieces and sunglasses. It looked, in all of its unfiltered drudgery, like a scene from a bad 1970s cop show.

Rather than rendering feelings of smug superiority, I was morbidly fascinated by the place. I wanted, for a small pocket of time, to be Albanian; albeit grossly unaware of what being Albanian during that era meant or involved.

My two greatest interests have always been football and places. The more remote and unreachable a place is, the more interested I am. And if they have a football team, well, even better.

Over the subsequent years, I became an Albanian football voyeur, following their league and national team by the means available – chiefly via the dual vehicles of *World Soccer* magazine and the *European Football Yearbook* – as an outsider curiously peering in.

With a paucity of prominent teams, recognisable players or any physical access to a reliable, consistent, authoritative stream of information during the 1980s and early 1990s, researching stories about Albania was tantamount to hunting down unicorns.

Any stories tended to be aired from the standpoint of Western teams and players who had endured poor experiences when visiting the isolated Balkan republic.

And there were some dark, alluring tales to be told and they will all be accommodated within these pages. Yet, as entertaining as these stories are, they engender a condemnatory, negative image of an Albania that existed under the strictest duress – a collusion, an illusion – orchestrated by one man, the Machiavellian leader of the Party of Labour of Albania (commonly known as The Party), Enver Hoxha. Lamentably, it remained a pretence in which many of the country's three million-strong populace were – for nearly five decades – wholly complicit.

For 50 years, Albania was subject to the harshest and politically repressive most totalitarian regime a European nation has ever endured, an era where self-expression, individualism and dissent were brutally purged and where friendships and familial ties counted for nothing.

Hoxha – doppelgänger to the creepy Lord Summerisle character portrayed in the 1973 film *The Wicker Man* – relished the power he wielded, embedding in his subjects a repetitive, anti-humanist message that was high in vitriol and low in substance with an assurance and zeal that served as testament to the Albanian proverb, 'The weaker the argument, the stronger the words.' The Albanian leader would greet his enemies – perceived or otherwise – with a smile, before giving an order of execution in their absence; one of history's consummate back-stabbers.

It was an era where the blurred margins between morality and obedience were exploited by The Party (in Stalinist Albania, The Party and Enver Hoxha were indivisible) and its minions, where a populace both shackled and motivated by fear chose to do what they were told rather than what was right.

In viewing Albanian football during this period from the outside in, we see a reflection distorted by the influence of a regime that endeavoured to make every facet of life joyless and political. Football, at its very best, in theory at least, is neither of these things.

With greater availability to archives, information and research resources, it's now possible to turn the mirror in on itself; to view football during those dark years from the inside out, celebrating the great players, teams, coaches and stories that were lost behind an iron curtain constructed by a cruel, deluded regime.

As with all football stories, there are joys and sorrows to be explored, but in writing a book about football in the door-bolted Stalinist dystopia that was post-World War Two Albania, it feels a little like giving a voice to an infant that's never spoken up for itself before.

In researching the book, I uncovered many incredible stories dating from Albania's footballing inception in 1908, through the formative part of the 20th century into the early 1940s; a period of fascist–communist transition in Albania. The journey takes in in the 'golden era' of Albanian football – a period that only Albanians living in the country at the time are privy to – and charts the 'unswinging' socialist '60s and '70s before heading into to the 1980s, when the full scope of the country's unique, hard-line variant of Marxism–Leninism had been fully realised and imposed. It also details the wind-down years of the late 1980s and early 1990s peering, briefly, beyond the dark, wasted years of Stalinism into the nation's, comparatively, bright footballing future.

These are football stories from inside the Hermit Kingdom; previously rendered mute, now given the means with which to communicate themselves.

Chapter One

Footballing Beginnings: 1908 to 1938

WHEN THE second wave of Christian missionaries arrived in the tribal backwaters of Shkodër in the early part of the 20th century, they must have been comforted by the sight that greeted them.

The trip, almost certainly, was an arduous and energy-sapping one, weighed down with the ecclesiastical baggage of their profession on this perilous, weather-battered traipse through the rockiest climbs in what was still, in essence, a medieval country.

Shkodër was a city lurking in the shadows of the Bjeshkët e Nemuna – the Accursed Mountains; great name, terrible portent – flanked by its steep canyons and wide valleys, accessible only via its precipitous, upwardly spiralling pathways. It was a region also beset by the constant threat of banditry.

Often romanticised in the works of English artist, Edward Lear, the Shkodran peninsula remained a fiefdom ruled by the dictums of the Kanun of Lekë Dukagjini; an archaic law system harking back to the 15th century which blended Christianity with primitive elements.

The Kanun propagated the cult of the *gjakmarrja* – the blood feud – with families granted permission, by tribal elders, to rain gory revenge on enemies who'd transgressed upon them. Also, it was notoriously demeaning in its treatment of women. After a wedding ceremony, the father of the bride would present the groom with a bullet wrapped in straw, giving his new son-in-law permission to kill his daughter if she defied him.

Gjakmarrja was outlawed by the regime, but returned unabated when Stalinism fell, a much-publicised incident occurring in Tirana in February 1992, when a man was beheaded with an axe in a hotel lobby for a killing his father had committed in a northern village over 40 years before. Primitivism, to the present day, continues to find the oxygen to survive in the mountain fiefdoms.

Despite the hazards of their journey, the missionaries arrived in a thriving city, replete with opportunity, its marketplace a hub of traders selling textiles, crafts and silverware.

The first wave of missionaries, arriving in 1905 from Malta, established several Catholic schools geared towards the religious and educational modernisation of old Shkodër, complementing the teachings of the large Islamic community already present in the city. But they'd also brought with them something else.

On the sparsely grassed terrains, children played a rough-hewn variant of a game resembling football called *top e kambë* – ball and leg – the balls fashioned from rags bound with string. It was an import that was to strike a lasting chord with the people of Albania.

A Maltese priest named Father Gut Ruter, a patron of Shkodër's Jesuit-run Saverian College, sought to harness the religio-social aspects of football under the banner of the Christian faith, assembling a team called Indipendenca – the first stand-alone football *klubi* in Albania – in 1912.

Indipendenca played friendlies against any local outfits willing to take to a pitch with them, but they were lauded for commendable performances against the Austrian army sides serving in Albania; a 2-1 defeat in 1913 constituting the first international fixture played on Albanian soil.

Captained by Palok Nika and featuring Kolë Hila, Kolë Gjoni, Gjon Pashkja and Pashko Fishta, the club – boasting players regarded as mavericks in Albanian football's evolution – saw their history-making exploits documented in the Austrian-Hungarian press, adding further legitimacy and contour to an emergent sport.

Football thrived as a purely recreational pastime, until a merger between two familial societies in the city – the Mustafa Pasha society and the Vaso Pasha society – in February 1919 spurred the foundation of Albania's first official sports club and academy, Shoqëria Sportive Vllaznia (Vllaznia Sports Society), an organisation geared towards the betterment of Shkodër's youth, not only via the vessel of football but through the combined teachings of literature, culture, theatre, music and gymnastics.

Vllaznia Sports Society was at the core of its community, offering opportunities to young people in pursuance of a proper education and development of untapped creative skills. As a result, Shkodër was rapidly earning external recognition as the intellectual and religious centre of a new, progressive Albania.

Taking a lead from their Shkodran forebears, other societies in Albania founded organisations promoting similar virtues, proactive in the advancement of Albanian intellectualism and well-being; Elbasan, Tirana, Korçë and Delvinë all forming sports clubs similar to the Vllaznia model.

In August 1920, Sport Klub Tirana was formed, and briefly changed to Shoqata e Futbollit Agimi (Agimi Football Association) before the founders settled on the name Futboll Klub Tirana.

Albanian football had been represented by a team from Tirana since 1911, a predecessor of KF Tirana competing in, and winning, the Fier Fair Football Tournament – Turneu Futbollistik i Panairit të Fierit. The eight-team competition including sides from Elbasan, Kavajë, Berat, Peqin, Vlorë, Fier, Lushnjë and, of course, Tirana saw Peqini thumped

6-1 in the final. It is Albania's oldest recorded football tournament.

Newly founded KF Tirana pitted their talents against the gifted Juventus of Shkodër at the Shallvare Grounds twice in October 1920, and it was these well-attended friendlies, high on incident and excitement, that showcased football as a viable, profitable phenomena within Albanian popular culture.

New clubs Adriatik of Kavajë, Luzemi of Durrës and Tomori of Berat were hastily inaugurated, supporting the need for a competitive league structure.

During the November of 1920, the first football regulations were penned in Shkodër; a clarion call summoning forces together in order to pursue a mutual goal – the formation of a bespoke national championship.

However, the game was condemned by the ruling Zogist regime for, purportedly, 'causing acts of aggression amongst Albania's youth', and was forbidden from being played in the 1925 rewriting of the constitution.

Zog was forced to retract the decision after a spate of public outrage, possibly on the advice of Mussolini, whom Zog had aligned Albania with during the spring of 1925. *Il Duce* was a fan of the game, harbouring a deep understanding of its propaganda potential.

So, in 1926 and 1927, the games continued, Korçë touring northern Greece and Tirana and the university side of Shkodër both playing matches in Yugoslavia against teams from Cetinje and Podgorica.

In 1928, the Zog–Mussolini axis welcomed Italy's most distinguished specialists into Albania, to assist with the development of Albanian sport and, in particular, football.

In June 1930, after the founding of the Albanian Football Federation – the Federata Shqiptare e Futbollit (FSHF) – English influence was called upon too, former British intelligence agent Colonel Hill taking on triumvirate duties as refereeing regulator, match official and nominated chairman of Albania's technical commission in time for the inaugural National Championship in 1930.

The first edition of the Albanian National Championship – Kampionati Kombetar – was contested by six clubs: Sport Klub Tirana, KS Skënderbeu Korçë, KS Urani Elbasan, SK Vlorë, KS Teuta Durrës and a rebranded version of Vllaznia Sports Society named KS Bashkimi (Union) Shkodër.

With meagre funding from Zog's government, clubs were forced to provide their players with kit, finance training, arrange facilities and foot travel costs out of their own pockets.

In spite of this, and due to mushrooming support at the Shallvare and the nascent popularity of the game in both Korçë and Shkodër, football was proving a success despite its lack of subsidy. However, the final of the first edition of the Kampionati Kombetar was never played, with the *Juglindorët* – the South Easterners – of Korçë refusing to participate, citing bias by the FSHF. SK Tirana – who'd finished level on points with the dissenting Skënderbeu *klubi*, albeit with a significantly better goal difference – were crowned inaugural champions by default.

Teething problems were something that football would outgrow, yet the government's want of interest in Albania's new national sport created the anti-establishment vacuum that Zog must have feared when inking the 1925 constitution.

Football-loving Albanians despised the regime and their snobbish non-involvement. With SK Tirana's success and their ability to draw big crowds, bolstered by a growing fan culture in the other competing cities, football became a forum for anti-Zog resentment which, dually, guaranteed the league's future.

The 1931 Kampionati Kombetar welcomed a further team, KS Muzaka of Berat. Formed in 1923 under the moniker Tomori (a name that the *Mistrecët* – the Captious – would return to in 1935), the new boys joined the Kampionati's increasing fold. Their first spell in the top tier was short and they were relegated at the season's end; SK Tirana were the champions, again, securing a 4-2 aggregate victory in the final versus KS Teuta.

Being in proprietorship of their own league, the FSHF were inaugurated as a member of FIFA in 1932, and thus invited to participate in both the 1934 World Cup finals in Italy – a mere skip across the Adriatic – and the France World Cup of 1938.

On both occasions, a lack of backing from the Zogist regime rendered entry to the competition a financial impossibility. It was very much an opportunity lost for the newly invested Albanian national side who would, resultantly, have to wait another 16 years for their first competitive international.

The Kampionati Kombetar campaign of 1932 rolled on irrespective of Zogist lethargy with Tirana again the winners, this time finishing ahead of KS Bashkimi by two points in a newly adopted league format.

In danger of becoming a one-horse race just three years in – Tirana winning all three titles thus far – 1933 was grateful to welcome a new champion to the fore, KS Skënderbeu of Korçë, the perennial bridesmaids, eventually taking their first title crown.

Buoyed by the goals of Teufik Agaj, the *Juglindorët* romped to success ahead of KS Bashkimi having scored and conceded fewer than all of their opponents – worthy *kampione*. Tirana finished a disappointing fourth, way off the pace.

The remaining years of the 1930s saw a return to dominance by SK Tirana, winning the title in 1934, 1936 and 1937 – there was no championship in 1935 – Mark Gurashi and two boys from Kosovo, Riza Lushta and Naim Kryeziu, proving potent new weapons in the *Tirona* machine.

Football had blossomed during the pre-war years. Budding from its humble beginnings in the stark mountain territories of the north merely 30 years earlier, the game had bloomed apace. Even in the wildest imaginings of the deepest sceptic, it was a growth that could not have been foreseen or logically charted. Football, in spite of its detractors, had taken its hold upon the Albanian people.

However, a change was coming, and not exclusively for Albania, but for the whole world, although it would be felt most sharply in the pocket of continental Europe that divided the Aryan north from the Asiatic east. And it would be a pinch that would last.

April 1939 presaged a new chapter in the dark, bloody history of the Albanian diaspora, an era that not only altered the nation's footballing direction but everything that its beleaguered people held dear.

In the forthcoming years, the championships – from 1930 to 1937 – would be expunged from the history books as 'the championships of the bourgeois regime and the reactionaries'. The Party's mission to edit the past in order to fit their abridged version of Albanian history had begun in earnest; the mere mention of the formative years of the Kampionati – in print or in conversation – liable to get you in serious hot water with the local authorities.

The promise of independence came at a heavy price. It was *Revolucioni* time in Albania, and not in a good way.

Chapter Two

Speaking the Language: Football Vernacular in the Hermit Kingdom

TO APPRECIATE the culture of a place, it's important to understand the language. Language, more than anything else, is the characteristic that distinguishes one set of people from another, forged by the geography, history and ethnology of the region.

Expressions, terminology and linguistic quirks are cornerstones of national identity, offering a window of insight into a country's shared being. In short, language is culture, and this chapter explores a glossary of terms used by Albanian football fans.

Geographically, Albania resides in the southern Balkan peninsula and, during the timeframe of the book, was neighboured along its north and north-east border by the Federal People's Republic of Yugoslavia and by Greece to the south and south-east. Its western coastline was – and still is – met by both the Adriatic Sea (north) and Ionian Sea (south) with Italy, separated by the Adriatic, less than 400 miles away.

Between 1945 and 1991 the Albanian border, on all sides, was an impenetrable gauntlet of barbed wire, electric fences, minefields and hillside bunkers erected to keep invaders out and dissidents in. In the southern coastal city of Sarandë, a mere eight miles from the Greek island of Corfu, searchlights criss-crossed the heavily fortified beaches and Albanian soldiers, on orders to 'shoot to kill', manned the trenches and concrete pillboxes that pockmarked the landscape.

There was no interaction with foreigners (markedly, the word for 'foreigner' in Albanian also means alien, strange and incompatible), no public debate, no social dissent and no analytical thought. In a setting where the regime and its numerous adjutants forced people to shut their mouths and switch off their brains, one can only surmise that the native tongue regressed as a result; Marxist–Leninist slogans and repetitive 'ear-to-mouth' diatribe halting the progressive use of language thus hindering its ability to grow. An ancient vernacular was transformed from its open, emotive template to an abbreviated dialect, worded almost entirely by verbs: eat, work, obey – functional, with no adherence to human expression.

Language stood still everywhere in Stalinist Albania. Except, it would seem, within the free-form, carte-blanchery of the football stadium where dissidence, in both word and deed, continued to exist in a hushed, yet potent form.

The Albanian language – Shqip, or Gjuha Shqipe – is one of the oldest European languages, deriving from the tribes of Illyria (an enclave in Roman-ruled Dalmatia), and has been spoken, in its primitive form, since the second century, gazumping English (and its Germanic brother tongues) by 350 years and predating modern Spanish by 700 years.

Shqiptar – Albanian language – appeared in written form for the first time in 1555, in a book entitled *Meshari* – Missal – scribed by Catholic cleric Gjon Buzuku. Just short of 200 pages in length, it contains translated Bible scripture, liturgies of the main annual religious holidays and the doctrine for performing Catholic rituals. The only existing copy presently resides in the Vatican library; scribed testimony to the age and heritage of Albania's mother tongue.

In modern Albania, there are two distinctive dialects still spoken, Gheg and Tosk. Gheg is predominant in the north of the country, Tosk in the south.

For the purposes of the book, it is important to differentiate between the two as – during the Stalinist era in Albania – language became a divisive measuring tool used to separate good, ideologically sound Albanians from potential class enemies.

The dialect I will be using for this glossary is the Tosk variant, as it was the prescribed language of the Albanian communists during Enver Hoxha's reign.

I will begin by listing the positions of players on the pitch, moving on to the generic Albanian words describing incidents within a standard game of football.

As I continue, I will translate place and competition names that will figure heavily in this tome.

I will finish with a few popular slang terms used on the terraces by fans to denote the *futboll i mirë/futbollistë të mirë'* (good football/good footballers) from the *keq* (bad) and – for the purposes of frankness – the *keq* from the plain *blozë*:

Positions/roles on a football pitch

Goalkeeper:	*Portier*
Left-back:	*Mbrojtësi i majtë*
Right-back:	*Mbrojtësi i djathtë*
Central defender:	*Qendërmbrojtësi*
Left midfielder:	*Mesfushori i majtë*
Right midfielder:	*Mesfushori i djathtë*
Central midfielder:	*Mesfushori qendror*
Attacking midfielder:	*Mesfushori sulmues/Mezalla*
Left attacker:	*Sulmuesi i majtë*
Right attacker:	*Sulmuesi i djathtë*
Central attacker:	*Sulmuesi qendror/Qender pyk/Sulmues pyka*
Substitute:	*Zëvendësues*
Head coach:	*Kryetrajneri*

Referee: *Arbiter/Referia*

Linesman: *Arbiter anësor* (Side referee)/*Gardalina*

Football terms

Kick-off: *Nis/Nis loja/Fillon loja*

Full time: *Rezultati përfundimor*

Penalty: *Penallti/Njëmbëdhjetëmetresh* (Eleven yards)

Goal kick: *Rivenie fundore* (Restart from the end)

Free kick: *Goditje dënimi* (Punishment kick)

Corner kick: *Goditje këndi/Korne*

Throw-in: *Rivenie anësor*

Foul: *Faull*

Red card: *Karton i kuq*

Yellow card: *Karton i verdhë*

Booked: *Merr kartën*

Offside: *Ofsait/Pozicion jashtë loje* (Out of position)

Out of play: *Aut/Jasht*

Fan/fans: *Tifoz/Tifozët*

Organisation/place/competition names

Albania/Albanian: *Shqipëria/Shqiptare*

Albanian national football team: *Kombëtarja e futbollit*
                                                                      të Shqipërisë

Albanian Football Federation (FSHF): *Federata*
                                                                      Shqiptare e Futbollit

Albanian national team nicknames: *Shqiponjat* (the Eagles)/
                                                                      Kuqë e Zinjtë (the
                                                                      Red and Blacks)

17 Nëntori/SK Tirana/KF Tirana: *Tirona*

Qemal Stafa national stadium: *Stadiumi*
                                                                      Kombëtar Qemal Stafa

23

Dinamo Stadium:	*Stadiumi Dinamo*
National Championship:	*Kampionati Kombëtar*
Republic Cup:	*Kupa e Republikës*
Balkan Cup:	*Kupa e Ballkanit*
European Cup:	*Kupa Evropiane*
UEFA Cup:	*Kupa UEFA*
European Cup Winners' Cup:	*Kupa e Fituesve të Kupave Evropiane*
World Cup:	*Kampionati Botnor i Futbollit*

Slang terms/terrace talk

They were awful/horrible:	*Ishin për ibret*
They were rubbish:	*Ishin bloz* (They were 'soot')
A team without shame/integrity:	*Ekip pa seder*
A team without energy/a tired team:	*Ekip I lodh*
A waste of space:	*Humbje hapësire*

Chapter Three

Every Given Sunday: the Matchday Experience in Stalinist Albania

'Fans wild with delight, children, smokers, drunks, cops, spies, vendors selling seeds and dates – there was room for everyone and everything! The stadium was magically transformed from 20,000 to 30,000, with a little courage and some strategic ass-placement.'

Gezim, Tirana

FOOTBALL IN Albania is, without recourse to understatement, a national obsession. Yet between the late 1960s, and until Stalinism's slow, lingering death in 1991, football became more than mere fixation.

In a country where the 1967 rewriting of the constitution denied people their freedom of faith, football became the new religion with pilgrims from Gjirokastër to Shkodër, Lezhë to Sarandë, filling stadia every Sunday afternoon in worship of their new, auxiliary gods.

I'd regularly dared to imagine how football looked and sounded during the closeted years of the Hoxha regime; what were the behaviours, the rituals and traditions of the typical Albanian football fan on every given Sunday?

It was only when my preoccupation with the history of football in Albania afforded me the fortune of meeting Irvin, that I was able – at long last – to add flesh to the allegorical skeleton that I'd imagined football in Albania to be during this veiled, blurred timescape.

Sure, I'd watched YouTube content of the Kampionati Kombëtar and Kupa e Republikës; vignettes – generally 15 minutes in length – depicting the best of the action from the important games of the day, redolent of the Pathé newsreels popular in-and-beyond World War Two.

Despite their grainy monochrome, the mini-films give a clear insight into what football meant to the average Albanian fan: all of the requisite passion, outrage and joy visibly etched in the faces and embedded in the reactions of the *tifozët* in direct retort to what is unfolding on the field of play.

And in those moments of ordered chaos, Albanians appeared free from the trials and injustices of their moribund, regime-subscribed lives, transported – via the vehicles of football and shared human experience – to a higher plain; a vista of harmony and liberty.

The chapter will try to examine and expand upon the Sunday matchday experience in communist-era Albania: What did football look like? Where did the fans go before and after the game? How would football of that era stand up against its modern variant? And, probably the most pertinent question of them all: how did football make Albanians feel?

Çdo të dielë të dhënë – Every given Sunday
'Work, work day and night, just to see a little light.'

Albanian proverb

For the well-briefed football fan living in Tirana during the Stalinist era, preparations for matchday began on a Wednesday afternoon.

At 5pm, Monday to Saturday, Skanderbeg Square ebbed and flowed with a tide of human traffic as the workers of Albania departed their city jobs as functionaries of the regime, making their short walks – or bicycle rides – via the tree-lined boulevards of inner Tirana, to their Soviet-built prefab apartments on the outskirts of the town.

There were no cars back then, aside from the funereal trundle of the black-windowed state vehicles dispatching dignitaries to their Party offices, or the intemperate growl of GAZ-69 trucks on their daily munitions runs. Buses were few; taxis non-existent.

Natives blithely recall the fizz of bicycle tyres on tarmac as the post-shift workforce traversed the roadways surrounding the square on their way home; a nostalgia lost in the clank and commotion of the modern, Mercedes-Benz-riddled matrix of 'new Tirana'.

Life was an outdoor experience in old Albania – city dwellers chatted in the parks while eating ice-cream, families enjoyed their ceremonial evening stroll – maybe a symptom of the oppressive nature of apartment living or perhaps a basic human want for thought time; a need to decompress. Modernist pursuits negate the need for interaction and the transitory freedoms that being outside afford. It's an irony that, in the context of the country's history, isn't lost on the elders of Albania.

Wednesday, bi-monthly, was payday. After receiving remuneration for the hours invested in performing their bit-part roles in the realisation of Hoxha's socialist dream, the workers of Albania would – as is ritual in all societies; Marxist, capitalist or otherwise – spend.

Wages would vary. In Stalinist Albania, although all people were equal, it would seem that some were more 'equal' than others with menial workers earning 2,000 old Lek per month and teachers and doctors receiving 8,000 Lek – roughly translatable to £5 per month.

Of course, avenues for the expression of self-enjoyment were limited; a packet of cigarettes, a magazine of choice maybe, but for the avid sports fan in Albania's biggest city, payday was usually preceded by a visit to Gimi's kiosk, a short distance from Sheshi Skënderbej – Skanderbeg Square – beneath the shadow of *Ushtari i panjohur*, the Unknown Soldier.

The monument of the Unknown Soldier, dedicated to the martyrs of fascist resistance, and its adjoining *sheshi*, were installed during the post-World War Two years on the site of the Kapllan Pasha Mosque – built in 1614 by Tirana's founding father, Sulejman Bargjini Pasha – which was demolished in 1967 as part of Enver Hoxha's anti-religious crusade. Fist raised, readied for a battle to the death, *Ushtari* is the visual antonym to the pastoral serenity of Islam. Maybe that was the point.

Gimi, a partisan from the days of the revolution, ran the vertical, oblong, metal kiosk – roughly the size of a standard telephone booth – 30 metres west of the *sheshi*.

The *kioskë* was implanted there by the government in the late 1960s. Gimi's war injuries rendered him unable to walk without the use of crutches, the product of some undefined wound harking back to the days of fascist occupation; a sedentary, cushy role assigned to Gimi as reward for being a good soldier and compliant comrade.

Despite being a regime-owned concern, it was very much Gimi's kiosk and was known as such by everyone; Gimi being a much-liked character throughout Tirana, his rotund, heavy-set frame and constant cheer, less an upshot of satisfaction with the ruling regime than the product of the ever-present bottle of raki concealed beneath the counter.

Embossed with the words *Gazeta Revista* – newspapers, magazines – the kiosk sold precisely that; copies of the national broadsheet *Zeri i Popullit* and recreational periodicals such as *Ylli*, *Pionieri* and *Shqiptarja e Re*, but for sports fans in the know it also served as a government-approved ticket office for the Albanian Football Federation.

Football became an essential social release for the Albanian male, particularly, and stadiums – without exception – were full, with the majority of fans obtaining their tickets from Gimi days in advance. It was common for a supporter to block buy, usually five tickets at a time: three for the buyer plus friends, two to 'flip' on matchday – generally with the addition of a five Lek commission. Free enterprise, albeit on a minute scale, was still alive in Stalinist Albania. You just had to ensure you didn't get caught.

Tickets were generally available for the three sections of the stadium: behind the goals and one pitchside stand, with the remaining stand – the *Tribuna* – a covered area, exclusively reserved for army, police, and Party members.

The wooden-benched stands occupied by the proletariat were called *njëzet* – 20 – as tickets cost 20 Lek. In the *njëzet*, seat rows and numbers were disregarded, the pre-match tussle for the best seats a weekly act of putative anarchy. In the regimented environs of Stalinist Albania, with all of its rules and restrictions, nobody ever bought into the concept of queueing.

The only place seat numbers were observed was in the *Tribuna*. From the *njëzet*, the workers could watch the *Tribuna* occupants: virtuous, upstanding ambassadors of The Party, attired in their good coats and Italian shoes, protected from the elements by the overhead canopy; the echoed promises of Hoxha's fair, classless society dissolving in the enveloping wind and rain.

For those imprudent enough not to buy tickets pre-matchday, there ensued a mandatory Sunday scramble for the remaining cache available via the small hatch at Gimi's kiosk. The scenes – although contextually unfitting of the time – resembled opening hours at the New York Stock Exchange. In Stalinist Albania, where public discord was well-nigh absent, fights regularly occurred in the *sheshi* as in excess of 1,000 fans clambered for the weekly privilege of watching their footballing heroes in action.

Arrests happened, but not as regularly as you would expect, the *Sigurimi* (Albanian secret police) choosing to turn a blind eye to non-ideologically motivated acts of mob misconduct.

Those unsuccessful in their matchday quest for tickets would have to try their luck at Tirana's only other vendors: the tiny portholes in the wall, under the staircase at Stadiumi Dinamo or Stadiumi Qemal Stafa.

Tickets for games at Stadiumi Qemal Stafa were generally prized above those at Stadiumi Dinamo, the latter perceived as a secondary venue where games of lesser importance featuring smaller clubs or early round cup ties were played. And, in general opinion, the atmosphere was never considered quite as good at the Dinamo; the stadium's openness allowing fan noise to escape, as opposed to the tight, concrete cauldron of the Qemal Stafa which amplified every whisper.

Despite the fervent nature of the *tifozët*, there has never been a collector culture in Albania. Football clubs in Stalinist Albania didn't print match programmes and match tickets were torn in half by ground staff upon entry into the stadium, so they couldn't be thrown over the wall and reused by fans outside the ground. As a result, these torn stubs were never kept as souvenirs by the Albanian football fan.

Come Sunday, Tirana came alive; a palpable buzz of collective excitement encompassing the city. Friends and fellow fans would congregate in Skanderbeg Square hours prior to the 3pm kick-off to smoke cigarettes and speculate on the outcome of the day's game.

Cigarettes were an integral part of communist Albanian life at all societal levels; almost everyone was a committed smoker. Enver Hoxha is thought to have smoked between 60 and 80 cigarettes a day. During the era of his despotic regime, what was good enough for Comrade Enver was pretty much good enough for everybody.

Produced cheaply in factories in Tirana, Durrës, Shkodër and Gjirokastër for domestic consumption and export to

Poland, Czechoslovakia and East Germany, squares, parks, streets and stadiums were suffused with the miasma and plumage of cigarette smoke. Indeed, it wasn't uncommon for coaches and their backroom staff to spark up a Dajti, a Labinoti or a Rozala – leading brands of the day – during regulation time. The latter – Rozala, named after a Shkodran fortress – purportedly had the taste and odour of burnt rubber and was considered the most injurious to Albanian health.

Within the remit of Albanian fan culture – as with fan culture anywhere else – there existed an ethos of one-upmanship. In Britain during the 1980s specifically, the need to fit in while standing out manifested itself in the attire fans wore to 'the game'; a pre-prescribed outfit that included a collage of accepted, 'cool' brands.

In Stalinist Albania, aside from the privileged few, everybody wore the same clothes and the same shoes sourced from the same factories and shops. Opportunities to impress your peers did not exist.

Yet, in the spirit of Albanian guile and entrepreneurism, a shortage of an opportunity didn't necessarily mean there wasn't an opportunity to be had.

Western cigarette boxes were highly prized status symbols in Albania and young Albanians, under cover of darkness, would congregate outside the bin rooms of the big Tirana hotels occupied by foreign guests and upper Party members.

Loitering in the service area of a main hotel where foreigners stayed, a surveillance hotspot for torch-wielding *Sigurimi*, was a risk that, at worst, could get you a black mark on your 'biography' – the file Albania's secret police compiled on every one of its citizens. A 'bad bio' – *biografi e keqe* – was considered a disgrace severely limiting an individual's chances of future progression. At best, you'd leave with a chastening word or a slap or kick from a *Sigurimi* agent. But due, in part, to the folly and ambivalence of youth, the kids did it anyway.

When the bin bags were brought out by hotel staff, they'd be summarily ransacked in search of empty packets of Marlboro and Camel Merit. Cheap Albanian cigarettes were then transferred to the empty boxes, as the cartons themselves – to cod-aspirational young Albanians – were considered an indicator of wealth and status.

By way of evidence, in August 1992 I took a day trip by ferry from Corfu to Sarandë. Communism had fallen the previous year, and Albania was now partially open for business. Sarandë was a city that was beautiful but in need of care. On arrival, our group had a drink at one of the newly appropriated port-side *kafeteri*. We were swarmed by locals, friendly and inquisitive, but also looking to inherit some small souvenir from us day-trippers.

I smoked at the time; Marlboro Red. I sipped a local beer and lit a cigarette, spiking the interest of three teens to whom I offered a 'smoke'. The genuine enthusiasm and gratitude the boys expressed at receiving this small token of Western consumerism actually caused me to laugh, so unexpected was their fervour.

Interestingly, not one of them smoked their cigarette, preferring to place it behind their ear or in the top pocket of their shirt, a status symbol to be flaunted, not used.

Western cigarette packets became commonplace at football games, lending their owner an air of bizarre, superficial kudos that can only have existed in Hoxha's Albania, a place where people had nothing.

Upon meeting in Skanderbeg Square and with pleasantries dispensed, fans excitedly strolled the short distance across the ornately tiled concourse of Tirana's central *sheshi* to Stadiumi Qemal Stafa, their spirits elevated.

Matchday brought with it a sense of celebration born from the thrill all workers the world over feel on their day off. Sunday was also recognised, by the proletariat, as *Dita e Popullit* – the Day of the People – when the functionaries of

The Party would recede from view, back to their apartments and houses in the incestuous milieu of *blloku* (The Block); a gated, impenetrable, mile-square city-within-a-city in the heart of suburban Tirana where only the privileged hierarchy resided.

Yes, Sunday was party time in the 26 districts of Albania, a shared mood neatly parcelled in the Shqiptare axiom, 'He who is not drunk on a Sunday, is not worth a greeting on Monday.' When football, and the human interaction it invariably brought, was supplemented to this equation, it made for heady, raucous enjoyment.

The walk to Albania's national stadium from the city centre took fans down Rruga e Elbasanit – Elbasani Street – a rare oasis where there were *pastiçeri* (patisseries) and *byrekore* (pie shops) selling *ravani* (sponge cake), *shendetlie* (honey and nut cake), *bakllava me mjaltë* (honey baklava), *qofte* (meatballs) and *byrek* – the traditional Albanian pie stuffed with spinach, cheese or both. The shops still remain, run by the children of the people who owned them during the communist years.

There were no food outlets at the football grounds, the only option for sustenance inside the stadium being *fara*: grilled sunflower seeds wrapped in paper cones sold from *tezga* (usherette trays). Elbasani Street, therefore, offered the best chance for a pre-match bite.

Eating was a function in Albania, a chore undertaken to preserve life, with any residual pleasure purely accidental. However, the *restorantet* – restaurants – that lined Elbasani Street kept a dormant food culture alive in Stalinist Albania; a venue where people could go to enjoy food for enjoyment's sake instead of merely reaping the benefits of its life-preserving properties. But the intake of some *qofte*, a *byrek* or a sweet *pastë* – pastry – also served a secondary and more vital purpose.

After eating, fans would converge on a *Lokal* (the government-approved bars present in all Albanian cities) where they could partake in the drinking of *raki*, Konjaku

Skënderbeu (Skanderbeg Cognac) in its hand-decorated bottles, or Fernet: a cheap, bitter Turkish aperitif, similar to Vermouth, imbibed with the sole purpose of getting drunk.

Indeed, alcohol was a part of the daily routine in Albania, with people of all professions and standing – teachers, lorry drivers, students even – indulging in a pre-work Fernet accompanied by a Turkish coffee to kick-start their day. And a generous tipple certainly added texture and fun to the matchday experience.

Tifozët were the same as they are now: passionate, verbose, full of intensity, with the marked difference being the lack of violence at games – a feature of ultra culture widely prevalent in modern Albania.

At derbies between the three Tirana clubs, there would be a palpable undercurrent of animosity, *Tirona* fans, especially, still charged with feelings of hatred towards Dinamo and Partizani, their aggrievement born from the unfairness the club suffered during the superclubs' formative years.

Tirona fans, emboldened – possibly – by the effects of *raki* and Fernet and in spite of fear of arrest, were known to berate the players of their Tirana rivals, Partizani's Loro Boriçi the subject of recurring abuse due to his unmarried status and the persistent rumour that he'd sired a bastard son with a woman in wedlock. However, the promise of a stretch in Spaç, Burrel or Gjirokastër, the *kampet e punës* – work camps – of Stalinist Albania, usually provided sufficient deterrent to any sustained acts of public insubordination.

And at 3pm, the stadium full to bursting, the football community of this fun-starved Balkan garrison would wage their own communal protest against oppression and servility. Amid the clamour and anonymity of the crowd, football-crazy Albanians could get lost in the joy.

But how did games look during these dark, oblique times? My friend, Irvin, told me, 'Although the pitches were shit the football was beautiful, highly competitive, full of quality, intelligence and skill. And the atmosphere was always amazing; we practically lived for the weekend. It was the only 90 minutes of the week that people could be themselves; forget about life and everything else, and scream and sing their hearts out.'

Joy, however, was always tempered with caution, as a stray, adverse comment could carry dire consequences.

'If you made a negative remark about the government, a spy in the crowd would call a *Sigurimi* agent who would intervene,' Irvin said.

Even celebration demanded moderation.

Partizani, Dinamo and 17 Nëntori all boasted near-exemplary home records. Albanian football – akin to their Italian and Yugoslavian neighbours – tended to be the territory of the home win with away sides generally faring badly. So, when the goals flew in (and they invariably did) the fans celebrated them euphorically; an antidote to an otherwise stolid existence. Irvin elaborates, 'The coffee shops and bars on Elbasani Street would donate a few till rolls or toilet rolls, or fans would cut up newspapers into confetti to throw when their team scored. But the most imaginative form of celebration was pigeons. Every household in Albania keeps racing pigeons to this day, and many fans would attach ribbons in their team colours to the pigeons' ankles and release them at the stadium. They would be waiting for you in their pigeon loft on your arrival home.'

The visits of Partizani or Dinamo to any city in Albania always added niggle and needle to a game; their successes seen as a contradiction to the tenets of equality and fairness preached by The Party.

Despite being disliked, Partizani remain the best-supported team in the country; an Albanian equivalent to Manchester United or Juventus, with supporters' clubs in all 26 districts. They are the team of the army and the army are always there, a presence that even the most ardent military objector is wont to tolerate. Dinamo's popularity, however, has withered considerably; everybody hated the *Sigurimi* then and nobody mourns their memory now.

The respected teams of the communist era were 17 Nëntori, KS Vllaznia, Labinoti, Lokomotiva Durrës, Besa and Flamurtari, although the latter had a reputation for being a rough, direct team – an Albanian Wimbledon – known for stretching the parameters of fair play and for doctoring their pitch to hinder visiting sides who played good football.

Fans would tune into the goings-on at grounds around the country by taking the Albanian-made, silver, lozenge-shaped transistor radios – about the size of a house brick – to the games; primitive contraptions with long antennae that stuck out like duelling swords threatening to injure unexpectant, neighbouring fans. In the video archives of the era, you can visibly see a legion of upright spokes glistening in the mid-afternoon sunshine. It's easy to envisage how so many hapless supporters suffered the painful wrath of a stray *radio tranzistor* aerial.

Word of developments in other games in other cities and towns would quickly pass around the stadium; small pockets of celebration an indication that a rival team had conceded a goal in some far-flung municipality.

Yet despite the fanaticism of the home support, an away-day culture struggled to thrive in Stalinist Albania. Unless connected directly by railway, travel proved troublesome, but not impossible.

When 17 Nëntori or Partizani travelled to Durrës on the coast to play against Lokomotiva, the train carriages were full to the point where some fans would clamber through the window and ride on top of the train.

But domestic trains only connected the cities of Tirana, Durrës, Vlorë and Shkodër. Travel to Kavajë, Lushnjë or the more distant reaches of Korçë or Berat would involve a three- or four-hour bicycle ride through the agricultural heartlands along the pitted, cratered roadways of old Albania. Others, with friends or family in the military, would hitch a lift on the army trucks moving soldiers and munitions from city to city.

Consequently, unless the game was in Tirana or other connected cities, away support was minimal, and if a team involving one of the capital's 'big three' was played in the highlands of the north or the arid flats of the deep south only diehard supporters would follow their team.

With away travel so inaccessible, RTSH – Radio Televizioni Shqiptar – was an essential accessory to domestic football support in the Hermit Kingdom; the voice of Ismet Bellova, an Albanian John Motson, an authority on, and a treasure of, the national game.

And after the *referia* whistle blew at *rezultati përfundimor* – full time – fans would pack away their radios and walk back to town, possibly returning to Elbasani Street to toast '*gëzuar!*' on a home victory or to drown away the sorrows of defeat, before filing home to revisit the trials of the day on the Sunday night football show, *Rubrika Sportive* – Sport Bulletin – the televisual mouthpiece for Albanian football.

Few Albanians knew of football outside of the country's hermetically sealed borders. Some whispered knowledge of Yugoslavian and Italian football existed; homemade antennae fashioned from sardine or shoe-shine cans offering insight into a world beyond the bunkers and the barbed wire. One fan from Durrës even recalled watching Italy win the 1982 World Cup Final with his family.

However, the threat of capture and internment by Albania's nefarious *Sigurimi* for attempting such a treason meant that foreign football was strange fruit tasted only by a courageous, foolhardy few.

Aside from the meagre TV coverage afforded by *Rubrika Sportive*, matchday was a thoroughly indigenous, Albanian experience to be lived out on the streets and in the stadiums of the cities and towns spread across the nation's 26 districts.

A celebration of an Albanian game that, in spite of all its requisite controversies and anomalies, captured the latent spirit of a people who'd become accustomed to doing what they were told. Children of a republic who, once a week, were allowed to come out to play, to be a genuine version of themselves. And it happened every given Sunday.

Chapter Four

Two Boys from Kosovo

ON 7 April 1939, Benito Mussolini's Italian imperialists invaded the Kingdom of Albania, forcing its ruler King Zog I into exile, thus annexing the country and expanding Italy's growing fascist empire.

There was scant resistanc – only pockets of dissent from individual partisans, landowners and piqued civilians. One such micro-rebellion delayed Italian military transit from Durrës to Tirana for two days, with its participants surrounded and slain. Durrës was seized on 7 April, Tirana the following day, Shkodër and Gjirokastër on 9 April, and all the significant centres of the country on 10 April.

Il Duce's troops were in full command of Albania by the time the 1939 Kampionati Kombetar rolled into life on 1 July.

Its format took the shape of an eight-club knockout tournament, with the quarter-finals played over two legs, a one-off semi-final and final at the Shallvare Sport Ground in Tirana to decide the victors.

The Shallvare quickly became the spiritual home of Albanian football, yet – despite its regal status – the facility wasn't even owned by SK Tirana or FSHF. It was hired from Italian-based landowner Miltiadh Shallvari. After his death in 1933, the ownership was contested by the Turks, who claimed that they had leased the expansive strip of turf to Shallvari's father, Konstandin. On his demise, Konstandin had bequeathed the territory to his son in a will. In the flux of change that preceded and followed World War Two, the Shallvare was finally absorbed by Hoxhaist Albania.

The Albanian footballing powerhouses of the 1930s, SK Tirana – champions for the previous two seasons – and Vllaznia from the northern city of Shkodër, eased past inferior opposition to contest the decider played in the failing sunshine of an Albanian autumn.

SK Tirana were coached by the generous, wealthy and charismatic Selman Stërmasi – a *Tirona* man to his core who'd invested untold funds and time into his passion project.

Stërmasi was born in May of 1908, the same year that football was introduced to Albania; a resonant pointer to the influence he would imbue upon the early development of the Albanian game.

He was a member of the *Agimi*, the society that founded *Tirona* in 1920 and co-founded SK Tirana in 1926, before he departed Albanian shores to study at the Academy of Physical Education in Rome.

Stërmasi had been a player of pedigree too, wearing the shirt of AS Roma between 1928 and 1930 before returning home to his beloved Tirana; seven seasons in the Kampionati Kombetar as a player yielding six titles. Blessed with strength, elegance and excellent technique, Stërmasi was an integral part of the engine room in a fine side.

When Stërmasi wasn't playing football, he was representing Albania on the athletics field, appearing at the 1933, 1934 and 1935 editions of the Olimpiadën Ballkanike – the Balkan Olympics – as a talented long-jumper and national record holder.

This remarkable man, whose career was embellished by a truly extraordinary roster of achievements, became the president of *Tirona* in 1937. The 1939 final against Vllaznia at the Shallvare would mark another notable success for Stërmasi.

Among the crowd at the Shallvare were scouts from the biggest hitters of Italian *calcio*: Roma, Bologna, Lazio included, there at Stërmasi's invitation. Since the annexation,

Albanians became de facto Italians with the clubs of their Adriatic neighbours viewing this newly appropriated hunk of soil as fair game for the shameless pilferage of the finest in previously un-mined Albanian talent.

Stërmasi, confident that many of his squad were good enough to cut it in Serie A, remained gritty in his resolution that the monied Italian clubs observe some semblance of financial fair play. The footballers of SK Tirana had their price. If the Italians were interested in making a purchase, that price would have to be right.

Wearing the pale blue and white stripes of SK Tirana that day were two players, both in their early 20s, who were fixtures in Stërmasi's successful *Tirona* side.

Naim Kryeziu and Riza Lushta both hailed from settlements in the Albanian-occupied old Kingdom of Serbia (now independent Kosovo): Gjakova and Mitrovicë, to the north of Albania.

Despite the boys' shared heritage, as footballers they were very different animals. Kryeziu was lithe, skilful, athletic and whip-sharp; able to cover 100 metres in 11 seconds, the consummate right-sided forward. Lushta was muscular and tough with two great feet; able to mix it against the most cynical and unforgiving of opponents – a formidable and fearless target man.

In acts of almost-perfect historical alignment, the two boys from Kosovo made their individual journeys to Tirana to study at its university in 1933 and 1934 – Lushta, the older of the pair, as a physician; Kryeziu as a PE teacher.

Both were spotted by the club while playing football for the university, promptly signed and by the 1934 season were – aged 16 and 18 – winning league titles for *Tirona*; Lushta heading the league scoring charts during the triumphant 1936 and 1937 seasons.

The final at the Shallvare proved to be something of a classic, with *Tirona* surging into a 6-2 lead on the hour – Kryeziu (two) and Lushta among the scorers – prior to a late hat-trick by Vllaznia's supremely talented forward Loro Boriçi reducing the deficit, the game ending 6-5.

An Italian sports professor present at the game recommended Kryeziu and Lushta to Roma, with Kryeziu – aged 21 at the time – joining *i Giallorossi* while 23-year-old Lushta headed 270 miles further south to SSC Bari. The clubs offered Stërmasi a 60 per cent commission fee which he gave to Kryeziu and Lushta in order to set up their new lives in Italy; a kindness that the boys were never able to repay.

When the communists exerted their control over Albania in 1944, Selman Stërmasi and *Tirona* were attacked by the incumbent regime. In March 1946, at a conference announced to the utter disdain of Stërmasi, the *Politburo* ordered the club to change its name to Puna Tirana (literally 'Work' Tirana) and latterly 17 Nëntori – 17 November – honouring the date of the communist liberation of Tirana. Stërmasi, present at the meeting that observed *Tirona*'s communist baptism, exited the hall denouncing the edict – and The Party hated him for it.

After refusing to collaborate with state security – the dreaded *Sigurimi* – in 1949, Stërmasi was liquidated and expelled from the club, forced into menial labouring work until his death in 1976. His legacy endures. KF Tirana (*Tirona*'s new moniker) named their stadium, built on the order of the *Sigurimi*, in his honour after communism's fall in 1991 – an irony that the jovial Stërmasi would have enjoyed.

In Rome, via an astonishing turn of fate, Kryeziu and Lushta's debuts saw Roma and Bari paired against each other at the Campo Testaccio on the opening day of the 1939/40 Serie A season. When the final whistle blew both players had reason to be content: Lushta scoring a debut goal for *i Galletti*, Kryeziu providing his first assist in a 4-2 win for the Romans.

The 1939/40 season proved a case of 'bedding in' for the young Kosovan-Albanians, Kryeziu making five first-team appearances for *i Giallorossi* with Lushta making 16 starts and scoring on three occasions in Puglia.

By the start of the following season, Juventus were alerted to the talents of Lushta. He signed for the Turin giants in the summer of 1940.

Both players established themselves as first-team regulars during the 1940/41 season, Kryeziu netting three times in 20 starts for Roma and Lushta plundering ten goals in 26 appearances for *i Bianconeri*. At the season's end, Juventus were fifth and Roma 11th.

The 1940/41 Serie A champions, Bologna, also boasted an Albanian footballer in their ranks. Sllave Llambi, a hard-as-nails central midfielder, is considered to be the first Albanian *Scudetto* winner, although he failed to feature in any league games in *i Rossoblù's* victorious season. He'd moved to Ambrosiana-Inter – latterly Internazionale – by the following campaign.

Prior to the 1941/42 season, Kryeziu, Lushta and Llambi were joined in Serie A by countryman Loro Boriçi, whose hat-trick had almost dug Vllaznia out of a hole against *Tirona* during the 1939 Kampionati Kombetar Final. He'd finally been lured across the Adriatic by the deep-pocketed affluence of SS Lazio. Boriçi would serve as an understudy to *Biancocelesti* legend and *Azzurri* 1938 World Cup winner Silvio Piola, before returning to Albania in 1943.

The 1941/42 campaign is where this story really begins. Kryeziu and Lushta, now accepted parts of the furniture at their respective clubs, would create history during the Serie A season, establishing themselves as Albanian footballing legends.

Juventus and Roma embarked upon 1941/42 with disparate aims for the season. Juve president Piero Dusio sought to revive the dwindled fortunes of the slumbering giant, elevating Giovanni Ferrari, winner of five consecutive *Scudetti* with the club as a player between 1930 and 1935 and a further three titles with Inter (1937/38 and 1939/40) and Bologna (1940/41), to the managerial post.

Roma appointed Alfréd Schaffer as coach prior to the 1940/41 season. Schaffer led an exciting Hungary side to the 1938 World Cup Final – a 4-2 defeat to the Italians in Paris – earning him global kudos.

Schaffer had been a magnificent footballer too, winning league titles in three different countries – Hungary, Germany and Austria – with MTK Budapest, 1. FC Nürnberg and Amateur Vienna. The wily Hungarian also represented the *Magyarok* – the national side – himself, scoring 17 times in 15 internationals between 1915 and 1919 and was voted Hungarian Footballer of the Year in 1915 and 1916.

Roma chairman Edgardo Bazzini pulled his coach aside pre-season, sceptical at the lack of transfer activity. Schaffer assured his boss that only a few tactical additions were required; with one or two tweaks, his Roma squad would be good enough to win the *Scudetto*.

Bazzini's incredulity had basis; Schaffer's first year in the capital – an 11th-place finish – had hardly set the world on fire, but *i Giallorossi*'s competitive style and Schaffer's status as a coach bought the Hungarian another season at the helm.

Any reservations Bazzini may have harboured dissipated by early November when Roma – unbeaten – faced Juventus at the Campo Testaccio, romping to a resounding 2-0 victory in front of 28,000 baying *Romani*. The mercurial Kryeziu opened the scoring inside 20 minutes with Argentine Miguel Ángel Pantó delivering the killer blow shortly after the break.

The Italian sporting broadsheets revelled in Kryeziu's performance, christening him *La Freccia* – The Arrow – fast and injurious to opponents. A solitary loss in a dozen matchdays had set up the *Capitolini* for a potential history-maker of a season.

Juve's opening dozen games – despite the regular goal contributions of Lushta – included five tame defeats, which was instrumental in the forced departure of coach Giovanni Ferrari, *i Bianconeri*'s season prematurely unsalvageable.

As Schaffer's *Giallorossi* continued their ascent to the acme of Serie A, Ferrari was replaced at Juventus.

Luis Monti, a veteran of 200 games for *i Bianconeri*, had represented both Argentina and Italy at the 1930 and 1934 World Cups. Nicknamed *Doble Ancho* – the Two-Door Wardrobe – for his robust, agrarian method of play, Monti was tasked with rescuing something from what had been, thus far, a wretched season.

Despite erratic league form, Juventus were showing flickers of potential in the Coppa Italia. A 5-0 tanking of Pro Patria beneath the shadow of the columbine at their Benito Mussolini Stadium in the round of 32, illuminated by a powerful 11-minute second-half hat-trick by Riza Lushta, offered Monti and Dusio a glimpse of gilt amid the darkness.

Juve followed this with a tough, tight 2-1 victory over title-chasing Genoa in the last 16, Lushta bagging a brace, his 81st-minute winner sending the Turin faithful into raptures.

As *i Giallorossi* arrived at the seasonal spring break off the back of a home victory over Atalanta, ahead of the chasing Torino, Venezia, Genoa and Lazio, Juventus were trouncing Modena 4-1 at the Benito Mussolini, setting up a Coppa Italia Final date with northern neighbours Milan.

The Romans, assisted by the considerable skills of the brilliant Kryeziu, re-emerged from their spring hibernation in resplendent fettle and won five of their last eight games – drawing the other three – to ease to their first *Scudetto*; a 6-0 battering of Ambrosiana-Inter in front of their own fans sealing the deal with two matches to play.

They concluded their campaign on 14 June 1942 with a routine 2-0 victory against Modena, crowned *campioni d'Italia* before their own adoring legion of fans. It was the first time the Italian title had been won by a club from the south.

Benito Mussolini's agenda to evince the supremacy and symbolism of the ancient city of Rome in the new age had been fruitful. *Il Duce* believed that *calcio* was an allegory for his utopian vision of a fascist Italy, with Rome at its centre. Roma had done their bit for the regime.

Meanwhile, Juventus approached the first leg of the Coppa Italia Final at the Arena Civica, Milan, having fallen into bad habits since the spring *intermezzo*, losing to Torino, Lazio and Napoli – the latter tilting on the very apex of Serie A relegation. Juve limped over the line in a wholly unsatisfactory and distant sixth place.

The solitary spark of light in Juventus's doomed season had been the form of Riza Lushta. At the close of 1941/42 he was the top-scoring foreigner in Serie A, plundering 17 goals in 28 games; his guile, intelligence and firepower establishing him as a favourite among the Juve *tifosi* and earning Lushta the sobriquet *La Bombardiere* – The Bomber.

On 21 June, Luis Monti's beleaguered Juventus arrived in Milan out of form and out of favour, yet escaped the cauldron of the Arena Civica with a 1-1 draw courtesy of Savino Bellini's first-half shot.

With honours even, Milan travelled to Turin for the deciding leg, and beneath the dark sentinel of the Columbine over-standing Stadio Benito Mussolini, Juventus – and in particular Lushta – produced a wonderful performance, belying their dismal season.

Within five first-half minutes, *i Bianconeri* assumed total command of the contest: Lushta's opportunist strike putting Juve ahead on 29 minutes and Vittorio Sentimenti, a talented *mezzala*, slamming home a penalty in the 34th minute after a foul on the Albanian.

Milanese goal machine Aldo Boffi briefly made a fight of it shortly after the break, before Lushta fired in two in 120 seconds either side of the 70th minute to win the Coppa for Juve. It failed to rescue Luis Monti from the ignominy of dismissal as coach.

The 1941/42 season made champions of two sides. Roma had proven worthy, deserved *campioni*; Juventus had succeeded in spite of themselves. It had also been a coronation of sorts for the two boys from Kosovo, who had ventured across the Adriatic with heady aspirations – and exceeded them.

Naim Kryeziu and Riza Lushta remained in Italy, forging long, successful careers. Kryeziu remained at Roma until 1947 before moving to Napoli, where he would spend a further five years. He returned to Rome in 1956 as part of the club's backroom staff prior to serving as head coach of *i Giallorossi* in 1963.

Kryeziu would continue to work for Roma as a scout into his 60s, discovering a young Giuseppe Giannini.

When Kryeziu – the last surviving member of Roma's first *Scudetto*-winning team – passed in 2010, their players wore black armbands during their game against Udinese in his honour.

Lushta stayed with Juventus until 1945 and was a continued source of goals, before spells at Napoli, Alessandria, Siena, Forlì and Cannes of France, retiring from the game in 1954.

Lushta died in Torino in 1997 aged 81. In Mitrovicë, Kosovo – his birthplace – the city stadium currently bears his name.

Neither player returned to their homeland.

The Albania they departed in 1939 was a very different place to the one liberated by the communist partisans in 1944, etching a further bleak chapter in the ongoing dark saga that is the history of Albania. But for a short time, two boys from its shores became champions in the country of the world champions.

Everything changed inside the Hermit Kingdom in the two years that straddled 1945. A country persecuted by foreign fascist invaders now underwent a subtle, burgeoning oppression, subjugated by enemies from within, every arena of society – football included – used as a political tool in its regime's warped apparatchik.

Chapter Five

The Boy Who Came Home

WHEN LORO Boriçi returned to Albania from Italy aboard the Brindisi–Vlorë ferry in the late summer of 1943 – Italy's fascist regime consigned to history's landfill along with its deposed dictator – it was a journey imbued with equal measure of frustration and relief.

Boriçi's two years at SS Lazio were tainted by a palpable lack of completion. Arguably Albania's most gifted footballer of his generation, Boriçi's stay in Italy's capital could never be interpreted as a wholesale failure; he had garnered a reputation as a fine player among the Lazio *tifosi*. The simple fact was the Italian chapter of Boriçi's career had been starved of opportunity.

Born Lorenzo Boriçi on 4 August 1922 in Shkodër, the prodigy was only 15 when he played for the Vllaznia first team in 1937, leaving Albania in 1941 to study jurisprudence – the philosophy of law – at La Sapienza University in Rome.

Boriçi was a player of vision, technical ability and prodigious work-rate, with a propensity for the spectacular. On joining *i Biancocelesti* from Vllaznia Shkodër in the summer of 1941, it had appeared that the tall, elegant Albanian would be imparting his enviable gifts on a larger, more discerning audience.

Over the course of two maddening years, Boriçi was reduced to a standby role, shadowing Silvio Piola, the Lazio legend and Italian World Cup winner in 1938.

When given a chance to breathe – the sustenance of game time – Boriçi impressed in the pale blue, scoring six goals in 19 appearances for *Le Aquile*. However, by the close of the 1942/43 season, Piola had picked up the *Capocannoniere* crown, the prize afforded to Serie A's top goalscorer. Boriçi's chances of being anything other than a benchwarmer for the greatest player in Italy had robbed him of his enthusiasm for Italian football. Homesick and disillusioned, he caught the boat home.

In a cruel caveat, the folly of fate relieved Boriçi – still only aged 21 – of what may have developed into an outstanding career in Rome. Within a month of his return to Albania, Piola was gone, snapped up by northern behemoths Torino.

The Albania Boriçi returned to was a land of renewed promise. A wave of anti-fascist sentiment pervaded throughout the villages and towns of the nation, spurred by the revolutionary activity of Lëvizja Nacional-Çlirimtare – the National Liberation Movement – fronted by activist and committed Stalinist, Enver Hoxha.

Hoxha spoke of 'liberation' and 'independence', using the words to oil the wheels of rebellion. What he failed to impart was that these worthy soundbites didn't necessarily equate to freedom.

By the time football resumed in 1945, Hoxha had been installed as president. Huge cash sponsorship from Titoist Yugoslavia and Stalinist Soviet Union ushered in a new age of modernisation throughout the country; times were a-changing.

However, in the football heartlands of Albania, time seemed to have stood still with Vllaznia and *Tirona* contesting the first post-war Albanian National Championship Final, just as they had the last one, three years earlier.

It was a final of two legs, played on 23 and 26 December, a politically motivated decision rubber-stamped by The Party to devalue the status of Christmas in the country's two main

Catholic centres, Tirana and Shkodër. Hoxha would go further. In the 1967 rewriting of the Albanian constitution, he would ban religion totally, making Albania the world's first atheist state; a dystopian wilderness where the leaders expounded the virtues of socialism while extracting all of its humanist content.

Boriçi returned to Vllaznia and was the key instrument in the domestic resurgence of the *Kuq e Blute* – Red and Blues – creating and scoring goals with regularity on the way to the final. Vllaznia would win both legs by the same 2-1 score, Boriçi earning his first domestic honour after two influential, energy-infused displays.

Seven months later, the club from Shkodër did it again. *Tirona*, persecuted by the regime and forced to adopt a new name, Puna Tirana – latterly 17 Nëntori – wouldn't feature this time. They would wait two decades to win another title with Vllaznia's opponents this time manifested in the shape of KS Flamurtari of Vlorë.

The northerners of Shkodër blew the Vlorë southerners away, winning both legs in a resounding 5-0 aggregate triumph, Boriçi supplying the assists for Vllaznia's exciting young striker, Pal Mirashi (nicknamed *Djaloshi i Malit* – Mountain Boy) who originated from the precipitous tribal fiefdoms of Dukagjin and had recently secured his berth in a provisional national squad list.

The champions also included a cluster of other soon-to-be Albanian internationals: goalkeeper Dodë Tahiri, midfielder Bimo Fakja and the defensive pairing of Muhamet Dibra and Bahri Kavaja – the latter invoking national outrage in September 1950, defecting on a journey back to Albania after an international fixture in Budapest against Hungary. Kavaja fashioned his escape by swimming across the width of the Bosporus during a brief stop in Istanbul. He evidently didn't fancy the post-match governmental inquiry; Albania had lost 12-0 against the Hungarians.

They were joined in a talented Albanian national squad by Sllave Llambi (another returnee from Italy where he'd played for Bologna and Ambrosiana-Inter); Qamil Teliti, a regular goalscorer for Besa Kavaje regarded as the most feared striker in Albania; Rexhep Spahiu, an adaptable defender who'd go on to partner Boriçi as joint coach of Partizani Tirana in the late 1950s; and the youthful bustle of *Tirona* midfield pairing, Aristidh Parapani and Vasif Biçaku.

With the 1946 edition of the Balkan Cup – Kupa e Ballkanit – to be hosted by a positive, new Albania at the recently completed Stadiumi Kombetar Qemal Stafa (a project conceived during Italian fascist occupation but birthed via the voluntary sweat and graft of 1,000 comrades seven years later) it was amid a miasma of optimism and interest that the country approached this landmark sporting event.

The job of guiding *Shqiponjat* – the Eagles – through their inaugural troika of competitive internationals against powerful opponents in Yugoslavia, Bulgaria and Romania fell to the charismatic Serbian, Ljubiša Broćić.

Broćić, aged 35, would later win league titles with Red Star Belgrade in 1951 and 1953 and Juventus in 1958 before managing PSV Eindhoven and Catalan giants Barcelona, but this was his first meaningful appointment.

He had impressed the Yugoslavian Sports Council while managing the Belgrade Trade Union side. When, in 1946, a treaty of co-operation was signed between Albania and the Yugoslavs, marking an influx of technical advisors of all professions into Albania, Broćić was tasked with managing the national team.

After observing a clutch of Albanian league games, Broćić picked a side he believed best equipped for the forthcoming Balkan Cup, instilling Boriçi, a youthful 24 years of age, as his captain and leader.

His first task was to embed in this newly acquired squad a style of play widowed of fear; attacking, competitive, based on teamwork and hard work and, after building this side, testing them out against credible opposition.

Afforded two weeks in which to prepare, Broćić's *Shqiponjat* met Montenegro at the Campo Sportivo, Shkodër, on 22 September 1946 before 7,000 feverish Albanians – the country's first official international. Uninhibited in mood, playing fantastically offensive football they ruthlessly unpicked the hapless Montenegrins and won 5-0. Boriçi provided the inspiration, Qamil Teliti two of the goals.

Over the following fortnight, Broćić refined his system, drawing upon Albanian footballers' natural parallels with their Italian neighbours; flair and pragmatism adjoined, while adding to the mix the technical, tactical know-how of the Yugoslavian game. By the eve of the Balkan Cup on 6 October 1946, the Albanians were ready.

The tournament took the shape of a mini-group with each side playing each other once.

It is easy to underestimate the difficulty and significance of the Balkan Cup tournament without affording it context. The teams that Albania would face in Tirana over the subsequent week were seasoned international outfits.

Yugoslavia, Albania's first opponents, had played competitive international football since 1920. Already World Cup semi-finalists and two-times Balkan Cup winners (they would go on to win Olympic football silver in 1948), *Plavi* – the Blues – now boasted the prodigious talent of Stjepan Bobek, Yugoslavia's all-time top international goalscorer.

Bulgaria and Romania were the most dangerous of dark horses. Both technically excellent, Bulgaria had won the competition twice in the early 1930s, and Romania three times interspersed by World Cup appearances in 1934 and 1938.

Albania, international virgins, would find themselves profoundly tested by powerful and experienced rivals.

On 7 October 1946, Tirana arose, excitedly, from its collective slumber, supporters converging early on Stadiumi

Qemal Stafa – so current its completion that the dust of post-construction billowed across the concrete terraces carried on the breeze of a balmy late-autumn morning.

However, by the afternoon the weather had changed; thunder rumbled in the hills that peered over Tirana's new stadium, the heavens opening with rare violence.

After a rain-hindered opening ceremony, including a rallying speech from Enver Hoxha, the comrades within the Qemal Stafa – 20,000-strong – readied themselves for the main event.

The ensuing game was played out beneath a shroud of black umbrellas. Albania could only hope that the inclemency of the weather wouldn't prove a dark portent for the forthcoming tournament.

The Yugoslavia that Albania faced in their first competitive fixture were of a particularly fine vintage. Led by the coaching duet of Milorad Arsenijević and Aleksandar Tirnanić, team-mates at the enormously successful BSK Beograd in the 1930s (latterly renamed OFK) and veterans of Yugoslavia's 1930 World Cup campaign, *Plavi* boasted the defensive bornite of captain Miroslav Brozović and Ivica Horvat and the attacking thrust of Frane Matošić and Stjepan Bobek; footballers of vast experience and pedigree.

However, Broćić identified a lack of pace at the heart of the Yugoslav defence which his side sought to exploit. The results were utterly spectacular. On an uneven, patchy, muddied pitch, Boriçi's sharpness of thought and deed released both Pal Mirashi and Qamil Teliti within the first eight minutes to establish a quite incredible 2-0 lead.

Anton Mazreku, commentating for Radio Tirana, Albania's first analytical football voice, conveyed the glorious news to the population huddled around radios in the 26 districts beyond the walls of the Qemal Stafa, his delivery a mix of jubilation and disbelief.

Amid the deluge, Albania continued to tease the shell-shocked Slavs, Boriçi adopting the role of chief matador in a first-half humiliation of stunned opponents. When Boriçi spun his marker Dragutin Lojen once too often, the chastised defender unleashed his fury with a tackle that, in modern times, would've earned ten red cards. Lojen remained on the field, while Boriçi – unable to continue – was substituted at half-time and replaced by the infinitely less gifted defensive anchor, Bahri Kavaja.

Shorn of their creative lynchpin, Albania wilted post-break. Their 2-0 lead quickly became 2-2 within three minutes of the restart, Matošić and Bobek levelling. When Partizan Belgrade midfielder Zlatko Čajkovski forced home what proved to be the winner in the 57th minute, not even the most iron-clad Albanophile could argue that it wasn't deserved.

The hosts, sting drawn, blunt with shock, lacked the know-how to respond, playing out the remaining half an hour in a haze of passivity; a muted doppelgänger of their first-half selves. When Romanian official Radu Istrate blew time on this consummate game of two halves, defeat was met by the home support with disappointment and a shared sense of what might have been.

Rather than dwell on the hard truths of the defeat – Albania shrewdly undone by a guileful and practised Yugoslavia – Broćić congratulated his players on what, for 45 minutes, had been a splendidly inventive performance. The nature of the defeat would prove a stark lesson in the art of recovery for his raw Albanian upstarts.

The following day Romania and Bulgaria played out a tough 2-2 draw at the Qemal Stafa, Matyas Toth's late equaliser completing the comeback after the Romanians had found themselves two goals adrift inside half an hour.

Albania's chance to offset the blue mood of their opening reverse came a day later, Bulgaria afforded only 24 hours to recuperate from the excesses of their battle with Romania. Boriçi had undergone rudimentary repairs and was pronounced fit for the Bulgaria game, and it was his involvement that would have a profound bearing on the destiny of the contest.

The Bulgarian side that faced Albania on 9 October 1946 contained a core of established campaigners sourced from the country's top, Sofia-based clubs, SC Lokomotiv, PSP PSC-Levski and FC Sportlist.

Amid their squad, Albania's opponents boasted terrific footballing technicians including Bozhin Laskov, a tall, physically daunting forward with superb heading ability who would represent both Bulgaria and Czechoslovakia; Vasil Spasov, sharp and fast, and the finest of their current crop; and Krum Milev, a captain and general on the pitch who would later transpose his tactical brilliance to management, coaching CSKA Sofia to 12 league titles while dually overseeing the national team for six years.

Again, the Qemal Stafa was a white-hot cauldron abundant with a heady miasma of freshly excavated national pride, only this time the umbrellas were gone and a bright winter sun illuminated proceedings.

Ljubiša Broćić adjusted his side nominally in the wake of their narrow opening loss; the only change being the inclusion of Vllaznia's Bahri Kavaja – ahead of Xhavit Demneri – from the newly formed Partizani club.

A spirited Bulgaria started well, testing Albanian resolve with quick, incisive football. The *Shqiponjat* had opened superbly against the technical might of the Yugoslavians, but the reverse was evident against a lesser threat; the hangover of painful defeat married with the weight of national expectation inhibiting their early play.

Vasil Spasov took advantage of the hosts' lethargy after five minutes, shooting beyond an at-fault Dodë Tahiri in the Albanian goal to make it 1-0.

Rather than capitulate as they had against the Yugoslavs, Albania rallied and went close twice before Boriçi rewarded home fervour with a deserved equaliser on the half-hour, Albania entering the break the better side.

Bulgaria were a body of souls exhausted from their exertions against Romania the previous day, and 20 minutes into the second half tired legs and minds combined to gift Albania a penalty that was slammed home, right-footed, past keeper Simeon Kostov with rasping aplomb by the brilliant Boriçi.

Within three minutes, Boriçi had fed the boy from the mountains, Pal Mirashi, who nervelessly added a third. The Albanians held their 3-1 lead until the final whistle, which was greeted with wild celebration by jubilant fans at the Qemal Stafa – a *stadiumi* that already felt very much like home.

Two performances heralding an age of positivity and possibilities, orchestrated in equal measure by Boriçi and Broćić, adopted exaggerated significance when Romania tore up the script by beating Yugoslavia 2-1 at the Qemal Stafa two days later. *Plavi*'s loss meant that an Albanian victory in their final game against the Romanians could feasibly result in the hosts actually winning the tournament, a prospect assumed impossible prior to its start.

Two days later – 13 October 1946 – Skanderbeg Square and the Italianate tree-lined *bulevardis* that fed the concourse of the Stadiumi Qemal Stafa babbled and effervesced with cacophonies of human excitement.

One afternoon, two games of football that would establish the destiny of the eighth edition of the Balkan Cup.

Bulgaria faced off against Yugoslavia in the midday kick-off, *Plavi* easing into a 2-0 lead via a brace from Božidar Sandić before a late consolation by Bozhin Laskov with two minutes left saw the game end 2-1 in favour of the Yugoslavs. More importantly, it meant that an Albanian victory, by any margin, versus Romania would make them, after three competitive fixtures, recipients of a first internationally recognised honour.

Adversely, it also meant that a Romanian win would see the *Tricolorii* crowned champions. The stage was spectacularly set.

Virgil Economu's side created a shock by inflicting a rare defeat upon Yugoslavia and, in their role as holders, were expected to see off Albania with some degree of comfort. The experienced Nicolae Reuter of the CFR Timisoara club had planted a marker by scoring in both of Romania's games and, with support from the dual threats of the youthful Iosif Fabian (who'd go on to win Serie A with Torino in 1947/48 and a Portuguese double in 1953/54 at Sporting CP) and Francisc Spielmann (integral in firing Nagyváradi AC to their recent Hungarian title), this offered Broćić much pre-match food for thought.

The importance of the fixture hung like a weight over the two teams, the first half passing in tense, insipid stalemate. It was a game badly in need of inspiration.

Urged on by expectant home support and buoyed by the attacking triumvirate of Boriçi, Teliti and Mirashi, the *Shqiponjat* found their rhythm and delivered the game's deciding moment on 55 minutes.

Chasing a long, hopeful ball down the left channel, Qamil Teliti overtook full-back Ferenc Mészáros and hooked a hopeful cross into the Romanian box where Pal Mirashi out-muscled his marker, arcing an angled, near-post header over keeper Gheorghe Lăzăreanu from seven yards.

Thirty-five minutes of anxious attrition followed before Yugoslavian referee Marijan Matancic called time on the contest, the Qemal Stafa ascending into a raucous, unbridled human carnival.

Loro Boriçi, the on-pitch general and orchestrator of the victory, received the trophy from Hoxha atop a rickety wooden podium adorning a laurel crown, looking every bit the Roman hero he almost became at Lazio. He would go on to win a smattering of trophies as a player and coach, managing Albania on four separate occasions, but – from a national team perspective – it never got this good again.

As coach, Ljubiša Broćić had masterminded a success as superb as it was improbable, his popularity among his players documented in Belgrade newspaper *Politika* on 14 October 1946: 'When the referee blew the whistle at the end of the Albania–Romania match, the stadium was buzzing with the cries of 30,000 spectators [official records list the attendance as 20,000]. The Albanian players rushed to the gates where their coach, Ljubiša Broćić, stood, taking him by the hand and raising him to triumph. A charming gesture by the Albanians; in their moment of great victory, they did not forget their coach, Broćić – a triumph to which he contributed on a large scale.'

With the Albanian national team's beginnings kickstarted by glorious success, led by a young coach capable of forging an exciting and winning side, the future appeared to be bright for Broćić's *Shqiponjat*. But within months Broćić was gone, a tectonic shift in the relationship between Tito and Stalin – in which Enver Hoxha sided with the latter – leading to his premature return to Belgrade.

The *Shqiponjat* would perform well under Broćić's successor, Adem Karapici, at the 1948 Balkan Cup, a 1-0 win against Romania in Bucharest with Mirashi scoring the winner, tailed by a 0-0 draw in Tirana against a Hungary side that would, under Gusztáv Sebes, soon become the finest in the world, followed by another scoreless draw in Belgrade versus the Olympic silver medallists, Yugoslavia.

But years of societal restriction, augmented by a lack of connection with the outside world, starved Albania and its footballers of the chance of testing their abilities, regularly, against better opposition.

Albania's club sides would play in European competition intermittently during the 1960s, the national side competing in the World Cup qualification stages for the first time in 1966.

When Loro Boriçi sailed into the port of Vlorë in 1943, his return hinted towards a successful footballing future for Albania, partially realised in 1946. By the 1960s, Albanian football had lost ground with the rest of the world, the foundations laid and bridges built by Broćić, Boriçi and the Balkan Cup-winning side of 1946 wastefully dismantled.

This sense of unmet potential would weigh heavier on the emergent nation, as the 1950s and 1960s boasted many of the finest footballing talents in Albanian history.

National energies were geared towards worthier socialist goals; the socio-economic progression of Albania from primitivity to modernism. For 15 years, post-war, the regime would – albeit utilising Yugoslav and Soviet money – successfully drain the marshlands, eradicate malaria, champion literacy, introduce subsidised health care and develop industries. Superficially, Albania appeared to be taking the great leap forward, living the Marxist–Leninist dream. But at what human cost?

In tandem, the subsequent decade and a half would herald the politicisation of all aspects of Albanian life, with football playing its own bit part in the execution of The Party's virulent agenda.

Chapter Six

The Rise of the Superclubs

THE YEAR of 1946 observed a continuance in the domination of northern Albanian *klubi*, Vllaznia Shkodër. Post-war champions in both 1945 and 1946 and boasting six starters from the triumphant Balkan Cup-winning side, the expectancy was that – domestically, at least – the wheels would continue to trundle in a similar direction.

However, inside the Hermit Kingdom wheels were revolving within wheels, the course of the national game altered inestimably by the interference of the regime and its keystones of dictatorial power – the army and police.

Tuesday, 1 January 1946 saw the dissolution of two military football clubs, Ylli (Star) Shkodër and Liria (Freedom) Korçë on the edict of the regime's Ministry of Defence, with their best players joining a new entity, originally christened Ushtria – the Army. Twelve days later, Ushtria played their first match, pitted against champions-elect Vllaznia in Tirana. During a scoreless draw, they wore a signature all-red kit, a constant that would remain into the post-communist era.

On 4 February 1946, subject to the hastiest of rebrands, Ushtria became a KS – *klubi sportiv* – renaming themselves after the Albanian partisans who fought for the country's liberation during World War Two, harking the official birth and baptism of Albania's original superclub, KS Partizani of Tirana.

Initially sourcing their pool of players from the Shkolla Ushtarake Skënderbej – Skanderbeg Military School – it soon became obvious to the junta that an injection of weathered, experienced footballers would be required for their project to bear fruit.

Key performers from Partizani's competitors were transferred to play for the army side by order of Hoxha's ruling regime. A veritable tsunami of talent flooded into the club from the persecuted *Tirona*. Indeed, when Partizani faced *Tirona* in their first match in 1947, eight of the 11 Partizani starters were players hijacked from *Tirona*.

Northern heavyweights Vllaznia and Besa – 'Besa' being the cultural precept meaning 'to keep the promise' and 'word of honour' – hailing from the sea port city of Kavajë on the Adriatic coast, also witnessed their finest crop of footballers wantonly gobbled up by Partizani.

The regime despised *Tirona* for their perceived grandiosity and bourgeoise history, while Shkodër – under Hoxha – was the alleged centre of Gheg-speaking, anti-communist intellectualism and religiosity, divergent to the newly preached canons of Marxist–Leninism and contrary to Albania's Tosk-speaking, atheist Party invective.

The Tosk-speaking community, indigenous to territories south of the Shkumbini River, were seen as the true partisans and upholders of communist/nationalist values, whereas the Ghegs to the north were observed with suspicion by Gjirokastër-born Tosk, Enver Hoxha and his innately distrustful regime.

Tirona and Vllaznia were ethical foes in urgent need of breaking. Besa Kavajë of Kavaja, a run-down industrial city where the regime disposed of the ideologically impure (exile to Kavaja the Albanian equivalent of being 'sent to Coventry') were equally unfortunate, having reared two of Albania's finest forwards, Zinhi Gjinali and Qamil Teliti, both brazenly pilfered by Partizani.

In a period spanning less than two years, Partizani acquired the services of Alfred Bonati, Rexhep Spahiu, Sllave

Llambi, Sulejman Vathi, Vasil Biçaku, Aristidh Parapani and Besim Fagu from *Tirona*; they all were, or would soon become, full internationals.

Partizani then appropriated Besa's potent striking duo, Gjinali and Teliti, and incumbent talents Muhamet Dibra, Bimo Fakja, Xhevdet Shaqiri, Hamdi Bakalli and, most tellingly, Loro Boriçi from champions Vllaznia.

With their pick of national talent, Partizani eased their way to the Albanian title in 1947, one point ahead of second-placed Vllaznia with *Tirona* – now 17 Nëntori – 14 points adrift and a very distant fifth.

The following season was a rewriting of the same story, Partizani winning the championship play-off against Vllaznia 6-2, Xhevdet Shaqiri, Vasif Biçaku and Zinhi Gjinali (four) providing the goals – players sourced from *Tirona* and Vllaznia – in a one-sided contest. They reaffirmed their dominance in the Kupa e Republikës Final, beating *Tirona* 5-2 at the Qemal Stafa, thus becoming Albania's first 'double' winners.

1949 heralded a double-double as Partizani – fuelled by the goals of league top scorer Loro Boriçi – were victorious in both national competitions; the runners-up spots taken, again, by Vllaznia and *Tirona*.

In a country that noisily expounded the virtues of social democracy and equality, sport was heading down an exceedingly rum, undemocratic path. The army club were in danger of monopolising domestic football in Albania. It was a trend that hadn't escaped the attentions of the leadership of The Party.

Whether The Party understood the adversities of one-club dominance within Albania's rigid socialist structure – especially as it was domination born of anti-socialist principles – or simply wished to reinforce control by making the dual bedrocks of their despotic rule ever more visible, is a point for debate.

Either way, conversations were had in the national power centres that would see Albanian football both improve aesthetically, while simultaneously descending into an eddy of Orwellian paradox.

On 3 March 1950, a new football club representing the Ministry of the Interior of Albania and its nefarious state security/secret police subdivision, the *Sigurimi e Shtetit*, was founded.

The new team would wear an admiral blue – the hue favoured by its uniformed hierarchy and donned by its operatives. Tirana joined a roster of cities boasting both red and blue football clubs, akin to the established European metropolises of Milan, Munich, Liverpool and, more tellingly – given Hoxha's post-war penchant for all things Soviet – Moscow.

When Dinamo Tirana were birthed, their fathers at the Ministry of the Interior had yet to evolve into the monster they would soon become, Blutë's christening welcomed by a populace still revelling in the enjoyment of a freshly carved and apparently meaningful independence.

The *Sigurimi*, created in 1944 with implicit instructions to quell counter-revolution and suppress opposition to The Party, were Hoxha's 'dear and sharp tool', afforded the autonomy to imprison, disenfranchise and murder as long as it maintained the nation's dreadful status quo.

Initially, the *Sigurimi* used brutality to send a message to dissidents wishing to test their stomach. In the north, two men got into a fight in which one man died. The survivor was buried alive on top of the dead man he killed in front of appalled villagers forced to watch. It never happened again.

In Erla Maranaku's essay, *A Social History of Socialist Albania, 1975–1991*, Arben Zenelli, a survivor of the regime, elaborated on the *Sigurimi*'s mundane yet terrifyingly effective recruitment and modus operandi. Many years prior to 1975, the *Sigurimi* agents had ceased to wear their tell-tale blue uniform, the invisibility of agents being key to their impact. Arben explained, 'You had no idea who they were. But you knew they were everywhere. It could be your father, your brother, your teacher, or anyone else. They worked their regular jobs while also being members of the *Sigurimi*. They told the government what they heard.'

Based within the Shtëpia me Gjethe – the alluringly named 'House of Leaves' (headquarters to the Gestapo during the Nazi occupation of Tirana) – the measures the *Sigurimi* imposed inside its ivy-covered outer walls would serve to enslave Albanians physically, spiritually and psychologically for 48 years.

The fear the *Sigurimi* instilled in the populace was all-encapsulating; absolute, their greatest success – and greatest failure – being their very real campaign to eradicate freedom of thought.

In the winter of 1972, in an era when Albania drew its ideological lead and financial resource from Maoist China, a myth was peddled that the *Sigurimi* – buoyed by Sino scientific aid – had invented a device that could read minds.

Sceptically, I drew on the experience of an Albanian friend, who lived through the Stalinist era. I was told, 'It wasn't a myth. It was a progression of brainwashing techniques the *Sigurimi* already had in place. They [the *Sigurimi*] built a chair with hundreds of cables coming out of it. Enemies of the regime, during interrogation, were told that the machine could read their mind. Immediately, they would sign confessions for any trumped-up charges, fearful of what the machine might say.'

It was subjugation *par excellence*; the *Sigurimi*'s power so complete that the people of Albania were even denied the solace of their own thoughts.

Sigurimi power in Stalinist Albania did not, however, equate to the immunity of their own staff; eight of the *Sigurimi*'s nine directors between 1943 and 1991 were imprisoned and executed by the regime on a variety of contrived charges.

In 1950, plans were enacted for a stadium to be built in Tirana that would serve as a base for the team of the *Sigurimi*. After the war, Albania inherited only rudimentary sports grounds, such as the Shallvare. The Qemal Stafa – completed in 1946 and Albania's first bona fide *stadiumi* – was the home to Partizani, 17 Nëntori and a clutch of other Tirana-based sides leaving the venue ridiculously over-subscribed.

In an interesting side-story to this, 1952 observed the Qemal Stafa add another *klubi* to the burgeoning gaggle of teams that called it home.

At the beginning of 1951, leader Enver Hoxha joined the in-crowd of sponsors inside The Party who shared a vested interest in the Kampionati when he formed the long-windedly monikered Luftëtari i Shkollës së Bashkuar e Oficerëve Enver Hoxha Tiranë – Fighter of the Enver Hoxha United Officers School of Tirana – or Luftëtari Tiranë ('Fighter' Tirana) as they were otherwise known.

Hoxha's offspring competed in four Kampionati in 1952, 1953, 1954 and 1955, reaching the Albanian Cup semi-finals in 1952 and 1954 before their disillusioned benefactor dissolved them in 1955 for their failure to become serious challengers to Partizani and Dinamo's title crown.

Fixture congestion, a genuine need for a second footballing venue in the capital, married with the *Sigurimi*'s strong desire to see their Dinamo team housed in a customised stadium, similar to the model perfected by the Russian police clubs, prompted the regime into rapid action.

But unlike the Qemal Stafa, completed by willing communist volunteers, a celebration of national emancipation – the Stadiumi Dinamo in the west of the city – was erected by political prisoners under the watchful tutelage of armed militia. Many innocent Albanians died from exhaustion and the injuries sustained during its construction.

It is notably ironic that, post-communism, the stadium was renamed after Selman Stërmasi, in honour of the

Albanian martyr that Hoxha's dead regime had mercilessly endeavoured to destroy.

From their outset in 1950, Dinamo Tirana sourced their best players by using the same method as their predecessors Partizani; *klubet e vampirëve* – vampire clubs – sucking the life force from immediate rivals.

The mechanics of club transfers were thus. Good players were removed from their parent clubs on the premise of military service. While active in the 'services' the player would represent one the clubs of the regime, Partizani or Dinamo. This would free a player of any ties they had to their previous club.

After military service, the superclubs would offer these 'free agents' improved housing in the better suburbs of Tirana along with cushy, well-paid, undemanding part-time jobs in one of the city's many administrative offices or faculties as an incentive to join their team on a permanent basis.

It was a honeystick that the majority of Albanian footballers willingly grasped. Yes, you were 'free' to return to your parent club after your service – at least that was the rhetoric – but those who didn't take the bait were often victimised, liquidated and imprisoned, or worse. More later.

Vllaznia were forced to surrender Bahri Kavaja, Muhamet Vila, Hamdi Bakalli (back in Shkodër after a season with Partizani) and the wonderfully gifted forward Pal Mirashi to the Dinamo cause.

Prior to the 1950 edition of the Kampionati Kombetar, before a ball was kicked in anger, Partizani – under the duress of the *Sigurimi* – released four of their footballers to the fledgling Dinamo club: Sulejman Vathi, Xhevdet Shaqiri, Qemal Teliti and Zihni Gjinali, who assumed the role of player-coach.

Partizani were suffering the same indignities that had befallen *Tirona*, Vllaznia et al after their own formation in 1946; quality players unethically absorbed by a direct sporting competitor.

Circumstance suggested the regime wanted Dinamo to be crowned champions in their inaugural season. A Dinamo win, from an outward viewpoint, would go some distance in rebuilding trust and credibility in the domestic game, while pushing the regime organ, the fledgling *Sigurimi*, into direct, national focus.

If this was the plan, it was executed with an unfairness and essence of conspiracy that pervaded both society and sport in Albania.

Having finished the 1950 season level on points – Dinamo scoring 60 goals and conceding six, Partizani scoring 77 times while conceding 10 and both with identical records of played 16, won 14, drew one, lost one – modern rubrics would have established Partizani as champions, their goal difference hugely superior to that of their new city rival at + 67 compared to +54.

However, Dinamo were awarded the 1950 title using the deeply contentious method of goal ratio, which plotted the number of goals scored divided by the number of goals conceded.

The same method would be exploited five years later, when Partizani and Dinamo were again level on points with the former's goal difference equating to +81 while the latter's stood at +65; Dinamo were again, improbably, crowned champions.

The flawed nature of FSHF's decision-making process, coerced by regime interference, tainted what had promised to be an exciting era in Albanian football.

Despite moral anomalies surrounding the national game, *stadiumet* throughout the country were full as football consolidated its status as the sport of choice among the natives.

Dinamo Tirana won four consecutive titles between 1950 and 1953, but they failed to win the hearts of Albanians. They were a functional, efficient side with good players, but the finest player in the league – the true legend-maker – evaded their slipstream in the early part of 1950, falling into the waiting net of Partizani.

In the winter of 1931 on Xhamija Sherif (now Rruga e Ali Demit), east of Tirana town centre, a child was born into a *Tirona*-supporting family who has since become the yardstick by which all forwards – Albanian or otherwise – are measured.

The boy grew up watching the great *Tirona* sides of the 1940s play at the Shallvare and dreamed of keeping goal for his beloved club, practising the skills he'd learned while watching his favourite stoppers, Flamurtari's Dodë Tahiri, Niko Dovana of Teuta Durrës and *Tirona*'s own Giacomo Poselli.

Bearing more than a fleeting resemblance to American cinematic anti-hero James Dean, Refik Resmja joined *Tirona* – renamed Puna at the time – aged 15, debuting in February 1948 in place of his idol, Poselli.

During a fated training session months later, Resmja took respite from goalkeeping duties and played in a left-sided forward role, so impressing Selman Stërmasi that *Tirona*'s coaching luminary started him in the next league fixture as a striker. He would score four times in six outfield games for *Tirona*, but his strength, guile, intelligence and ability to score goals would quickly earn him a reputation as a player of uncommon potential.

Prior to the 1950 season, Resmja served a short term of national service before Partizani robbed *Tirona* of their new-found asset. Partizani afforded the 19-year-old the tactical freedom that enabled him to thrive in an already powerful, attacking side.

Despite Dinamo's dubious title success that year, the season concluded with Resmja as the league's top scorer. It was merely an appetiser for what unfolded during the unbelievable, record-shattering season of 1951.

The 1951 Kampionati Kombetar commenced clouded by the shadow of a recent defection scandal. Two Dinamo first-teamers, Bahri Kavaja and Sulejman Vathi, absconded to the West during a short stay in Istanbul after representing Albania during the 1950 international winter tour that took in games against Czechoslovakia, Hungary and Romania. It would be the Albanian national team's last excursion outside its borders for seven years.

When the season began, it did so amid an avalanche of goals; Resmja netting six times against Puna Berat in an 14-0 annihilation and adding a further seven during yet another double-figures tanking, 11-0 against Puna Fier.

The goals continued to flow effortlessly, Resmja completing the 1951 season having scored a barely conceivable 59 times in just 23 league games at an average of 2.7 goals per game – still the highest seasonal goal ratio ever in world football. It remains the most goals scored in a season by an individual player in the Albanian top tier. Resmja's goal haul included ten hat-tricks, the most in a league season. Resmja would be the Albanian league's top scorer for six years consecutively between 1951 and 1956. He is Partizani's all-time top scorer with 180 league goals.

After watching Resmja play in a friendly against a Magyar Select XI in 1952, legendary Hungarian coach Gusztáv Sebes spoke of his ability, 'Refik Resmja is worthy of playing alongside the great Ferenc Puskás.'

Resmja also earned a notable admirer in Bulgarian international and national team coach Stefan Bozhkov. 'Refik Resmja,' Bozhkov announced, in no mood for understatement, 'is among the greatest.'

Despite Resmja's omnipotence – Partizani finished the season having scored 136 while conceding only ten – they failed to hoist any silverware, finishing second by two points to a Dinamo side buoyed by the abundant talents of Pal Mirashi, player-coach Zinhi Gjinali, Qamil Teliti and the brilliant fluidity of Skënder Jareci, a recent acquisition from Ylli I Kuq (Red Star) Durrës, who were soon to become Lokomotiva.

To add insult to injury, *Dinamovitet* – dynamism; their adopted epithet – also captured the Kupa e Republikës and secured back-to-back doubles by beating Partizani 3-2 in the final at Stadiumi Qemal Stafa.

1952 and 1953 observed further double-doubles for Dinamo under Gjinali. A key performer in these successes was the shrewd, intelligent *mezalla*, Shyqyri Rreli, acquired from *Tirona*, another highly skilled addition to a Dinamo squad caulked with creative ballast. Rreli would go on to manage the national under-21 and senior side – twice – before returning to 17 Nëntori as coach in 1987, steering *Tirona* to successive titles in 1988 and 1989.

The regime's creation of a duopoly of socialist-branded superclubs was, again, losing kudos among serious football fans and academics with Dinamo winning everything domestically.

In 1954, Partizani appointed Myslym Alla as manager. Alla had been part of Selman Stërmasi's hugely dominant *Tirona* side of the 1930s and early 1940s, which included Naim Kryeziu and Riza Lushta.

Partizani's youthful new boss – a mere 35 years old when he took the reins – had enjoyed a successful spell as national team coach, masterminding two outstanding victories at the Qemal Stafa in November and December of 1952 against a Czechoslovakia side that would later qualify for the 1954 World Cup in Switzerland.

The former *Tirona* stalwart looked to impart the innate attacking philosophies instilled in him by his mentor, Stërmasi, on to a Partizani team in serious need of a lift – and a trophy. And Partizani, playing a brand of football rich in imagination and potency, subsequently re-found their groove during the 1954 campaign.

Resmja, augmented by the technical mastery of Loro Boriçi and rich skills of another recent recruit, ball-playing *libero* Roza Haxhiu – a cultured defender-cum-midfielder who'd garnered the attention of Italian club Lazio, earning the Romans an icy rebuke from FSHF and The Party – guided *Demat e Kuq* to their first title in five years.

Born Abdurrahman Haxhiu in 1930, the technically faultless Roza had been such an attractive child that his looks prompted a local nun to exclaim, 'Bello come una rosa!' Her comments translated to, 'As beautiful as a rose!' Haxhiu, a man with undeniable film-star looks, went on to become something of a national pin-up, retaining the pseudonym Roza until his premature death in 1964.

It was Resmja's first Albanian league winners' medal, Partizani collectively scoring 93 times in 22 games, 37 more than their closest rivals, Dinamo.

Notwithstanding a narrow Republic Cup loss to Dinamo, Partizani had found a way to become winners once more. They would've retained their title in 1955 too, but for the egregiously partial re-use of the dreaded goal ratio method.

The disappointment of relinquishing their crown in such profoundly unfair circumstances, for a second time, weighed heavy on Alla's men and, for the first time in six years, Partizani surrendered meekly to an imperious Dinamo in 1956 despite outscoring them – again – in the league.

Failure cost Alla his job. He was replaced at the season's end by Rexhep Spahiu, a veteran of Albania's Balkan Cup triumph ten years earlier.

It proved to be Loro Boriçi's final season at Partizani in a playing capacity. He would return, intermittently, from his player-manager role at Spartaku Tirana and, later, as the national coach (1957–62) to assist with training before rejoining the club as the coach on a full-time basis in 1962.

Aside from the predatory brilliance of Refik Resmja, Spahiu inherited from Alla a team filled with an abundance of extraordinary talent.

Lin Shllaku, acquired from Vllaznia at the end of the 1956 season, was a creative midfield technician with vision, skill and a range of passing that would see him win 14 trophies with Partizani and captain the national team for seven years.

Kolec Kraja, a striker and product of a now-embedded youth system, was nimble and fast with a cultured right foot. Kraja would later become the first Albanian to score in the European Cup during a 1962/63 home tie against the Swedes of IFK Norrköping, a game spoiled by repeated incidents of stone-throwing.

The diamond in Partizani's gem-encrusted crown was Robert Jashari – *Bert* to the Partizani *tifozët* – a forward of flair, pace and astounding close control.

Jashari, Tirana-born to Italian-Albanian parents, was another Albanian footballer with cinematic looks, and he would prove to be the generational glue that bonded the Partizani greats of the 1950s and 1960s. *Bert* replaced the departed king, Loro Boriçi, in the forward line alongside Resmja, later providing support for another footballing colossus in Panajot Pano, Albania's player of the 1960s. He would also score Albania's first goal in a World Cup qualifying campaign, against Bertie Peacock's Northern Ireland in Belfast in May of 1965.

It's said that before stepping aboard the team bus at Partizani's Palace of Pioneers training facility prior to away games, Jashari would serenade his young wife, Evin, promising her, 'I will score a goal for you today, my love.' Even in dystopian Albania, romance still found the air with which to sustain itself.

Akin to Pano, Jashari as a player was compared to the great Ferenc Puskás – the go-to, Stalinist-friendly footballing comparison in Albania during the post-war era – and, latterly, to Louis van Gaal as a coach due to his adherence to 4-3-3 and focus on the interchangeability of player roles; an Albanian variant of *totaalvoetbal*.

It's commonly extolled that Jashari never smoked a cigarette or took a drink in his life; a purist in impure times.

Yet when it came to winning, Jashari wasn't impartial to moral compromise.

At the tail-end of the 1981/82 season, during his tenure as coach of 31 Korriku Burreli whom he led to promotion as Division Two champions in both 1981 and 1983, Jashari demonstrated a penchant for the dark arts; the overtly un-socialist concept of gamesmanship.

Burrel was known for two things aside from football: its political prison and its apple trees. Eventually, all the trees were shorn to fire the nearby ferrochrome plant. The prison continued to clip its inmates long after the trees were gone.

Thrust into a two-way relegation dogfight involving his 31 Korriku side and Labinoti, with Jashari's charges desperate for a win, the club from *qyteti i mollëve* – the city of apples – embarked on their penultimate game of the season, at home to Flamurtari. Their opponents required points to bolster a title charge that had seen them rise to second place in the Kampionati Kombetar, behind leaders *Tirona*, trailing only on goal difference.

Labinoti, in an end-of-season twist that couldn't have been more dramatic if it had been Hollywood-scripted, faced *Tirona* at Stadiumi Qemal Stafa.

As Sul Trumci, the groundsman at Stadiumi i Burrelit – Burrel Stadium – performed his pre-match duties, he was approached by Jashari, who instructed Trumci to hang the old goal nets up.

During the warm-up, the match officials deemed the nets unfit for purpose; the kick-off was delayed by 30 minutes while Trumci put new nets in place. This halt in proceedings enabled Jashari and his Burreli team to keep track of happenings in the *Tirona*-Labinoti game on Radio Tirana. 31 Korriku beat Flamurtari 2-1, while Labinoti lost 2-0 in Tirana. Jashari's side were relegated, but the incident was indicative of the great man's win-at-all-costs mentality.

For the two seasons that followed, Partizani dominated the domestic game, beating Dinamo 3-1 in the 1957 league play-off while comfortably ousting Puna Durrës 2-0 in the Kupa e Republikës Final, both at Stadiumi Qemal Stafa.

In 1958, Partizani took the title ahead of Besa with Dinamo finishing a lowly fourth – the worst league performance in the *Blutë*'s short history – tightening their stranglehold on both trophies by hammering the re-emerging south-easterners of Skënderbeu Korçë 4-0 in the cup.

In late 1958, Rexhep Spahiu took his confident group of Partizani players to the Spartakiad Football Tournament in the German Democratic Republic (East Germany), contested between army-affiliated clubs from the communist countries of the world.

Albanian clubs had never played competitively outside of the country's hermetically sealed borders – *Demat e Kuq*'s first European Cup appearance was still four years away – due, in part, to the defection scandal of 1950, with the Spartakiad, featuring a surfeit of talented, tough opponents, providing a taster of things to come for Partizani.

The hosts were keen to display their credentials as a self-reliant, socialist nation. The GDR's economy had rapidly grown and – as was the case in Albania – were still riding the upward cusp of the Marxist–Leninist wave.

This was reflected in the GDR's painstaking preparations for the tournament. The games would be played at East Germany's triad of recently constructed stadia, which represented new bastions of socialist architecture: Walter-Ulbricht Stadion in Berlin, Magdeburg's Ernst Grube Stadion and the visually arresting, cavernous behemoth, the Zentralstadion, Leipzig.

The roster of teams included CCA București – the precursor for Steaua (pronounced 'Stair-wah' for those in the know) – already established as the finest club side in Romania; Dukla Praha, recently crowned champions of Czechoslovakia;

Bulgarian champions CDNA (CSKA) Sofia; and the GDR's representatives – and DDR Oberliga title holders – ASK Vorwärts Berlin.

All of the aforementioned teams would evolve into serious competitors in European football. For Partizani, it signified a first chance to test their ability against credible foreign opposition.

However, their opening fixture would pair them against opponents less fancied than themselves: the Vietnamese army club, Cong Hanoi, in Magdeburg.

Partizani's coaching team, Rexhep Spahiu and Sllave Llambi, afforded their side licence to have fun against the South-East Asians, Partizani storming into a 4-0 lead within 20 minutes through Gani Merja, Kolec Kraja and Refik Resmja (two) to effectively end the contest before it had really started.

The Albanians eased up on their inferior rivals, Robert Jashari completing a 5-1 rout with ten minutes left on the clock.

Their second game, also in Magdeburg, decided who would progress beyond the group stage; Partizani facing CCA.

In a far more evenly contested encounter that could've edged either way, Miço Ndini, Partizani's tireless left-winger, conjured the winner on 70 minutes, hammering home from inside the box for 1-0.

Partizani would remain in the familiar environs of Magdeburg, where they would be paired with Dukla Praha in the quarter-final.

The Czechoslovakians contained free-scoring Jaroslav Borovička, midfield anchor Svatopluk Pluskal and the brilliant Josef Masopust, all of whom would make key contributions when leading their country to the 1962 World Cup Final in Chile.

The Karel Kolský-led side that travelled to East Germany were fresh off the back of winning the Czechoslovak First

League title, finishing ahead of Spartak Prague Sokolovo (Sparta) on goal difference, and were overwhelming favourites to progress to the semis.

But Partizani blunted Dukla's weapons, tenacious hard work and no shortage of talent taking the tie into scoreless extra time. Lifted by their successful, collective act of attrition, Partizani grew, Refik Resmja sending the Albanians and their small entourage into raptures by rifling in the only goal of the game with just seven minutes remaining.

Partizani's imperious journey was predicted to end, victory over Dukla sending the Albanians to Berlin for a semi-final *tête-à-tête* with the representatives from the host nation, ASK Vorwärts.

On home turf, Vorwärts were an irresistible force. Unbeaten throughout the 1958 DDR Oberliga campaign, *Die Gelden und Roten* – the Yellow and Reds – featured regular performers from the East German national side in goalkeeper Karl-Heinz Spickenagel, midfielders Werner Unger and Lothar Meyer and the formidable, rough-and-tumble strike partnership of Horst Assmy and Günther Wirth.

The first half at the Walter-Ulbricht ebbed and flowed with Vorwärts, roared on by an all-East German home support, the better side without seriously threatening enigmatic keeper Sulejman Maliqati's goal.

Tall, lithe and spectacular, Maliqati was a stark, visual presence arrayed in black jersey and shorts, reminiscent of the great USSR stopper, Lev Yashin. It was an image choice that earned Maliqati the sobriquet *Mace e zezë* – the Black Cat – his wiry, long-limbed, feline elasticity perfectly attuned to the role of goalkeeping.

Maliqati suffered the ignominy of keeping goal during the ill-fated 12-0 defeat to the emergent powerhouse of international football, Hungary, on his full international debut in 1950; the *Shqiponjat* destroyed in Budapest by the superb *Aranycsapat*. As an introduction to international football, it couldn't have got much worse. But he was well protected by a diligent and determined Partizani rearguard action in Berlin.

In the 35th minute, and against the run of play, Partizani launched a breakaway assault on the Berliners' goal, Resmja's pass finding Mico Ndini who guided a left-footed finish beyond Spickenagel to give *Demat e Kuq* a flattering half-time advantage.

Post-break, Partizani yielded to a concentrated wave of East German pressure, Wirth temporarily freeing himself from the shackles of Fatbardh Deliallisi and Roza Haxhiu to head beyond a rooted Maliqati to level the score at 1-1.

Any anticipation of a total Vorwärts turnaround was muted by a Partizani side that remained calm, an imperious Robert Jashari bossing the hole linking midfield to attack; Jashari's assurance in possession, coupled with his insatiable work ethic transmitting to his team-mates.

The East Germans, increasingly frustrated at their lack of tangible progress, pushed too hard, leaving areas of space that a technician of Jashari's copious ability was wont to exploit.

With 11 minutes remaining, Jashari skipped his marker and squared the ball to Simon Dëda, who planted a decisive finish past Spickenagel; 2-1 Partizani.

Vorwärts, fatally wounded, offered little in the way of resistance, Partizani completing the shock of the tournament in the hosts' own backyard. As the Albanians celebrated, home fans in heavy, green army coats filed from the stadium in a shared state of bemusement and shock. Rexhep Spahiu and Sllave Llambi had effected a tactical miracle.

Vorwärts ran away with the 1958 DDR Oberliga title, scoring more and conceding fewer than any of their rivals, finishing a convincing six points ahead of second-placed SC Motor Jena – latterly Carl Zeiss Jena. They would become regulars in European competition, beating Wolverhampton

Wanderers, Bologna, Benfica, Feyenoord, Juventus and PSV on home soil in subsequent years, but Partizani's tenacity and canny intelligence had wrestled the East Germans into submission in their hometown of Berlin. They would travel to Leipzig to face Krum Milev's CDNA (CSKA) Sofia at the magnificent Zentralstadion in Leipzig.

Milev captained Bulgaria during the 1946 Balkan Cup. Already established as a club legend having led CDNA to eight Bulgarian titles since 1948, Milev comfortably guided his side past the Korean Army Club of Pyongyang and Beijing Army Club in the Spartakiad group stage, seeing them ruthlessly dispatch CCA București 4-0 in the quarter-final before edging past USSR's CSKA Moscow by the odd goal in seven in a thrilling semi-final.

On 28 September, Partizani Tirana and CDNA Sofia stepped on to the pitch at Zentralstadion before 100,000 expectant spectators. It is, to date, the largest attendance *Demat e Kuq* have played to.

Sofia were a capable unit, Bulgarian internationals Kiril Rakarov, Manol Manolov and Nikola Kovachev providing a solid defensive base, Gavril Stoyanov, Stefan Bozhov and Georgi Dimitrov shoring things up in the middle of the park with Krum Yanev, Panayot Panayotov and Dimitar Milanov offering a reliable steam of goals.

As a contest, the game was high in technique, keenly fought and incredibly tight. Its destiny hinged on a one-minute spell shortly after the break, Refik Resmja – later voted Player of the Tournament – manoeuvring the ball on to his favoured left foot before smashing a 25-yard strike against the underside of the Bulgarian crossbar.

A minute later, the ball was in the Albanian net, Rakarov thrashing a free kick from distance past a motionless Sulejman Maliqati.

Rakarov's splendid strike, despite forlorn Partizani attempts to restore parity, proved the winner, *Demat e Kuq* falling a small distance short at the final hurdle.

Despite their loss they returned home as heroes, spiking a national hunger to see Albanian footballers compete on an elevated European and world stage.

Sadly, the talented *libero*, Roza Haxhiu, would play no further part in the Partizani story. He sustained a severe head injury during a friendly tournament in Pleven, Bulgaria in late 1958. Complications caused by the injury would end his career and, six years later, his life aged only 33; a crushing loss to Partizani and to Albanian football.

Without Roza, Partizani would achieve comparable success at the 1963 Spartakiad in Vietnam, under the joint tutelage of Loro Boriçi and Rexhep Spahiu, beating their 1958 victors CDNA Sofia in the opener 2-1 before hammering Honvéd 4-0 – a Panajot Pano strike followed by a Robert Jashari hat-trick doing the damage – to comfortably navigate their group. Despite rarely sharing jokes on or off the field, Pano and Jashari enjoyed an on-field telepathy born of professionalism, intelligence and a mutual will to win.

A hat-trick by Pano saw off Vorwärts 3-1 in the quarter-final before Pavllo Bukoviku's solitary goal accounted for Honvéd – again – in the semi. As in 1958, the final was to prove a game too far for Partizani, losing 2-0 after extra time to CSKA Moscow in Hanoi.

In the 17 years since their formation, Partizani and Dinamo had dominated the domestic league in Albania; Partizani winning ten titles to Dinamo's seven, changing the landscape of the national game.

Via an era ushered in by the iron will of Enver Hoxha and The Party, Albanian football was no longer a democratic pursuit; favouritism, nepotism and political intervention was robbing the sport of its integrity and purity.

Yet due to the fortitude and perseverance of the old guard of the national game, all of this was all about to change. Briefly, at least.

Chapter Seven

That's Not My Name: the Great Club Name Cull of 1957

'Ti Shqipëri, më jep nder, më jep emrin
Shqipëtar' – 'You Albania, you give me
honour, you give me the name Albanian'

Motto of the People's Socialist Republic of
Albania (1946–91)

IN 1948, tensions between the USSR and Yugoslavia saw Albania detach itself from Yugoslavian freehold, allying with Joseph Stalin's Soviet Union and the other eastern European communist satellite states.

For Enver Hoxha, a Stalin devotee, it heralded an era when Albania faithfully imitated Stalinist dogma. Huge purges and heavy Soviet-funded industrialisation became Stalin's great legacy to Albania.

In the arena of physical recreation, sport clubs were founded to a Soviet template adopting Soviet-style names.

After Stalin's death in 1953, and subsequent denouncement by incoming leader Nikita Khrushchev, the relationship between the new Soviet premier and Stalin fanboy, Hoxha, steadily eroded until its total collapse in 1961.

Hoxha argued that Khrushchev was trying to build a Soviet-led communist empire, wishing to convert autonomous socialist countries into Soviet provinces, a view that shaped the Albanian leader's behaviour during the ensuing fallout.

In April 1956, the communist parties of the Warsaw Pact convened in Tirana tasked with a Soviet-led agenda demanding the swift removal of any remnants of Stalinism from eastern Europe. Hoxha, the obvious target, responded by purging The Party of any Soviet influence, promoting only friends and accomplices to the Albanian Central Committee and Politburo.

Khrushchev was incensed, setting in motion a sequence of events that would urge Albania's departure from the Eurocommunist clique and force Hoxha into alliance with Maoist China.

By the close of the 1957 Kampionati Kombetar, a wave of Albanianisation engulfed the country, with a widespread renaming of anything that failed to conform with Hoxha's imaginings of what was Albanian. Street names were removed from the walls of the big cities in an act borne of paranoia designed to confuse map-wielding invaders in the event of a potential attack, and The Party pocked the landscape and roadsides of inner Albania with concrete bunkers and border reinforcements.

Hoxha's Albanianisation policy proved inherent from the womb, with The Party submitting a list to the people containing regime-approved child names either of Illyrian descent or newly constructed monikers deemed suitable for the country's new generation of Marxist–Leninist revolutionaries.

The same would apply to the football teams competing in the Kampionati. Of the eight clubs in the 1957 championship, discounting Partizani and Dinamo, five used the prefix Puna, meaning work, a tag derived from Soviet influence – those from Korçë, Vlorë, Durrës, Kavajë and Tirana (*Tirona*).

All five had their names compulsorily changed to embody the credo of Albanianism. Puna Korçë reverted back to their pre-war name of Skënderbeu (Skanderbeg), named after the

Albanian national hero, Gjergj Kastrioti, who was known as Skanderbeg.

Vlorë also retook their original name, Flamurtari (Flag Bearer), as did Besa (Honour) of Kavajë. Durrës adopted the name Lokomotiva in a nod to their new-found post-war identity as the centre of Stalinist Albania's railroad industry.

Puna Tirana – *Tirona* – were renamed 17 Nëntori to denote 17 November, the date of Socialist Albania's Liberation Day.

The eighth club, Spartaku Tirana, the team of the Albanian Trades Unions, diffusing a strong after-scent of Sovietisation, were later disbanded in 1959.

A further nine clubs outside of the top tier surrendered their Puna prefix to adopt more socialist-friendly names, with a further Spartaku club – Pogradec – changing theirs to Ylli I Kuq (Red Star). The process of Albanianisation, in all aspects of national life, was ascendant.

Comrade Enver's attention to what many would deem superficial detail was the sharpened tool that knitted the tightly woven fabric of Albanian society, binding and snaring its people. In changing the names of people, places, even football teams to something wholly Albanian, Hoxha was systematically erasing a history when Albania at least played some part in the world's bigger picture.

In 1992, contained within the extensive library in Enver Hoxha's house in Blloku, Tirana, amid the former leader's personal library containing over 70,000 books, a copy of George Orwell's dark parable, *1984*, was uncovered.

For those who haven't read the book, it contains a chilling citation that defines the toxic nature of misappropriated power, 'He who controls the past controls the future. He who controls the present controls the past.'

It isn't beyond reasonable reckoning to imagine that Hoxha read Orwell's bleak, prophetic words, using them as his maxim rather than dispelling them as egregious components of a dark, cautionary tale. Hoxha understood that by changing the names of a few football teams, he was – in small measure – controlling the present and the past while steering the future.

It wouldn't be the last time football would be used by The Party to meter control, causing Albania's past, present and future to sneak into a blunt and ugly focus.

Iconic Games

Partizani 1 Dinamo 0

Kampionati Kombetar play-off final replay

2 July 1961

Stadiumi Dinamo, Tirana

Attendance: 15,000

Partizani: Sulejman Maliqati, Fatbardh Deliallisi, Miço Papadhopulli, Iljaz Dingu, Miço Ndini, Gani Merja, Kolec Kraja, Pavllo Bukoviku, Panajot Pano, Tomor Shehu, Sotir Seferaj

Head coach/*Kryetrajneri*: Rexhep Spahiu

Dinamo: Qoshja, Çaushi, Skënder Halili, Qamil Halluni, H. Verria, Skender Jareci, Lorenc Vorfi, Nikollë Bespalla, Mehdi Bushati, Stavri Lubonja, Fiqiri Duro

Head coach/*Kryetrajneri*: Zyber Konçi

Referee/*Arbitri*: H. Hysenaj

1961 witnessed Albania in a state of transition. From a footballing aspect, it was the last season in which the spring-to-autumn schedule would be adhered to. The 1962/63 edition of the Kampionati Kombetar observed a change to the autumn-to-spring season widely accepted by the rest of the European continent.

For the years that had preceded 1961, a whiff of uncertainty had pervaded regarding the country's relationship with their Soviet allies. When the Sino-Soviet split created a rupture inside the global communist community in 1960, Albania sided with the Chinese, becoming Beijing's only European ally.

Comrade Enver saw de-Stalinisation and Moscow's subsequent thaw with Titoist Yugoslavia as a danger to both his rule and Albanian national security. Hoxha had good reason to be wary of Khrushchev as many of the reasons the Soviet premier used to condemn Stalin were pertinent to his own reign.

The Soviets, in a last-ditch attempt to keep Albania's errant leadership onside, issued a loan of over £84m to Albania in late 1957 to subsidise The Party's forthcoming Third Five-Year Plan, chalking off further debts of £80m which Albania owed the USSR. Hoxha hedged his bets, taking Khrushchev's financial sweetener while awaiting further developments.

When China's fallout with the USSR became world news, Hoxha artfully seized his chance to join Beijing in unified defiance against what Chinese and Albanian politicians dubbed 'Soviet revisionism'.

With the Cuban Missile Crisis dominating the broadsheets, Khrushchev quickly lost his appetite to fight with nondescript Albania, removing Russian dreadnoughts and submarines from the Albanian naval bases of Sazan Island and the southern city sea port of Korca in preparation for more pivotal battles.

For Chairman Mao, it offered the prospect of a tactical base in Europe from which to challenge Soviet political dominance. For a vulnerable Hoxha, it provided another 'big brother' who could fight his awkward battles. Just as quickly as the Soviet armada had fled, the Chinese fleet arrived.

It was against this backdrop of political intrigue, bluff, counter-bluff and downright mistrust that the 1961 season began in the spring. Dinamo, double winners in 1960, were rightly regarded as the favourites for the forthcoming campaign, Zyber Konçi's *Blutë* having lost just once – 3-1 to Partizani – during the previous season.

For Rexhep Spahiu-led Partizani, champions in 1957, 1958 and 1959, it offered the opportunity to reassert their dominance in wake of their rivals' emphatic triumph of 1960.

There was the promise of a realistic challenge from the club in East Tirana, 17 Nëntori, who were playing some delightful, expansive football under the tutelage of Myslym Alla. The *bardhë e blutë* were still a few seasons away from launching a serious challenge, although their time would soon come.

In the campaign prelude, the *Kupa e Kongresit* – the Congress Cup – Partizani expressed seasonal intent, tearing into *Dinamovitet* with vengeful hunger. Refik Resmja, still in wonderful fettle at the age of 30, banged in a splendid hat-trick to win the pre-season curtain-raiser 3-0 in *Demat e Kuq*'s favour.

Later, with eight weeks of the season played and Partizani and Dinamo neck-and-neck, it was the red side of Tirana that was celebrating again. Pavllo Bukoviku, Robert Jashari and Resmja added the goals to another dominant Partizani performance, Stavri Lubonja's consolation a mere statistic in a one-sided 3-1 triumph.

When the sides met for a third time on 11 June, in the late-afternoon balminess of a packed Stadiumi Dinamo – Comrade Enver himself present in the *Tribuna* seated alongside his 'faithful friends' Kadri Hazbiu (head of the *Sigurimi*; a Dinamo fan) and Petrit Dume (deputy minister of defence; an ardent Partizani supporter) – Dinamo were three points adrift of Partizani with two games remaining.

Ninety minutes later they had reduced the deficit to one point, a 2-1 triumph courtesy of strikes by Stavri Lubonja and Skënder Jareci – Sotir Seferaj replying – sending the Kampionati Kombetar to its final day.

Despite Dinamo trailing big on goal difference, the goal ratio anomalies of 1950 and 1955 had caused a rethink among the hierarchy at FSHF. Goal difference and goal ratio would no longer decide the destiny of the Kampionati –

points attained being the only measure of overall success. The logistics were simple: a Dinamo win married with Partizani's failure to win their final game against 17 Nëntori would leave the title race tied.

To add further old-school texture to the exhilarating mix, the games would take place on different days. Dinamo played first on 22 June, fulfilling their side of the bargain by walloping Labinoti 6-0 at Stadiumi Dinamo. A day later, with Dinamo's direct opponents knowing what was required of them, a late *Tirona* equaliser – earning them a 2-2 draw – robbed Partizani of the cut-and-dried conclusion they craved, leaving both teams level on points.

So, on 29 June – a Thursday – a play-off was arranged to be played at Stadiumi Dinamo deciding the 1961 edition of the National Championship.

The rules for the fixture were, in themselves, revolutionary. If the game remained tied after 90 minutes, 30 minutes of extra time would be played. If there was still no outright winner, a second match would be played. If the second match was undecided after 90 minutes and extra time, a second period of extra time split into two further 15-minute segments would be played; 150 minutes in total. The salient caveat was that if a 'golden goal' were scored in this extra period of overtime, play would end and the destiny of the title would be decided instantly. If the game remained level after 150 minutes, lots would be drawn. Penalty shoot-outs wouldn't be introduced for a further two years.

Anton Mazreku, head of FSHF and the organisational brains behind this format, also commented on this epic coming-together from his seat at the rear of the *Tribuna*. Mazreku, a seasoned sports reporter, cut his journalistic teeth as co-founder and the editor-in-chief of the *Sporti Shqiptar* – Albanian Sport – broadsheet (latterly *Sporti Popullor*), the first authoritative Albanian language sports publication. His calm, measured, informed opinions made him the perfect choice when Radio Tirana sought a commanding voice for its live transmissions.

Droves of Tiranian workers converged on the Stadiumi Dinamo post-shift to view a match that was as tense and tight as the Kampionati itself. In fading late-afternoon heat, the dual behemoths of the Albanian game locked horns.

In the opening moments of a titanic battle, Dinamo's Nikollë Bespalla skied a virtually unmissable chance over the Partizani crossbar. The air of profligacy continued, Partizani's Kolec Kraja's cross-shot somehow evading the oncoming traffic populating the Dinamo six-yard box. Even the usually efficient Refik Resmja and Panajot Pano were having an off-day, both squandering presentable chances, hindered – it must be acknowledged – by the notable contributions of Dhimitër Qoshja in the Dinamo goal.

After 90 minutes the game remained scoreless. Deep into the dying embers of extra time, with both sides visibly fatigued, the same applied. Yet, with three minutes left on the clock, Robert Jashari called upon his last reserves of energy, manufacturing half a yard of space on the edge of the Dinamo area prior to feeding Resmja's overlap to his left. Taking one touch to set himself, Partizani's legendary goal machine prodded an improbable late opener.

Partizani players and fans celebrated wildly, convinced they had regained their crown. But within a minute it was the Dinamo fans in a state of euphoria, Stavri Lubonja thrashing in a bobbling loose ball from 15 yards; 1-1.

When the final whistle blew moments later, both sets of players hugged in a show of mutual congratulation and respect rarely observed in the modern era. Partizani had been the marginally better side, but Dinamo refused to relinquish their crown without a hell of a scrap. The National Championship, still in the balance, would go to a second play-off.

Sunday, 2 July 1961 was prescribed as a suitable date for the second and, ultimately, deciding match of the 1961 title race.

The *sheshis* and *lokals* of inner-city Tirana were lit with excitement, debate and conjecture – who would be crowned the new *Kampionët e Shqipërisë*? It was a fervour that transposed itself to the Stadiumi Dinamo, an arena that, by the 5pm kick-off, was elevated to a heaving jeroboam of expectation, apprehension and dread.

Partizani's talisman, Refik Resmja, was consigned to the substitutes' bench by coach Spahiu, his exertions four days earlier rendering him unfit to start in this most vital of end-of-season encounters.

His omission served as fuel to a Dinamo side that started brightly, Skënder Jareci heading an early chance wide of Sulejman Maliqati's *gate*. Mehdi Bushati, well placed inside the Partizani box, wasted a further chance for the Blues minutes later, firing wide amid a melee of bodies. It heralded a reaction from *Demat e Kuq* that almost brought an opening goal, Panajot Pano and Sotir Seferaj both going close with speculative shots.

However, Dinamo largely controlled a tight opening half. When Pano, on the stroke of half-time, screwed his drive wide of the target with Qoshja beaten, the suggestion was that this was going to be *Dinamovitet*'s day.

The second half entered into a war of attrition with no quarter given or expected. Dinamo controlled possession with *libero* Skënder Halili instigating much that was good about their play, but their dominance failed to yield a goal. Extra time came and went, Dinamo ascendant yet toothless.

After 120 minutes, the final entered an exciting new phase – the domain of the golden goal.

For aficionados of the beautiful game, the golden goal was introduced – and became an accepted addition to modern football – at the World Cup hosted by France in 1998 after it was initially trialled in youth competitions in 1993. But the Albanian variant of *goli i artë* predated its inception by at least 32 years. And it was upon this wholly Albanian invention that the 1961 Kampionati Kombetar would hinge.

In the 122nd minute of the second match – the 242nd minute of this momentous contest – the championship was finally decided. A probing ball to the left of the field from the omni-sharp Kolec Kraja found Pano, the league's leading scorer that season, in a pocket of useable space. As Pano advanced, Dinamo's defence backed off, allowing Partizani's pocket Merlin licence to advance to the corner of the 18-yard box and smash an unstoppable left-footed drive beyond the desperate clutches of Qoshja.

Joyous scenes amid the Partizani contingent welcomed the peal of *arbitri* Hysenaj's final whistle, the Dinamo supporters – as is customary on such occasions – making a prompt, pained beeline for the nearest exit. The *Blutë* had been the better side in the second match, their on-field primacy cruelly unrewarded on the day, although only the most ardent, one-eyed Dinamo fan would dare argue that Partizani hadn't deserved their success over the seasonal *piece*.

For the scorer of the winning goal, 22-year-old Panajot Pano, it was his first of four Kampionati titles and it was a strike that would herald a return to Partizani supremacy, the army club retaining their crown in both 1962/63 and 1963/64.

For Dinamo, it signposted a title drought that would last for six years; a famine that would only be sated in the most dubious of circumstances.

It also presaged a change in Albania, in both society and in sport. Chinese communism would influence the decision-making of The Party, with Hoxha adapting many of Mao's preachings to his own monstrous template.

On the outside lane, in the race for football sovereignty, a dormant ghost had risen and was keen to haunt the 'New Firm' of Albanian football. And haunt it would, unleashing even darker spectres that would spook national football and The Party hierarchy in the coming decade.

Chapter Eight

1957–1967 – Renaissance and Retribution: the Giant and the King

WHEN *TIRONA* (under the guise of 17 Nëntori), tutored by ex-Partizani coach Myslym Alla, won the Albanian title at the close of the 1964/65 season – their first since 1942 – and retained it the following year, narrowly ahead of Partizani on both occasions, there was a suggestion that regime interference was on the wane and that equality, in sport at least, had returned.

Those with the acumen to look beyond the two-horse race that the Kampionati Kombetar had become foresaw a renaissance in the country's domestic game that had been in the offing since the latter part of the 1950s.

By 1958, definite markers had been planted indicating a revival in the *bardhë e blutë* corner of the capital, with a rebuild in place that promised to reseat *Tirona* at the top table of the Albanian game once more.

Nursery to a surfeit of outstanding young talent, Alla, in his role as youth coach of *Tirona*, was shrewdly cultivating a crop of players capable of challenging the 'New Firm' of Partizani and Dinamo for domestic honours.

Among their ranks, *Tirona*'s 'Academy of '58' boasted a roster including footballers who would become legends of the national game. Their number featured Pavllo Bukovicu – *Ben* to the fans – a nimble forward who scored lots of goals, Osman

Mema, known as *Finoku* – 'Clever, like a fox' – a feral defensive midfielder, elder brother of Ali and part of the Mema dynasty that continues to etch fresh chapters in *Tirona* history. There was Fatmir Frasheri – *Xhehariri* ('The Diamond') – a player who's name always enters the conversation when you ask an Albanian, 'Who's the best *mbrojtësi i djathtë* [right-back] to wear the national shirt?'

Yet there were two other players, both vital, composite parts of the envied *Tirona* Academy, who played in different positions on the field (each uniquely gifted in their roles), whose stories are intrinsically knitted into the sloe-black tapestry of Albanian history during the Stalinist era; a history beset with contradictions, absurdities, political interference and cruelty.

Panajot Pano and Skënder Halili are names rarely uttered in the same sentence when Albanians talk about football, so divergent their life paths that they almost defy association.

Pano and Halili were probably the finest Albanian players of the era – of any era.

Pano, born Panayiotis Thomas Pano on 7 March 1939 in the port city of Durrës of Greek Orthodox stock, joined *Tirona* in 1954.

Like the great Refik Resmja before him, Pano began his career as a goalkeeper. However, youth team coach (and former Albanian national team manager) Karapici saw potential beyond the mere prevention of goals, unleashing Pano on an unexpectant Albania as a *Sulmuesi i majtë* – left-sided forward – during a youth tournament in the July of 1956.

Halili was born on 20 August 1940 in Tirana of Muslim stock, playing his football on *Rruga Fortuzi* – Fortuzi Street – the kindergarten of Albanian football; a dust-strewn patch of hallowed, yellowed turf that has since produced fine players such as Indrit Fortuzi and Blendi Nallbani, which served as the early stomping ground to an infant Pano upon his arrival from the coast.

Halili, an excellent carrier of the ball with a sublime range of passes, was deployed into a *libero* role by Alla. With a mind as sharp as his features, Alla was a tactician and innovator of considerable nous; the *libero* role never previously being implemented in Albania.

Conventionally handsome, with blond hair and chiselled, Germanic features, it's oft said that Halili's style of play was comparable with that of the great West German *libero*, Franz Beckenbauer. Yet by the time Beckenbauer was enhancing his considerable reputation at the 1966 World Cup finals in England, Halili's career was already dead and buried.

After promotion to the post of first team coach in 1956, Alla was keen to blood his fledgling talents, with Pano and Halili – in spite of their youth – thrust into first-team action. Both players featured in a Republic Cup fixture against Besa in the October of 1957.

Pano and Halili then featured in a spectacular trouncing of *Sigurimi* club Dinamo at a packed Qemal Stafa the following May, a sensational 4-0 victory in *Dinamovitet*'s designated home game; Pano was unplayable, Halili unflappable.

In front of a rapt 30,000 baying *tifozët*, *Tirona*'s football was fast, dynamic, and loaded with spirit and tigerish determination. The beleaguered *Tirona* fans, shorn of their finest footballers for over a decade by the organs of the regime – Partizani and Dinamo – were dreaming of success again.

Even Radio Tirana mainstay Ismet Bellova voiced his approval. 'Pano,' enthused the man whose voice became synonymous with Albanian football for almost the entirety of the Stalinist era, 'is a young man of many aspects, with a distinguished career at Tirana ahead of him.' He would prove to be only half-right.

To add insult to injury, *Tirona* had the temerity to knock Dinamo out at the quarter-final stage of the Republic Cup two weeks later on a searingly hot day at the Qemal Stafa. A 0-0 draw after 120 minutes necessitated a further arduous 15 minutes of extra time (penalties were yet to be introduced as a method of concluding games) – 135 minutes in total. With both sets of players on the brink of physical exhaustion, *Tirona* were finally awarded the victory on a superior 8-4 corner count.

The double humiliation of a sporting pillar of the dictatorship indicated a power shift in the national game; a breath of life after 11 years of hegemony. The Party were unquestionably annoyed.

Tirona's second-placed league finish at the close of the 1959 season, narrowly behind Partizani; Dinamo finishing nine points astray in a distant third proved the final straw for their patrons. A plot was set in motion to halt *Tirona's* growing momentum.

When the season closed, all of the *Tirona* Academy side were conscripted for national service, their new crop of talent distributed among the superclubs; Bukoviku, Mema and Halili joining Dinamo, Pano to Partizani.

When Pano's two years of national service elapsed, Partizani made him an offer he could barely refuse: better housing, better-paid job – the usual regime schtick.

Pano would become a Partizani legend, winning four Kampionati Kombetar titles, six Kupa e Republikës, and a Balkan Cup as well as leading *Demat e Kuq* to a runners-up placing at the 1963 Spartakiad. He also won the Albanian league top scorer prize twice and was voted Albanian Sportsperson of the Year in 1960.

The little man from the port city, with his elusive size, low centre of gravity, powerful, dominant, aggressive play, rapier-like left-foot and very striking resemblance to an iconic Hungarian footballer of the era, earned himself one of the two sobriquets he was commonly associated with: *Puskás i vogël* – the Little Puskás. But to many, he was simply known as *Mbreti* – the King.

Pano, never scared to impose his game on even the loftiest of opponents, received a rave review from none other than *Der Kaiser* himself. Recollecting two tussles with his Albanian adversary during West Germany's 1972 European Championship qualifying campaign, Beckenbauer quipped, 'If Panajot Pano doesn't remember me, I remember him.'

Panajot Pano's was, unarguably, a career well lived. I strongly implore you to watch some footage of him in his prime. He was quite a player.

However, Skënder Halili's forced divorce from the club he loved took him down a far murkier path. Posted to a project for which he had little appetite – Halili wore the blue of the team of the *Sigurimi* with deep dissatisfaction and remorse – it is a testimony to Halili's quality and application that he still managed to win the 1960 Kampionati Kombetar with Dinamo.

When Halili's national service ended in 1961, Dinamo attempted to lure him into their fold permanently in the formulaic, accepted way. However, *Gjiganti* – the Giant – refused.

An ardent *tifozë e Tironës*, bred into a family *bardhë e blutë* to its marrow, Halili, as a boy, was raised on the stories passed down by his elders telling of the wrong-doings committed upon his beloved club by Partizani, Dinamo and their scurrilous overseers.

Understandably, at the end of this forced marriage, Halili wanted out of Dinamo. Free from the shackles of national service, the pathway was clear for his return to the *Tirona* fold. But in Stalinist Albania, where ambitions were culled and freedom non-existent, it wouldn't be that easy.

Dinamo staff, coupled with their masters at the Ministry of the Interior – and especially *Sigurimi* chief Kadri Hazbiu – were outraged by Halili's rebuke. The club issued a complaint to FSHF and Halili was subsequently banned from playing football at all levels for two years.

During the years of his ban, Halili was assigned to menial agricultural work in the fields of the cooperative farms, beyond the bustle of Tirana. These years harked a continuance in Partizani dominance, *Demat e Kuq* winning the title ahead of Dinamo in both 1961/62 and 1962/63. Robert Jashari and Pano proved a powerful, prolific partnership; Pano finishing as Kampionati Kombetar top scorer in 1962, Jashari taking the crown in 1963.

Yet in Halili's absence, *Tirona* were rising from the ashes of the 1959 fallout, winning their first domestic trophy – the Kupa e Republikës – in 21 years at the close of the 1962/63 season in a ridiculously thrilling two-legged final against Besa.

The first leg at Stadiumi Qemal Stafa saw *Verdhezinjtë* – the Yellow Ones – from the western lowlands of Kavajë steal an unlikely, and seemingly decisive, 3-2 away lead; Dimroçi, an Ikonomi own goal and Lilimani's late winner inspiring Besa to victory despite replies from *Tirona*'s Ali Mema and Ernest Gjoka.

With trepidation, *Tirona* travelled the 17 miles to Kavajë to contest the second leg at the compact show grounds that preceded Stadiumi Besa. Before a crowd alleged to have been near 10,000 in number, *Tirona* silenced the *Verdhezinjtë* home support, 18-year-old forward Bahri Ishka finishing neatly following an excellent pass from Mema after 12 minutes.

The final continued to ebb and flow, the perpetual sway of dominance between the two sides failing to yield any further goals. After 120 minutes, with the away goals rule years away from being introduced as a metric to decide a game's outcome, the tie succumbed to the newly levied decider of penalties, each team designated a solitary penalty taker tasked with the role of dispatching all of his team's kicks; five in total.

Besa elected T'habit Rexha as their penalty taker; *Tirona* opted for Pavllo Bukoviku, released from his 'military service' at Partizani.

In a bruising, competitive game both *Tirona* keepers, Metani and Bello, sustained injuries that prevented them from keeping goal in the decisive shoot-out.

More in desperation than hope, Alla handed the gloves to 20-year-old Ali Mema. Mema, born on Rruga Shyqyri Bërxolli in the heart of Tirana to a *Tirona*-supporting family, would later establish himself as a club legend; part of the aforementioned Mema dynasty.

Braziliani – the Brazilian – as he became known to his acolytes, due to a wily, creative verve and metronomic control of game-tempo, was taking his first steps on a journey that would elevate him towards club legend status. The 1963 final, and what would unfurl, provided a launchpad to a very special relationship shared between the player, club and fans.

T'habit Rexha, known locally as *Biti*, was a well-known singer in the city of Kavajë, but he hit all the wrong notes with his penalties, Mema saving his first three – while Bukoviku calmly netted *Tirona*'s – to seal a memorable triumph.

Skënder Halili returned to his *Tirona* family in time for the 1963/64 season. Short of fitness, limbs wearied due to exertions in the fields, he took his place in a side that was in transitory flux; a new batch of young players being blooded by the perennially brave, adaptive coach, Myslym Alla.

In truth, it was a season that disappointed, *Tirona* finishing sixth with all comers trailing miles behind a rampant Partizani side that ended the season unbeaten with Robert Jashari, again, leading the scoring charts.

But it was also pivotal, allowing *Tirona*'s fresh, new talent – and influential returnee – time to bed in, proving crucial to their subsequent ascent.

In the 1964/65 season, everything came together for Alla, Halili and the new wave of *bardhë e blutë*, an early cup exit away at Labinoti liberating *Tirona* from secondary distractions and leaving them free to fully concentrate on the important business of league form.

A youthful squad (Fatmir Frasheri, Gëzim Kasmi, Bahri Ishka, Skender Hyka and Ali Mema were all aged 24 or under) augmented by the weathered experience of Bukoviku and the masterly Halili – both 25 – outlasted older teams. With Partizani oddly profligate, losing away at Besa, Dinamo and Lokomotiva and drawing at home to Besa, Dinamo and Flamurtari, the door opened for *Tirona* to capitalise.

Despite losing home and away to *Demat e Kuq, Tirona* beat them in the pursuance of the ultimate prize, the Kampionati Kombetar, by the narrowest of one-point margins. It was the club's first championship since 1942 (and the first to be officially recognised by the regime), Halili immaculate throughout.

The 1965/66 title race was an even closer affair, although the season began inauspiciously. Not for *Tirona* or Partizani, who were both in thunderous form, but for the Stadiumi Qemal Stafa itself.

Sunday, 5 October saw the first Tirana derby in a Kampionati Kombetar season that was already shaping into a two-horse race between the previous campaign's main challengers.

When Partizani and *Tirona* met at Albania's national stadium, Radio Tirana commentator Anton Mazreku labelled the tussle the '*Tomxherristi*' – the Tom and Jerry – a cat-and-mouse battle between two tetchy adversaries recently popularised on Televizioni Shqiptar, both hell-bent on victory with neither yielding an inch. The Party may not have endorsed imperialist American ideology, but it seems they were wholly comfortable with the import of their cartoons.

The *stadiumi*, built two decades earlier, had been projected to hold 12,000 fans when Italian architectural drawings were submitted in the late 1930s. By the '50s, the Qemal Stafa regularly hosted games where crowds in excess of 20,000 were in attendance. Such was the want for tickets that, beneath the main *Tribuna*, two smaller wooden *Tribuna* were built to sate demand.

When the game commenced, there were as many fans outside the stadium waiting to enter as there were seated inside, several without tickets, some fuelled with raki and cognac from their pre-match libations on Rruga Elbasanit.

Minutes after kick-off, Partizani winger Ahmet Qojle manoeuvred himself into a dangerous position inside the *Tirona* box before arrowing in a fierce drive that rippled the back of the opponents' net.

Prompted by the raucous celebrations inside the Qemal Stafa, those remaining outside forced the stadium gates, hundreds of illegitimate entrants scattering to find vantage points in an already heaving arena.

The initial wave of alarm incited by the ensuing crush quickly escalated into widespread panic when the makeshift, portable, wooden stands, installed two years earlier, collapsed beneath the weight of bodies, taking its occupants to the ground with it. Within moments, a platform supporting the structure – 70 metres in length and the width of the *stadiumi* running track – collapsed too, resulting in further human injury.

Play was halted, briefly, although Radio Tirana chose to stay on air, a saturnine Anton Mazreku struggling to find the language to make sense of the chaos as players from both sides, aided by the army and military, offered assistance to the wounded and the dead. It is astounding to believe that play resumed, but resume it did, Partizani winning 1-0 – a frippery in wake of the carnage.

The number of fatalities isn't precisely known. In an era when death was a statistic, the loss of a few football fans counted for little. There was no public inquest and families of the dead were never compensated, with FSHF and The Party accepting no accountability.

Post-Qemal Stafa disaster, football – as it invariably does – found a way of healing itself simply by soldiering on regardless, providing a source of therapy in a time of deep, human despair. When the teams met again in the spring of 1966, Partizani led nominally, but *Tirona*'s key 2-1 win over Partizani at a newly restored Stadiumi Qemal Stafa placed Alla's side back in contention for the title. It proved vital, *Tirona*'s win squaring the Kampionati on points, although their goal difference of +39 was greatly superior to Partizani's +33.

Ironically, had the contentious method of goal ratio been used, as it was in 1950 and 1955, Partizani would've been crowned champions, *Demat e Kuq* robbed, yet again, by the application (or, in this case, non-application) of complex mathematics. However, by 1965/66 football had grown up and undergone modernisation, even inside the Hermit Kingdom. This edition of the Kampionati Kombetar would be decided by a play-off at the Qemal Stafa; a winner-takes-all contest to decide the destiny of the title.

Again, it would be *Tirona* who would rise to the occasion, Halili producing one of his finest performances in another 2-1 win.

Tirona applied themselves well in the European Cup too, knocked out at the preliminary stage by Scottish champions Kilmarnock 1-0 on aggregate in a tie that remained on a knife-edge to the last, Bertie Black's effort at Rugby Park late in the second leg taking Killie through by the narrowest of margins.

In both legs, *Tirona* recruited the services of old boy Panajot Pano on a short-term loan, a practice that was both questionable and rife in Stalinist Albania. And it had nearly paid off, *Mbreti* going close twice against Kilmarnock at the Qemal Stafa.

Halili and Pano – the Giant and the King – were to be paired together in the first round of the 1966/67 European Cup, *Tirona* again securing the 'loan' of Partizani's forward for, what appeared to be, an ostensibly winnable two-legged encounter against the Norwegian champions, Vålerenga.

However, it was a tie that would never take place. The evening prior to their projected flight to Oslo, the *Tirona* squad went to bed early after an evening spent unwinding in the foyer of the Hotel Durrës.

Just after midnight, the team were awoken by the sound of a commotion in the corridor. *Sigurimi* agents had entered the hotel, seized Skënder Halili and ghosted him away in a GAZ-69 truck.

According to *Sigurimi* records, Halili had been witnessed selling two wristwatches to a man in the Armenian Quarter of Tirana, on the east corner of Skanderbeg Square. A further search of Halili's apartment uncovered a small quantity of US dollars.

Guilty or not, Halili was harshly sentenced to 11 months' hard labour, after which he was deployed to work in the chrome mines of Bulqiza, located in the remote north-east of Albania. Despite coaching at youth level, Halili never kicked a ball competitively again, his brilliant career over at the age of 26.

As for *Tirona*, they were ordered by FSHF not to travel to Oslo, costing the club a two-year ban from European competition. It also prompted the slow dismantling of Alla's great side.

The sad epitaph to this tragic Albanian parable was added long after Halili's death on 13 December 1982; a demise resultant of back-breaking work conditions in the dark mines of Dibër County.

Gjiganti's funeral, despite a downpour, was attended by a 200-strong cavalcade of *Tirona* fans, a show of muted protest against the dictatorship. Whether myth or fact, it has been ventured by many close to *Tirona* during this time-period that Halili was ratted out to the *Sigurimi* by a team-mate back in '67.

Allegedly, within *Sigurimi* data – one million files in number – stored deep inside the House of Leaves, there exists a document attesting to this, naming the culprit who sold Halili out. Some *Tirona* fans believe that name to be Panajot Pano.

It's an ending to a story replete with the espionage, mistrust and double-dealing that, as Westerners, we believed characterised life in what was conveniently branded 'the Eastern Bloc'. It's a parody that, while existing within the realms of belief, is unthinkable; a fabled denouncement forewarning against the poisonous legacy of treachery.

True or otherwise, it is believable because it's symptomatic of the Albania that Enver Hoxha and The Party created: a continuous swirl of slander, half-truths and outright lies.

Yet, despite the belief that things couldn't really get much worse, socially as in sport, the regime was about to confound these notions, entering its people into another black phase in a history already steeped in blood and shame.

Chapter Nine

1966/67: The Championship of Coals
– *Kampionati i Qymyrit*

AS THE rest of the world indulged itself in the Summer of Love, 1967 in unhip and unhippied Albania witnessed an odious rewriting of the national constitution. Within its dictum (undoubtedly the most abhorrent piece of legislature in the nation's history) any semblance of Westernism was outlawed and all religious belief was made illegal with venues of worship desecrated, reappropriated and, in many cases, demolished upon its order.

Article 37 of The Party's poisonous manifesto was concise in its vulgarity, 'The state does not recognise any religion and supports atheist propaganda to inculcate the scientific-materialist vision of the world.' Enver Hoxha had knowingly – and willingly – unleashed a monster.

After Albania's rancorous split with Khrushchev's USSR in 1960, the dictatorship befriended Maoist China, and Hoxha, in an obsequious nod towards his new patron, sought to enact a cultural revolution akin to the upheaval that had taken place in China in 1966.

In Hoxha's warped imaginings, rogue reporters, civil servants, office workers and bureaucrats were responsible for a perceptible increase in public hostility towards The Party.

Many had been bold enough to criticise the social injustices perpetrated by the regime in the name of socialism.

Prices of basic goods were increasing as salaries froze, while the goods that could be bought were of a poor quality. Discontent bubbled in the 26 districts.

Hoxha waged bloody war on the 'journalists with pens for hire' and 'cafe politicians', all gripes ruthlessly silenced using the regime's sharpest tools: the army and the police.

In scenes redolent of the Khmer Rouge's emptying of Phnom Penh eight years later, white-collar workers were relieved of their administrative duties and marched to the cooperative farms to work the land, intellectuals were imprisoned for behaviours deemed 'anti-socialist' and the education syllabus was nationalised with Albania's history revised.

An extended period of xenophobic zeal heralded a further spate of mandatory name changes, in particular surnames perceived as unfitting or offensive from a nationalist, political, ideological or moral perspective. This included names that were Yugoslavian, Greek, Bulgarian or Italian in origin, with all remnants of foreignness summarily swept under the allegorical rug.

Prospective parents were now only allowed to source the first names of offspring from *Fjalor me Emra Njerëzish* – the regime-prescribed *Dictionary of Children's Names* – appellations devoid of overseas influence or religious connotation.

'Religion,' eulogised Hoxha, borrowing heavily from the works of Karl Marx, 'is the opium of the masses.' He bolstered the claim with his own infamous and recurrent maxim, 'The faith of the Albanians is Albanianism.'

Hoxha's words prefigured boom growth for the most definitive of oxymorons, Nationalist Stalinism, with religion its most loathed target.

It wasn't the first time that The Party had imposed heavy prohibitions on religion and its teachings. A steady stream of Catholic clerics and intellectuals were liquidated when the Hoxha administration rose to power in 1945. The 1967

103

National Constitution merely bound injustice and murder in the noxious, sugar-coated legitimacy of legislation.

Hoxha took personal responsibility for the diligent enactment of the Constitution's edicts, forwarding a letter to all local branches of *Partia e Punës e Shqipërisë* – the Party of Labour of Albania – which read, 'Be cautious, but ruthless, as religion is still very influential among the people.'

Hoxha assisted in the scripting of a propaganda film released by the State Film Archive and Atheist Museum entitled *E Verteta Mbi Fene – Truth Over Religion* – a 15-minute tirade depicting spiritual leaders as cowardly, manipulative supernaturalists. Footage therein of terrified religious heads subjected to verbal humiliations at predisposed kangaroo-court 'trials' is particularly difficult to watch. One can only presuppose the fate of these poor men after they were unjustly declared 'guilty'.

Martyrs to these hateful new laws were Catholic priest Rev. Shtjefën Kurti, executed for performing a baptism, and Arjen Arben, a 16-year-old boy interned in a hard labour camp for eight years for pointing his family's television aerial across the Adriatic towards neighbouring Italy.

Imams and dervishes of the Bektashi Islamic sect had their beards shaved publicly by the Red Guards of the Communist Youth, their cemetery summarily vandalised; the bones of the dead were thrown into the river, example to a plethora of horrors committed in the name of Hoxha's national constitution.

In an era of diminished faith, football, too, was to suffer its own crisis of confidence.

On 24 June, league leaders *Tirona* looked to consolidate their position at the top of the table in a crucial Tirana derby at Stadiumi Qemal Stafa against Partizani.

With *Tirona* leading on 33 points, Dinamo on 31 and Partizani very nearly out of contention with 25, defeat for *Demat e Kuq* would extinguish any hopes they harboured of wrestling the leaders' title away from them. With just four games remaining, the team the regime had tried to abolish were well on course for a hat-trick of championships.

Tirona were in a rich vein of form, a team at their peak, having navigated the season unbeaten so far, hammering Dinamo – their closest rival – 3-1 at home in a one-sided affair, drawing the return 2-2.

Although *Tirona* achieved their successes in spite of the regime and the obstacles it laid in their path, football fandom remained a refreshingly egalitarian affair with supporters of all clubs free to attend any game available every given Sunday. Yet, with Partizani inarguably the best-supported team in the country, *Tirona* would arrive at away matches – and those at home too – to be welcomed by chants of 'Partizani, Partizani'; a large number of the fans present at all *stadiumet* being followers of the army club.

The dictatorship actively disliked *Tirona*, its functionaries indignant that *Tirona* fans still called their team by the old name and not 17 Nëntori, the moniker the regime rechristened them in honour of the communists' liberation of the capital.

Tirona began their title defence in style, narking governmental hierarchy in the process. After an away win against Besa in January of 1967, *Tirona* fans travelling back from Kavajë by train converged on the Club of the Officers' House (now the Club of the League of Writers) in Tirana, and sang songs in praise of their football club.

General Petrit Dume, major general and deputy to the Minister of Defence, a humourless dolt of a man, was in the club at that time and was suitably unamused by the spectacle.

With the exception of Enver Hoxha, Mehmet Shehu and Hysni Kapo, bigwigs of the regime would congregate in the *Tribuna* every Sunday. And all of them, except for the head of the Ministry of the Interior, Kadri Hazbiu (a Dinamo fan), were avid Partizan *tifozët*.

But Dume was a different beast. He would regularly intrude upon the Partizani dressing room on matchday, volunteering opinions on tactics and team selection; a petty busybody in a position of critical, national importance. He once chased down the Partizani coach on the team's return from an away defeat in Korçë, flagging the bewildered driver over, jumping aboard and launching insults at their 'underachieving' players.

Due to the tenuous nature of the pocket rebellion outside the Club of the Officers' House, no action was taken against the *Tirona* fans, but Dume was a man with both a long memory and a particularly vindictive streak. He would wait patiently for an opportunity to exact his revenge.

The match itself, adjoining intense city rivalry with an unhealthy suffusion of political undertone, was a taut and nervous affair.

Since Partizani's formation in 1947, *Tirona* had only beaten them twice: both 2-1 victories at Stadiumi Qemal Stafa in the 1965/66 edition of Kampionati Kombetar. It was very much a game that was in the balance.

Tirona coach Myslym Alla, aware of Partizani's attacking threat of Lim Shllaku, Robert Jashari and Panajot Pano, a lethal triumvirate, opted for a considered approach hoping to exploit Partizani's need to be offensive. For *Tirona*, a draw would constitute a good result; for Refik Resmja's Partizani anything other than victory would leave them with no chance of lifting the title.

Pavllo Bukoviku, a servant of *Tirona* for 11 years, recalled an incident prior to the game that served as a portent to future events. On arrival at Stadiumi Qemal Stafa, the *Tirona* players were approached by three opposing fans who imparted an odd, cryptic message, 'Beat Partizani. We don't want this championship anyway.' Quite who these fans were and what they meant remains a mystery, but this peculiar constellation of words seemed indicative of foul play afoot.

Inside the Qemal Stafa, *tifozët* from both corners of the city created an atmosphere still prevalent in modern-day Tirana derbies, although the till rolls, shredded toilet paper and racing pigeons of the Stalinist era have now been succeeded by fireworks and smoke bombs.

With the game level at 1-1 and with eight minutes remaining – a Pavllo Bukoviku opener negated by a Rudi equaliser for Partizani – Bahri Ishka joyously slammed home a *Tirona* winner, sparking wild celebrations amid the *bardhë e blutë* contingent inside the stadium.

The revelries spread to the dugout, where *Tirona's* Niko Xhaçka – earlier substituted – enjoyed the moment vociferously. However, Xhaçka's wild celebrations attracted the considerable ire of Partizani and Albania captain Lim Shllaku, and an altercation ensued which *Tirona* captain Pavllo Bukoviku tried to defuse, Shllaku giving Bukoviku a slap for his troubles.

Referia Fidai Pupa, from Korçë, in a putative attempt to re-establish some semblance of control, sent both players off, Bukoviku's protests of innocence ignored by the ruffled official.

Minutes later, it was *rezultati përfundimor, Tirona* achieving a priceless 2-1 victory and keeping their dreams of a third successive Kampionati Kombetar title very much within their remit. With news of Dinamo's 0-0 draw against Vllaznia in Shkodër filtering through on fans' *radiot tranzistor, Tirona* now led the field by three points with just three games left to play.

The end of the match prompted the home support to break into enthusiastic choruses of '*Tirona, Tirona!*' and pigeons adorned with blue and white ribbons encircled the Qemal Stafa, much to the affront of the communist leaders perched in *Tribuna*. Hastily, sullen of face, they departed the stadium in their limousines, withdrawing back to Blloku.

Fans exited the arena – rapt after witnessing a robust and hard-fought Tirana derby – filing down the concrete staircases of the Qemal Stafa amid the animated hubbub of post-match chatter, making their way back into town before heading home, via Rruga Elbasanit, to their prefab domiciles.

In the corridor leading to the dressing rooms, Pavllo Bukoviku and Osman Mema celebrated *Tirona's* success. Both had previously played for – and won titles with – Partizani, but a victory for your team of choice, rather than one subscribed to you via national service, must've meant much more to these friends and team-mates.

Their old coach and mentor at Partizani, Refik Resmja, flanked by a representative from the Albanian Press Organisation (who was also a reporter for the *Sporti Popullor Shqiptar* newspaper) interrupted their post-match huddle.

Allegedly, the reporter (a Partizani 'sympathiser' – despite press affiliations – who will remain nameless) verbally insulted Bukoviku, calling him 'a rabid dog', to which Osman Mema retaliated by kicking the agitator.

After an exchange of choice words, police chief Qemal Balluku – brother to Beqir Balluku, Partizani patron and Albania's minister of defence – entered the fray to investigate. The *Tirona* players gave their version of events and that, seemingly, was the end of the matter.

The following morning, *Sporti Popullor Shqiptar* reported that FSHF had decreed that Partizani and *Tirona* forfeit the match 3-0 with their remaining two fixtures also to be forfeited by the same scoreline.

An 'official report' stated that a fight between players had taken place on the pitch, spurring violent conduct on the terraces. Despite there being no action on the field affecting the course of play with claims of resultant fan violence in *Sigurimi*-policed Albania patently unfeasible, *Tirona* and Partizani were both expelled from the 1966/67 Kampionati.

By punishing Partizani – a state club already out of the title race – FSHF clearly believed this hollow gesture added credence, externally, to what was a mockery of a decision.

It's commonly hypothesised that the decision to punish both clubs was orchestrated, an act of collusion, between the Ministry of Defence (Beqir Balluku and Petrit Dume implicated) and the Ministry of the Interior (Kadri Hazbiu cited), the outcome quickly delegated to FSHF, on Hoxha's approval, for them to enforce.

In 2007, the reputed Albanian writer, broadcaster and sports journalist Skifter Këlliçi attempted to uncover evidence of the meeting that decided the fate of the 1966/67 Kampionati Kombetar, sourcing the minutes from the General Directorate of State Archives and FSHF meetings of the time. His search unearthed nothing; all documentation of the scandal had conveniently vanished.

With Partizani already out of realistic title contention prior to the game, the punishment deprived *Tirona* of a possible six points (eight if you include the two deducted after the Partizani win). Dinamo won the title by five.

Even in the button-lipped environs of Stalinist Albania there were audible whispers; The Party didn't want *Tirona* to win a third successive title. It was feared that another *Tirona* triumph may shatter the myth of army/police invincibility. In a country that relied on the presence of these dual custodians to preserve power – thus assuring the complicity of its people – maintaining this veneer of impregnability was vital. To expel any miasma of weakness, the regime manufactured a scandal to deprive *Tirona* the opportunity of laying seed to such doubts.

The 1966/67 season has since been dubbed *Turpi i futbollit Shqiptar* – the disgrace of Albanian football – FIFA refusing to recognise the Albanian champions of that year. Dinamo were, in turn, denied entry to the European Cup in 1967/68 by UEFA.

It was a pity; *Dinamovitet*, equipped with a fine coach in Skënder Jareci and the predatory goalscoring craft of Medin Zhega, could've easily made an impression on the European Cup, their progress, ironically, hindered by the plots and fabrications of the regime that had birthed them.

In 2006, Jareci, in recollection of *Dinamovitet*'s 1966/67 championship 'win', expressed his feelings regarding the subsequent celebrations, 'When my football players ... cup in their hands ... started doing the lap of honour around Stadiumi Dinamo, it was very difficult for me. That trophy and the lap of honour belonged to Tirana and only Tirana.'

There's an Albanian proverb that reads, 'Stroke the dog and it will mark you with its dirty paws.' The *Kampionati i Qymyrit* – the Championship of Coals – had left its egregious imprint on everybody it touched.

From a sporting, political, social and spiritual perspective, 1967 was an unmitigated disaster for Enver Hoxha and his regime, internationally derided as cheats, liars and philistines by leaders of the global community. Hoxha and The Party's bigwigs would cease to receive invitations to important world events, having to content themselves with the dull, mock legitimacy of bespoke Party Congress and Politburo meetings.

As for Beqir Balluku and Petrit Dume: purportedly the instigators in the plot to dethrone the rightful champions of the 1966/67 season, they were arrested by the *Sigurimi* in August 1974 on unrelated charges of high treason. Assisting the regime in the enacting of their dark acts didn't necessarily buy you their loyalty. Both were executed in November 1975.

Their alleged collaborator, Kadri Hazbiu, lasted for a further seven years before meeting the same brutal end in 1982.

The murky goings-on during the 1966/67 season enabled change, partially through modest reform, but more prevalently due to national embarrassment. *Tirona* won the next two championships in the wake of 1967 and, in following years,

Partizani and Dinamo dominance – although still apparent – was never quite as pronounced as it was in the initial two decades of their existence.

As Albanian football emerged from the 1960s, the regime's manipulation of football as a political tool lost much of its edge; the game allowed to traverse a moderately standard course.

The superclubs still used the same nefarious recruitment policy they always had, and in doing so continued to regularly out-punch their rivals.

But, as the Albanian regime ran out of allies and funding for their failing socialist experiment dwindled, hurtling the country into penury and near-starvation, football's importance – from a governmental perspective – lessened, creating an oddly levelled playing field. And within that small window of opportunity, some wonderful football stories were born.

Iconic Games

Albania 0 West Germany 0

European Championship Qualifying Group 4

17 December 1967

Stadiumi Qemal Stafa, Tirana

Attendance: 21,889

Albania: Koço Dinella (KS Dinamo Tirana), Frederik Gjinali (KS Dinamo Tirana), Frederik Jorgaqi (KS Labinoti), Lin Shllaku (captain; FK Partizani Tirana), Teodor Vaso (KS Skënderbeu Korçë), Ramazan Rragami (FK Partizani Tirana), Ali Mema (KS Vllaznia Shkodër), Josif Kazanxhi (SK 17 Nëntori Tirana), Sabah Bizi (FK Partizani Tirana), Panajot Pano (FK Partizani Tirana), Medin Zhega (KS Dinamo Tirana)

Head coach/*Kryetrajneri*: Loro Boriçi

West Germany: Horst Wolter (BTSV Eintracht Braunschweig), Bernd Patzke (TSV München 1860), Horst-Dieter Höttges (SV Werder Bremen), Günter Netzer (VfL Borussia

111

Mönchengladbach), Willi Schulz (captain; Hamburger SV), Wolfgang Weber (FC Köln), Siegfried Held (BV Borussia Dortmund), Hans Küppers (TSV München 1860), Peter Meyer (VfL Borussia Mönchengladbach), Wolfgang Overath (FC Köln), Hannes Löhr (FC Köln)

Head coach/*Kryetrajneri*: Helmut Schön

Referee/*Arbitri*: Ferdinand Marschall (Austria)

When the qualification groups for the 1968 European Championship were drawn in Rome during the autumn of 1966, many of the entrants were looking to consolidate, or atone for, their performances at the 1966 World Cup finals.

The admirable performers at the World Cup, England as winners, semi-finalists Portugal and USSR, and quarter-finalists Hungary, were the expected qualifiers from the group stage, with footballing giants Italy, Spain and France – who'd failed extravagantly in England – looking to re-establish themselves as credible forces in world football.

The Soviets would find themselves pitched against Greece, a nation they had failed to annex to the communist Eastern Bloc a few years earlier in a messy altercation that still rankled within both camps.

There would be a tussle between ideological half-brothers, Hungary and East Germany, in Group 5, the Hungarians in a state of transition post-*Aranycsapat* up against a communist Germany hoping to build a side to match their neighbours both east and west.

However, it was Group 4 that promised to be the most problematic; the only three-pronged group of the entire eight. It contained the irksome troika of Yugoslavia, West Germany and Albania.

A simmering cauldron of potential volatility, Group 4 appeared to be the most unattractive of trysts; an unsexy threesome with no willing participant.

Despite a mutually peaceful post-war relationship, there existed a deep-rooted dislike between the Yugoslavs and the West Germans; the Nazis committing atrocious crimes upon the Serb, Croat and Chetnik communities in Yugoslavia during World War Two. And West German foreign policy remained bound by the tenets of the Hallstein Doctrine inked in 1955, legislature dictating that the German Federal Republic (West Germany) would not establish diplomatic relations with any nation that recognised the German Democratic Republic (East Germany) as a bona fide state. Yugoslavia had done so since 1957. The Yugoslavs had also defeated the West Germans 1-0 in the quarter-final of the 1962 World Cup in Chile, Petar Radaković's late strike sealing *Plavi* a berth in the semis of a tournament that their German opponents believed they should've won.

These snags were inherent yet manageable. However, the real dangers stemmed from Yugoslavia and West Germany's unstable – and awkwardly recent – history with Albania.

Memories of Nazi occupation between 1943 and 1944 still weighed heavy on the Albanian psyche. Hitler's alliance with Albania's anti-communist militia, Balli Kombëtar (the National Front), and their subsequent war crimes against the ethnic Serbs, Greeks and gypsies resident in wartime Albania remained a virulent focus of argument for Enver Hoxha. War may have ended in the field, but it was still being waged in the rhetoric of the Albanian regime.

Yugoslav–Albanian relations had been fractious since the Tito–Stalin split in 1948; all Yugoslavians living in Albania were immediately extradited and any Yugoslavian sympathisers still resident within its borders imprisoned or worse.

There was another perpetual bone of contention, too: Kosovo, an Albanian colony within the Federal Republic of Yugoslavia where – rumour had it – Serb-led Yugoslav forces were committing atrocities of their own on Kosovo's ethnically Albanian populace.

Albania was an irritation to both Yugoslavia and West Germany; an impertinent child in need of a punishment that – when queried on their behaviour – hid behind its untouchable big brother, China.

The three competitors in Group 4 embarked upon the six fixtures that would decide qualification with differing expectations and goals. For Helmut Schön's West Germany – World Cup runners-up in 1966 – a powerful, potent side, anything other than qualification for the latter stages of the competition would be deemed a huge failure.

Yugoslavia were undergoing a rebuild under the guidance of the wise and wily Rajko Mitić. Mitić had been the captain and leader of the great Red Star Belgrade side of the 1950s, driving *Zvezda* to five titles and three cups. He was also a regular starter for the national team, earning Olympic silver medals at London 1948 and Helsinki 1952 and netting the winning goal against England in Belgrade in a 1-0 victory in 1954. He would score an impressive 32 goals in 59 appearances for *Plavi*, competing at the 1950 and 1954 World Cups.

However, since their fourth-place finish at the World Cup in 1962, the national team had entered into a period of torpor, knocked out of the 1964 European Championship qualifiers by Sweden and losing 3-0 to Norway in Oslo during a dreadful 1966 World Cup qualification campaign that saw France win their group; Yugoslavia finishing an embarrassing and distant third. The appointment of Mitić by the National Team Selection Committee – which included, among others, the great Vujadin Boškov – sought to slam the brakes on this negative cycle.

Mitić inherited a talented squad containing some standout performers in Dinamo Zagreb's Slaven Zambata and Vojislav Melić, and Red Star's Ivica Osim and Dragan Džajić.

For Albania, under the tutelage of national footballing great Loro Boriçi – in his second term as *Shqiponjat* head coach – expectations were set at a moderate level. Indeed, Albania's only other full competitive qualifying campaign had been for the 1966 World Cup. There had also been a last-16 knockout two-legged tie against Denmark to decide a place in the 1964 European Championship quarter-finals; a 4-0 reverse at the Idrætsparken in Copenhagen preceded by a promising 1-0 win courtesy of Panajot Pano's early goal at the Qemal Stafa.

Professor Zyber Konçi, a sports scientist and co-founder of the Albanian Institute of Physical Culture and Sport, had overseen the 1964 play-off and much of the 1966 campaign, and both had offered tangible flickers of hope.

Despite registering five defeats in their World Cup qualifiers, there was much encouragement to be drawn from the nature of Albania's performances. Narrow defeats in Rotterdam and Geneva versus the Dutch and the Swiss evidenced a team playing with freedom and good movement, passing and speed at its core. However, full-time fisticuffs in Geneva after a 1-0 loss to the Swiss in May 1965 – Frasheri, Jashari and captain Shllaku attempting to wrestle the match ball from Swiss forward Jean-Claude Schindelholz as a keepsake – failed to endear the visitors to their hosts or to a native UEFA, but in the vast litany of Albanian discrepancies of the era this ranked low on the list.

During the campaign, Konçi blooded the youngsters, Iljaz Çeço, Medin Zhega, Nico Xhaçka, Ramazan Rragami and Ali Mema all profiting from their coach's bravery, foresight and scientific footballing philosophy. Upon his return to the Institute of Physical Culture and Sport in 1965, *Profesori* – the Professor – bequeathed a spirited crop of players to the newly appointed Boriçi in time for Albania's final World Cup qualifier against Northern Ireland in Tirana.

With Boriçi handing debuts to Partizani's Foto Andoni and Labinoti's Bashkim Rudi in a team featuring ten starters aged 25 or under – Lin Shllaku at 27 the only veteran – the new boss seemed to be embracing Konçi's predisposition towards youth.

A spritely Albania closed their campaign with a 1-1 draw against the George Best-inspired Irish at Stadiumi Qemal Stafa. Dinamo forward Medin Zhega's late equaliser not only secured his country's first competitive point, but also deprived the Irish of their 1966 World Cup place; Bobby Peacock's side finishing behind Switzerland by a solitary point. For Boriçi, it constituted a good start, providing hope for the forthcoming games against West Germany and Yugoslavia.

Albania's opener pitted them against the West Germans at the boxy Stadion Rote Erde in Dortmund. Again, Boriçi put trust in his young players with nine starters 25 or under, with only Fatmir Frasheri (26) and Panajot Pano (28) upping the average age ratio.

Die Mannschaft, with Franz Beckenbauer in the *libero* role, offered a competitive debut to *Der Kaiser*'s club team-mate – a muscular and aggressive 21-year-old forward who'd been rattling the net with mundane regularity all season for the newly emergent Bayern München. His name was Gerd Müller.

Boriçi, to his credit, fielded a team of attacking intent, Ali Mema, Ramazan Rragami and Sabah Bizi forming a creative midfield trio to feed Niko Xhaçka, debutant Skender Hyka, Bahri Ishka and Panajot Pano.

In the first half there were moments: Bahri Ishka seeing his shot headed off the line by West German captain Willi Schulz, and Niko Xhaçka drawing a flying save from World Cup keeper Hans Tilkowski.

However, good attacking work was undone by defensive fragility; two moments of hesitancy ruthlessly punished by West Germany's fledgling forward.

Chasing a 2-0 deficit, *Shqiponjat* wilted, Müller adding two further goals to his tally and FC Köln's left-sided forward

Hannes Löhr weighing in with a couple of rockets; the result a somewhat harsh 6-0 defeat.

Weighted by the ignominy of a heavy defeat and the public and media dissension it triggered, Boriçi approached the impending fixtures against Stalinist Albania's hated 'revisionist' neighbour, Yugoslavia, in the throes of an ethical and tactical quandary.

Further heavy defeats against the Yugoslavs – a historical and ideological enemy – would rain doubt upon Boriçi's managerial capabilities, from both FSHF and the press corps. Fear of failure, on Boriçi's part, led to a lack of moral courage and a reversion to the footballing conservatism that Zyber Konçi had strived to outlaw.

When Rajko Mitić's *Plavi* arrived at the Qemal Stafa in the death throes of spring 1967, they expected to be stretched and attacked. The Albanian team that Boriçi picked was built for attrition, playing a static Albanian variant of *catenaccio* that – while restricting chances for the opposition – offered the home side absolutely no goal threat whatsoever.

Yugoslavia took the few chances that came their way, Dinamo Zagreb's Slaven Zambata scoring either side of half-time to ease the visitors to a functional 2-0 win. When Cypriot referee Kostakis Xanthoulis ended a thoroughly moribund encounter, a resonant silence enveloped the Qemal Stafa, *tifozët* drifting joylessly home in their miserable droves.

The Albanian press were outraged, calling for the exclusion of Panajot Pano from the national team. 'He has lost all of his qualities,' argued *Sporti Popullor*, failing to identify that his ability to affect any facet of attacking play had been stunted by his manager's *Boriçian* tactics – *Boriçian* becoming a convenient buzz phrase in Albanian parlance of the day to denote tedious, defence-minded football.

Rather than tweak his losing formulae, Boriçi adopted the same tactics for the return at the tight, atmospheric Stadion Jugoslovenska Narodna Armija – Stadium JNA – in Belgrade.

As Albania sat, *Plavi* attacked, Željezničar's Edin Sprečo fortuitously opening the scoring after 44 minutes with a left-wing cross that drifted under debutant keeper Jani Rama's crossbar. With the deadlock broken Yugoslavia took full control, Red Star forward Vojin Lazarević's bullet header sandwiched between Ivica Osim's emphatic brace.

For the new *Shqiponjat*, it constituted a disastrous start to Boriçi's second reign; the man who'd excelled as a footballer calling upon all of the currency his past achievements afforded him to remain in the managerial role.

There had been drama in the other games in Group 4. Less than a month after their merciless destruction of Albania in Dortmund, the West Germans visited Belgrade to face the Yugoslavs at Stadion Crvena Zvezda. And it proved an awkward and testing battle for Helmut Schön's side, a physical Yugoslav back line shackling the attacking intentions of Hannes Löhr and Gerd Müller, the pairing that had proven so effective against the Albanians.

In a tough match of few chances, *Plavi* conjured the decisive moment, Branko Rašović's raking ball into the German box headed past the diving Sepp Maier by Olympique de Marseille striker Josip Skoblar. The goal saw him mobbed, on the pitch, not only by a cameraman positioned behind the goal, but by two girls in short shorts and white, knee-length PVC boots – visual proof of Titoist Yugoslavia's submission to Western influence.

Other notable trivia regarding the fixture was that it featured a 20-year-old Berti Vogts who would make 96 appearances for *Die Mannschaft*, this being his first.

The return, played at the Volksparkstadion in Hamburg in October 1967, inserted between Yugoslavia's two comfortable victories against Albania, was another fiercely contested game, Italian referee Concetto Lo Bello having to warn the Yugoslavs to refrain from some roughhouse treatment administered to their not-wholly-innocent hosts.

Hannes Löhr drove the Germans into a half-time lead that was equalised within a minute of the second half starting, Slaven Zambata profiting from a rare defensive lapse to poke home beyond Maier.

For 25 minutes the game remained in the balance, Dragan Džajić missing a chance to give *Plavi* the lead. It proved costly, with Müller and Hamburg legend Uwe Seeler scoring brilliant headed goals to punish Yugoslavian profligacy and turn the game in West Germany's favour.

The 3-1 victory temporarily placed them at the head of the table. Yugoslavia's win in Belgrade versus Albania the following month returned *Plavi* to the summit, above West Germany by two points with *Die Mannschaft* having a game in hand, but also boasting a far superior goal difference.

It all boiled down to the final game in Group 4, West Germany requiring a win – by any margin – against Albania in Tirana to progress to the knockout stages of the 1968 European Championship in Italy.

When the wheels of the Swiss Air flight hit the pitted runway tarmac in the alien landscape of Albania during the ides of December all semblance of autumnal warmth and sunlight had long since deceased.

The dull thud of rubber on asphalt was greeted with a sigh of collective relief by the footballers of the German Federal Republic. The plane had circled airspace above Rinas Airport twice already, allowing the underworked airport staff time to remove stray sheep from its runway.

As *Die Mannschaft* and staff waited for the step ladder to be positioned enabling them to disembark the aircraft, there must've been a collective sense among their band that the omens weren't good. Indeed, Wolfgang Overath and Wolfgang Weber had been forced to endure hospitality Stalinist Albanian-style years previously when they'd been part of the FC Köln team that faced Partizani in a 1963/64 European Cup tie; an experience they were not keen to relive.

After escaping the dead-eyed observations of passport control, the laborious bag checks and petty confiscations, their ramshackle *autobus* delivered them the 11 miles, beyond the sterile co-ops and concrete bunkers that punctuated the Albanian countryside, to the relative serenity of Hotel Dajti that straddled the east side of Rinia Park on Dëshmorët e Kombit Boulevard – Boulevard of the Martyrs of the Nation – where all the foreigners stayed. It was rumoured that its rooms were bugged, and the *Sigurimi* listened in from a sub-basement under the hotel. It was a rumour that was proven to be true after the veil of Stalinism fell in 1991.

Forced to represent their country in this joyless dystopia, the footballers of West Germany must have asked themselves the same imponderable question asked by the many Westerners unfortunate enough to get the same gig, 'How did we get here?'

It was a question that was all the more indefinable in 1967, the year that Enver Hoxha's regime banned religion, blew up the churches and mosques and murdered holy men and women. In truth, the question was in grave need of expansion and, to this day, still demands an earnest and thorough answer.

The West Germans had learned from the previous experience of their club sides; beards and hair were suitably shorn, clothing was staid and regimented, German food was brought in to Albania but it was prepared by an Albanian chef. The DFB – *Deutscher Fußball-Bund* – in their appetency to adhere to the rules, left no organisational stone unturned, taking every precaution possible to placate their capricious hosts. But it's said that an organisation is only as reliable as its representatives. After West Germany's arrival at the Hotel Dajti rumours were rife of a mini-scandal involving one of their footballers.

It was alleged that Gerd Müller, *DFB-Team*'s prodigious young forward, had spent an undue amount of time in the company of a female hotel maid named Hojna. Further to this, hearsay suggested that the two were in love. With the *Sigurimi* alert to the situation, immediate steps were taken to avert this wholly unwholesome frisson.

Despite the improbability of the union, shards of evidential proof do exist. Müller returned to the Hotel Dajti in 1971 for another Euro qualifier representing *Die Mannschaft* – in itself utterly circumstantial. Yet in 1985, Finnish cup winners HJK Helsinki, drawn against Flamurtari in the first round of the European Cup Winners' Cup, received a peculiar letter from a retired ex-footballing icon requesting to join the club on 'a single-match contract' demanding, 'Let me come to Albania with you. I want to see my girlfriend.' The author of the letter was, of course, Gerd Müller.

But the most telling piece of proof is probably the most mundane; a fully fit Müller – top scorer in the Bundesliga – was dropped for the Albania game.

On 17 December 1967, darkness descended on the Qemal Stafa; sable clouds loomed overhead and an all-enveloping cold gripped rain-threatened Tirana.

The visit of the West Germans to Albania was the hot ticket in the city. In the week preceding the game, Gimi's downtown kiosk, beneath the shadow of *Ushtari i panjohur,* became a hub of concerted push-and-shovery; Albania's football fans desperate to get their hands on the remaining tickets and be part of this shared, visceral experience.

The natives were buoyed by news that West Germany's influential *libero*, Franz Beckebauer, would not be in the line-up; an injury sustained while training at Stadiumi Dinamo ruling him out. No Müller, no Beckenbauer. Something weird was happening in the Albanian capital.

As the proles alighted the concrete staircases leading into the Qemal Stafa's cavernous bowl, the entitled 'stalwarts' of society took their place in the *Tribuna*; Party members joined by the large entourage of Chinese dignitaries present in the city for the biennial Albanian-Sino jolly-up.

Signwriters spent the week leading up to the West Germany game modifying the *stadiumi* billboards transforming the Qemal Stafa into a presbytery of Marxist–Leninist ideologue, espousing the virtues of socialist *modus vivendi* in unintentionally hilarious fashion.

'*Ushtroni Gjimnastikën ë Merditë*' (Do gymnastics in the afternoon) demanded one slogan. '*Galishmeni Revolucionar*' (Give revolution a try) implored another; a subtle reimagining of John Lennon's Westernist 'Give Peace a Chance' mantra. But the sign that amused and befuddled most read, '*Kalitja fazike është një detyrë patriotike*' (Phasic tempering is a patriotic duty) a message surely lost in the snow blizzard of meaningful translation.

Nis loga – kick-off – was projected to take place at 2pm Tirana time, but as the anthems blared and Austrian official Ferdinand Marschall exchanged handshakes with captains Lin Shllaku and Willi Schulz, the heavens hung heavy like a blackened shroud. Stadiumi Qemal Stafa was a rarity among European national stadia in the sense that it had yet to install serviceable floodlights. Indeed, the country wouldn't be fully electrified until the end of 1968.

Fortunately the darkness abated, flames of light piercing the murk, rendering the match playable. But the pitch remained uneven and rucked, sand caulking the holes where heavy rain had fallen; the ball rolling at a bobble – a naysayer to the tenets of attractive, controlled football.

Beneath the ominous skies, two teams of polar-opposite world standing played a kind of football; West Germany struggling to get their passing game going, Albania feeding on the plentiful scraps that their opponents' pitch-enhanced laxity afforded them. As the first half evolved, excitement began to swell on the terraces of the Qemal Stafa; the fans' beloved *Shqiponjat* weren't just holding their own, they appeared to be winning the battle.

When the half-time whistle blew, it was greeted with a mass roar of approval. The West German bourgeoisie hadn't laid a glove on Albania, their 20-year-old debutant goalkeeper Koço Dinella yet to make a save of note.

Direct from the restart, as if to signal Albanian intent, Panajot Pano – on receiving a short pass from Medin Zhega – ran directly at the West Germans; matador football, visibly unsettling Helmut Schön's men. Pano's endeavour and adventure set a pattern for the second half that his team-mates were at duty to follow.

Seven minutes after the break came the great 'what if' moment of the game; a moot point that's been at the core of aggravated discussion among Albanians for decades since.

Sabah Bizi, now wielding full metronomic control in the middle of the park, laid a short pass wide to his overlapping right-back, Dinamo Tirana's Frederik Gjinali – also making his *Shqiponjat* debut. Without taking a touch, the tall, slender defender drilled in a delicious low delivery – part cross, part shot – that swerved towards West German keeper Horst Wolter's near post. The Braunschweig stopper spread himself to prevent the cross from entering the net, but it appeared that he'd done so too late, batting the ball back into play from behind the goal line.

The spectators in the Qemal Stafa all screamed '*Gol*'. Wolter immediately raised both arms above his head – his face a portrait of concern – an unnatural response that, on review, seemed to be the action of a guilty man.

To compound this purveying air of conspiracy, the ball remained stationary, half a yard from the goal line, for a few seconds, neither Wolter nor his covering centre-half Wolfgang Weber attempting to either pick it up or clear it. They both, tellingly, turned in the direction of the Austrian referee. It was only when the official failed to signal for a goal that Wolter eventually clutched the ball in his arms.

A minute later, following splendid hold-up play by Pano, Gjinali struck a 30-yard howitzer that grazed the German bar.

This growing well of pressure appeared to signpost the coming of an Albanian opener, the home support lit with excitement. Wolfgang Overath and Günter Netzer, footballers used to bossing midfield flow, retracted, pushed deep into pockets of the pitch they were loath to go, forced acquiescence incited by the four-pronged vigour of Mema, Bizi, Zhega and Pano.

Then, with 20 minutes still remaining and West Germany struggling to make any kind of impression in a game they were desperate to win, Loro Boriçi gestured from the touchline, signalling that the creative midfield triangle with Bizi at its point be inverted to a negatory troika with Ali Mema at its base. He had lost his nerve opting, like so many Adriatic coaches of the decade, for solidity above flair. Boriçi's odd predilection for safety – *Boriçian* football – had re-emerged to blunt his team.

In spite of their coach-sanctioned lack of cutting edge, Albania held firm for the remainder of the game, sparking wild celebrations on the Qemal Stafa pitch. Hundreds of men in long coats invaded the field to hug and kiss their muddied heroes; captain Lin Shllaku was almost bulldozed to the floor by one joyously over-zealous supporter. Impromptu paper fires burned on the concrete terraces, ash spiralling into the late-afternoon sky; a homage to *Shqiponjat*'s glorious 'draw'.

Helmut Schön's tenure as West Germany coach hung by a thread in the wake of what the *Deutscher* press labelled '*Die Schmach von Tirana*' – the Shame of Tirana. Only following conciliatory talks with the DFB was his job spared. The rest, as they say, is history.

As Germany licked its wounds, Albania rejoiced. 'It was such a big upset that we celebrated for a month,' reminisced Panajot Pano in 2010. 'We won the game really [in reference to Gjinali's disallowed goal]. The papers said it was 0-0, but the Germans knew it, the referee knew it, we knew it.'

For *Shqiponjat*, it was a success steeped in irony. With *Die Mannschaft* ripe for the taking, Albania's opportunity to score an even more sensational victory had been prised from their grasp due to the tactical pragmatism of a coach who'd been fearless and attack-minded as a player. And while the stalemate deprived the Germans of their place in the European Championship quarter-finals in Rome, it also left the back door ajar for Albania's arguably greater enemy – Yugoslavia – to capitalise. Like so many triumphs of Albanian lore, this was a bittersweet story with a sting at its tail.

A further fateful twist of the knife saw Albania withdrawn from the qualifying campaign for the 1970 World Cup finals in Mexico by FSHF, any momentum gained from the West Germany performance and result senselessly annulled.

Further purges swept Albania between 1967 and 1970; evils committed reinforcing Party power creatively repackaged under the ugly misnomer 'consolidation of victories achieved'.

The one arena where a variant of democracy traversed its semi-normal course was on the football terraces of Albania, and on 17 December 1967 at the Stadiumi Qemal Stafa, in the face of a considerable and intimidating foe, those terraces had rocked.

Chapter Ten

Fatmir Shima – the Man
From Xhomlliku

IDEAS FOR the content of this book came to me in a variety of ways.

There were things that I already knew, things I discovered while ensnared in the rabbit hole of research, and things I thought I knew, yet didn't, but on which I was subsequently happy and grateful to be corrected.

This story falls into none of the above categories. It's one that I quite simply bumped into by accident.

As mentioned in the book's acknowledgements, much of the detail and shading was provided by my friend, Irvin, a *Tirona* and Spurs-supporting Albanian expat presently residing in south-west London.

I'd been speaking with Irvin for a few months, sharing ideas on the direction in which I wanted the book to go and deliberating on which stories merited coverage. After discussing the Albanian matchday experience with Irvin (covered in Chapter 3), I remarked – in an aside that was purely throwaway – 'I wonder what it was like to have played football in Albania back then?'

'Oh,' Irvin retorted nonchalantly, 'my dad played football in the old Albanian second division. Is that something you'd be interested in?'

'Erm, YES PLEASE!'

So, this is the story of Fatmir Shima, or *Salluku* (Leftie), *Kaçurrelsi* (Curly) or *Simpatiku* (Good Looking) as he was manifoldly known to the small enclave of committed *tifozët* who took their place on the terraces of Stadiumi Kamëz, Tirana County – home to KS Dajti Kamëz – during the club's 'golden era' between 1969 and 1975.

Kamëz, eight miles north-west of central Tirana, is a district drenched in footballing tradition. Formerly a small agricultural outpost, the town played host to the first official football match in Tirana on 26 July 1908: a celebration of the Young Turk Revolution, earning Kamëz enduring status as an Albanian football heritage site.

The fixture, organised by Refik Toptani of the Toptani clan – the leading Albanian noble family in Ottoman Albania, owning much of the land in the rural districts surrounding Tirana – brought together two societies: the *Tërkuzaj* from Kamëz and the *Agimi* from Tirana, a forebear of the modern-day *Tirona*.

The fixture took place on the grounds that presently house the Agricultural University of Tirana – *Universiteti Bujqësor i Tiranës* – founded in 1951 and originally named the *Institoruti i Lartë Bujqës* (the High Institute of Agriculture), an establishment which plays a central role in our protagonist's tale.

In excess of 1,000 Tiranians gathered from across the county to celebrate the Young Turk Revolution and attend the game, which kicked off at 5pm and culminated in a 3-3 draw.

Although the fixture wasn't in accordance with regulation rules which weren't yet formalised (there were no field markings or crossbars and the pitch was a yellowing dustbowl), it's considered to be the first game of football to be played in Tirana, and, as such, the first Tirana derby.

The *Tërkuzaj* society continued to play representative games until their official foundation on 10 September 1936, the new club christened Kamza.

With the advent of communism, Kamza were renamed Ndërmarrja Bujqësore e Shtetit Ylli Kuq Kamëz – Red Star Kamëz State Agricultural Enterprise – in 1949 (a tag that drew few fans and even fewer catchy terrace chants), reverting back to Kamza again in 1950. This lasted until 1953, when they became KS Dajti Kamëz – or KS Dajti – a name which stuck until 1993.

Born into a traditional Tirana family in 1951, Fatmir Shima heralded from the Xhomlliku district in the east of the city. The area is named after the glass-facade bar that existed in the district during communism, a place where functionaries of the system and its workers would mix for a post-shift libation; *Xham* meaning glass.

Xhomlliku was a former Turkish settlement, but many of its Ottoman buildings and mosques were demolished post-World War Two, replaced by prefabricated communist apartment blocks.

In a time of architectural flux, the sole fixture of permanency in the eastern suburbs of Tirana was the horizon-hogging, darkly verdant climbs of Mount Dajti further east, rising above the Xhomlliku district.

Young Fatmir and his family lived in a huge house with an Italianate garden; a remnant dating back to before the revolution, with the extended family all living in close proximity. Many of the Shima clan remain, the interwoven threads of family, tradition and habit binding them to Xhomlliku.

Over the elapsing years, government officials would visit the house regularly, siphoning away Shima-owned land, absorbing the family's hard-gained wealth into Hoxha's wasteful socialist machine with no talk of recompense, family heirlooms stolen without argument – any whiff of dispute and it could all end very badly for the Shima family.

Eventually, the old house was completely swallowed up by the regime and demolished; the Shimas were rehoused in one of the new state-assembled abominations.

In the late 1950s into the 1960s, Xhomlliku was a hub of human life, workers from the villages – reappropriated into Hoxha's new industrialist, trades-orientated Albania – flocking to the district to take up residence in the concrete behemoths of state-built housing.

People would congregate in the local *sheshi* to sit and talk, or sip *kafe* or *raki* and play *tavëll* or *domino* at the canopied *kafeteri* on the corner of the square. For Fatmir, the *sheshi* was a meeting place for friends, and – upon arrival – they would take their shared ball and head off in search of a strip of turf or tarmac on which they would relive the games of *Tirona*, Partizani and Dinamo until dusk fell.

Fatmir's ability as a talented *mesfushori i majtë* – left-sided midfielder – who displayed huge attacking prowess grew. The boy bounced between teams of minor note in both Xhomlliku and its surrounding environs, playing football, instinctively, as and where the opportunity arose. Yet that was about to change when – in the autumn of 1968 – the Shimas received a knock on their door.

1968 was a year in which Hoxha's regime completed their nationwide electrification programme, shedding artificial light on even the darkest corners of the country, Kamëz included.

It was also the year that Albania withdrew from the Warsaw Pact after it had been instrumental in its foundation in May 1955. Hoxha finally pulled the plug in the wake of an ongoing political dispute with Brezhnev-led USSR, citing the Pact's Soviet-fronted August invasion of Czechoslovakia as the final straw.

It was a mock-ethical stance that drew support inside Albania, but was greeted with howls of derision by sceptical Pact members, asking how could a country that butchered its religious leaders and interned its intellectuals have any allusions to moral grandeur?

Albania – now allied solely with Maoist China – had burnt their bridges with any remaining friends in the West.

In the first knockings of autumn, the *Sigurimi* were out in force, redoubling operations to remove any remaining 'undesirables' from society.

In the mid-to-late '60s, state security increased their staff number to peak levels with 16,178 collaborators, 1,088 agents and 12,332 informants all in the *Sigurimi*'s employ.

Paranoia, within The Party and on the streets, was rife. The cement factories at Elbasan, Berat and Krujë worked around the clock to produce the materials needed to build the (estimated) 750,000 mushroom-shaped bunkers that scarred the mountains and coastlines of Albania. It was rumoured that on completion, the *Sigurimi* got the engineers who built the bunkers to sit in them. They would then drop bombs on them to test their strength. The bunkers that the engineers emerged from alive were earmarked for The Party's hierarchy.

In this climate of fear, an unexpected knock on your front door was not something to get excited about.

But this particular visitor, contrary to the Shima family's bleak mood, was here to deliver good news. The suited man standing at the door was in the service of 17 Nëntori. Young Fatmir had been scouted while playing for a team in east Tirana and duly selected to train with the *Tirona* Academy; the fertile youth system that had birthed Pano, Halili, Frasheri, Bukoviku, Lushta, Kryeziu and multiple Memas, an opportunity that – despite his academic aspirations, for he was also a gifted student – Fatmir was eager to seize with both hands.

Training at *Tirona* Academy was well-structured and both tactically and technically excellent, overseen by Osman Reçi, the *bardhë e blutë* legend and distinguished performer for Partizan, Vllaznia, Dinamo and *Shqiponjat*.

Reçi, a football purist, played with culture and poise throughout the exciting era of the 1950s and served as an advocate and mentor to Fatmir Shima, blooding the youngster in key games culminating in a Tirana derby against Partizani

Academy at Pallati i Pioniereve – the Palace of the Pioneers – *Demat e Kuq*'s salubrious training facility inaugurated in 1958.

This high-profile youth fixture, played out before a packed Pallati, was the featured game of the day on Radio Tirana, commentated on by Albania's first great analytical footballing voice, Anton Mazreku.

Mazreku's appetite for and knowledge of all sports, but football chiefly, lent additional texture and legitimacy to the crackle of RTSH radio coverage, his commentary an essential part of the matchday experience for those unable to attend the game.

Mazreku was also the man who mentored and then unleashed a fledgling Ismet Bellova upon the Albanian football-listening public during the 1950 Kupa e Republikës Final between Dinamo and Partizani.

Albanian football fans were shorn of the national game's original voice following Mazreku's sad demise in August 1969. However, he'd implanted a natural successor into the void his loss created in the shape of Bellova.

Mazreku was very much taken by the talents of *Tirona*'s new left-sided midfielder, celebrating his second-half strike with an energetic rejoinder, 'Gol! Kaçurrelsi! Simpatiku! Fatmir Shima është e ardhmja e futbollit Shqiptar!'

Translated, roughly, it means, 'Goal! The curly one! The good-looking one! Fatmir Shima is the future of Albanian football!'

I'm not one to deprive a man of his moment and/or resort to flights of fancy, but this is what I'm reliably told – by the Shima clan – Mazreku allegedly bellowed when Fatmir scored. We will say no more and move on.

Despite being a player of recognised talent, Fatmir was ushered away from the academy fold. Football, during the Stalinist years, held no guarantee of rewardable success. The top tier of the profession afforded an individual and their family the comparative luxury of improved housing and an easier job, but it didn't seat them among the 'high earners' in the socialist pay structure.

Fatmir's elder brother, Gezim, had loftier ambitions for his younger, academically adept sibling.

Gezim remains a respected academic himself; an archaeologist of repute who still has his work published in French journals and magazines well into his octogenarian years. He was also the chief union leader after the fall of communism and was integral in the overthrowing of the Socialist Party of Albania during the 1998 protests that almost brought civil war to the country.

After the death of their father in the early 1960s, Gezim adopted the patriarchal role in the Shima household and, like the good elder brother he was, directed Fatmir down the academic path; a long-term, life-safe option.

In 1969, Fatmir was accepted at the High Institute of Agriculture in Kamëz, studying agronomy – the science and technology of producing and using plants for food, fuel and fibre. In a new, self-reliant Albania, agronomy was considered an important investment in the safeguarding of an autonomous, socialist future.

It was an area in which Fatmir would excel, becoming Albania's premier agronomist and in 1975 director of the Kamëz cooperative, the body that supplied meat, vegetables and milk to The Party in order to sustain the population. His residence in the role failed to dovetail with Fatmir's participation in competitive football.

Immediately after taking his place at the institute in the autumn of 1969, Fatmir spent much of his spare time, as he always had, playing football with a new clique of friends whom he'd met on campus. And again, Fatmir's extra-curricular kick-abouts alerted the university sports coaches who promptly added the youngster to their university academy. It wasn't long before Fatmir was plucked from their ranks by local side KS Dajti.

By September, Fatmir had already established himself as a favourite among the *Kamzalijnt Tifozët* – the hardcore hundreds who followed the club.

His first three appearances for *Blutë* brought with them three goals, two proving to be winners against KS Erzeni from the central-west town of Shijaku and at Minatori – Miner – Tepelenë in the Tosk southlands. *Simpatiku* was becoming a household name in the foothills of north-west Tirana.

In his five years with *Blutë*, Fatmir earned the adoration of the *Kamzalijnt*, Dajti's staunch student-based support, scoring 55 goals in five seasons from a left-midfield position. Never, during Fatmir's term at Dajti, did a season consist of more than 24 league games. In his final season – 1974/75 – *Blutë* played just 19 games (including the ill-fated 4-3 play-off final defeat to KS Luftëtari that denied Dajti promotion to the Kampionati for a first time amid dodgy refereeing and allegations of scandal). Ratio the amount of goals Fatmir scored against the number of games he played for Dajti and it's a quite phenomenal strike rate for a player in that role.

Fatmir quickly elevated himself to the position of senior player. In a modest side comprising footballers who, either due to lack of ability or alternate career choice, weren't able to get into the first teams at Dinamo, Partizani or *Tirona*, he was the star; a player of sublime skill, tactical nous and technical merit. He was popular with the fraternity girls too, due to his tousled black curls and chiselled Illyrian features. Or so I'm told.

Playing football for a second-tier side held no hard-currency reward for a footballer of the era. The only genuine benefits were that you worked five hours and got paid for the mandatory eight while Mondays and Fridays were spent in training for two hours. Club staff also received three meals a day at a designated restaurant, a luxury unheard of among everyday Albanians, who generally subsisted on one.

Training and matchday, for the players of Dajti, presented a triweekly chance for welcome social contact. Without fail, the whole group would arrive an hour early on training days to talk, occasionally about stories in the news, but more regularly about football and the latest songs on the radio. It was a normal, human coming-together set in what was an abnormal and saturnine place in time. Banter among mates.

Yet when training began, it was serious business: 100 per cent committed and focused, observed by Dajti's discerning and demanding troop of coaches and club directors. In spite of being meticulously watched and critiqued, training was an experience to be enjoyed, a glorious release from the mundanity of the administrative office or the factory floor.

Within five short years, Fatmir had risen from the ranks of unknown debutant to first-team regular arriving at the exalted plain of player most revered by the *Kamzalijnt*. But, aged just 24, when most players are yet to hit their footballing peak, his nascent career was over.

After graduating from the High Institute of Agriculture in 1975, Fatmir reluctantly accepted the advice of Gezim and pursued a career in agronomy; a second choice – by no small distance – for the man of many monikers.

His new post took him to the other side of the mountain, to a sedate agricultural co-op beyond Mount Dajti, miles from the bustle and commotion of Xhomlliku. The distance and difficulty of the terrain made weekend travel home tough, the upkeep of a footballing career near impossible.

Reflecting on his footballing past, Fatmir is whimsical, yet there remain pangs of genuine regret; lingering spectres of business unfinished. The end-of-days question we all wish to avoid endures, 'What if?'

The 1975 play-off final defeat against KS Luftëtari from the Tosk city of Gjirokastër still weighs on Fatmir's memory. The venue in the neutral wilderness of Korçë hindered the possibility of *Kamzalijnt* fans travelling to the game, with Gjirokastër significantly nearer. The referee was allegedly a 'ringer', appointed by FSHF to ensure that the club from Tosk Albania prevailed. After the relegation from the top flight of Skënderbeu Korçë and Punëtori – Workshop – Patos at the close of the 1974/75 season, the Tosk territories boasted just one surviving southern team in the top division; Flamurtari from Vlorë. If a Tiranian club were promoted, there would be five teams from the capital taking their place in Albania's first division at the start of the 1975/76 season – Partizani, Dinamo, Tirona, Shkëndija and KS Dajti. It presented a logistic that FSHF may have wanted to avoid.

Dajti's narrow defeat ended any forlorn hopes Fatmir harboured regarding a career in top-tier football; the result brusquely signposting his expected, yet unsought destiny. It still irks Fatmir as an opportunity missed.

Fatmir waxes lyrical about his coach's conveyance of tactics at Dajti; chess pieces planted on a felt pitch – Subbuteo-style – with chalk to mark movements on the field, echoes of receding nostalgia brought into sharp focus by an astute and agile mind.

But the greater feelings of loss stemmed from the realisation that his would be a life lived within Albania and her borders. Players played with a passion for the shirt and for their team-mates on pitches rutted and dust-ridden, with no financial incentive apart from the small concessions offered by the regime.

Any payment was earned from the feeling of personal and communal pride football offered and the adulation it garnered from the small pockets of support. But for players at all levels, there was always the gilt-glimmer of hope that they would be signed for a Dinamo or a Partizani; a government-subsidised team, heralding the ultimate reward that every Albanian footballer craved – a trip abroad.

A visit to a country beyond cruel constraints of the regime constituted the acme of Albanian footballers' expectations; a brief interlude from the governmentally prescribed toil of native life. Robert Jashari, the Partizani great, was so aggrieved by the regime's refusal to allow him to travel to a European Cup Winners' Cup tie versus Torino in 1969 (citing his Italian heritage as a possible reason to defect) that he immediately quit football; Jashari's story a mere aperitif to the insufferable distress Hoxhaism caused.

Italian clubs, especially, showed continual interest in Albanian footballers; Vogli, Frasheri, Halili, Pernaska and Ali Mema were all coveted by Italian suitors. Rragami, Ballgjini, Minga and Kola received offers from foreign agents. Legend dictates that Ajax coach Rinus Michels was actively interested in the acquisition of Panajot Pano, but was crudely rebuffed by FSHF.

Football, for all of the joy it afforded Fatmir, neglected to offer the one thing he craved: the opportunity to make a decision about his own future. He was a cog in a machine where the collective was all and individual ambition stood for nothing. The absence of rudimentary human freedoms meant that even the most talented subjects were bound to a life that was prescribed to them; a life that was often a consolation prize in the worldly gambit.

Shima's dual failings were that he was talented in too many areas and, more painfully, that he was born in Stalinist Albania, where talent was brokered; pigeon-holed to benefit the regime best – not the individual.

Fatmir Shima; *Salluku, Kaçurrelsi, Simpatiku* – a man of many pseudonyms, whom arguably Albania's greatest commentary voice once lauded as 'the future of Albanian football'. A man who craved the glory of his sport, yet was forced to settle for the functionality of agronomy. A noble pursuit and a worthwhile life, sure.

But it isn't football, is it?

Iconic Games

17 Nëntori Tirana 2 Ajax 2

European Cup First Round First Leg

Stadiumi Qemal Stafa, Tirana

16 September 1970

Attendance: 17,516

17 Nëntori: Mihallaq Konomi, Fatmir Frasheri (captain/*kapiten*), Gani Xhafa, Perikli Dhales, Gezim Kasmi, Skender Hyka, Ali Mema, Niko Xhaçka, Arben Cela, Medin Zhega, Iljaz Ceco

Substitutes/*Zëvendësues*: Josif Kazanxhi (Niko Xhaçka; half-time), Shpetim Habibi (Mihallaq Konomi; 61 mins)

Coach/*Trajneri*: Myslym Alla

Ajax: Heinz Stuy, Wim Suurbier, Barry Hulshoff, Velibor Vasovic (captain/*kapiten*), Ruud Krol, Nico Rijnders, Johan Neeskens, Gerrie Muhren, Sjaak Svart, Dick van Dijk, Piet Keizer

Substitute/*Zëvendësues*: George van Bockel (unused)

Coach/*Trajneri*: Rinus Michels

Referee/*Arbitri*: Peter Schiller (Austria)

When the draw for the European Cup first round took place in Basel, Switzerland, in June 1970, it threw together several interesting contests with many of the continent's elite forced to make uncomfortable journeys into uncharted territories to either protect or perpetuate their international reputations.

Newly crowned English champions Everton endured a chilly trip 'up north' to face Keflavík, the Icelandic league champions, with the previous season's tournament runners-up, Celtic, facing an equally brisk northernly sojourn to Finland where they'd been paired against the extravagantly monikered Kokkolan Palloveikot.

There was a potentially explosive face-off between the Irish and Northern Irish champions, Waterford United and Glentoran, that would keep the garda and military of both Irelands in a state of pensive alert.

The reigning champions of Europe, Feyenoord of the Netherlands, would visit Ceaușescu's Romania and the potential banana skin posed by UTA from the country's textile city of Arad.

Feyenoord had earned their place in the 1970/71 edition of the competition as a result of the final win at Milan's San Siro against an under-par Celtic, a 2-1 victory that had cemented Netherlands' reputation as an emerging force in world football. But it was the Rotterdam club's Amsterdam neighbours who had been drawn in the most intriguing of the first-round ties.

Ajax won the 1969/70 Eredivisie at a canter, five points ahead of second-placed Feyenoord, scoring 100 goals and conceding only 23 during the 34-game season. They'd shown glimpses of European pedigree too, reaching the final in 1968/69 and the quarter-finals in 1966/67. Yet 1970/71 heralded the augmentation of what would prove a great journey for Rinus Michels' wonderful side, playing the game in a new way – *totaalvoetbal* – executed by a group of players who were technically comfortable and competent with or without the ball.

The Dutch *kampioenen* were drawn against the Albanian *kampionë*, 17 Nëntori of Tirana, a tie that provided both the allure and subsequent difficulties that a trip to the continent's least obliging nation presented.

By 1970, a period of social and cultural change had been in progress in the Netherlands, the nation's youth engaged in the new-worldly pursuits of rock 'n' roll, drugs, informal clothing, sexual exploration and moral idealism. The contrasts between the Netherlands and Albania – mired in the aftermath of the 1967 constitutional rewrite and the toxic cultural revolution that preceded it – couldn't have been more starkly pronounced.

However, there was one social phenomenon in which both countries were mutually invested – bicycles. In the

Netherlands, a growing trend away from motorised transport was taking shape, Dutch people taking to the streets to protest not only against both the carbon emissions and huge traffic flows, but more pointedly to oppose to the high number of child deaths on the roads – over 500 children were killed in collisions with motor vehicles in 1969.

Whereas Dutch – and more pertinently, the Amsterdammers' – leanings towards this mode of transportation were prompted by the pervading air of ethical idealism that blew through the lowlands of progressive Holland, Albania's was born of social necessity. Either way, the results remained the same; bicycles reigned in Tirana as they did Amsterdam.

When the draw was made, the players and staff of 17 Nëntori were enjoying a shared club holiday on the beaches of Durrës on the Albanian Adriatic coast. Propping up the bar with beers in hand, the announcement – made during the midday news on Radio Tirana – was received with enthusiasm by the footballers of *Tirona*.

The team spirit and belief among Myslym Alla's group of players was equivalent to that of their Dutch counterparts. 17 Nëntori were locked into a cycle of recurring success between 1965 and 1970, a half-decade where the club, embodying the characteristics prevalent in *Tirona*'s finest teams – sacrifice, determination, positivity and beauty – were a dominant and foreboding force domestically, breaking the Partizani–Dinamo chokehold on the national game. They were confident of making an impact against *De Godenzonen*.

In the lead-up to the first leg in Tirana, the Albanian regime forwarded a letter to the Dutch club warning them that their players – the 'long-haired scum' – would not be allowed to enter the country if they had facial hair or haircuts measuring in excess of 3cm in length, thus generating a flurry of activity in the barbershops neighbouring De Meer.

A pithy response regarding the Albanians' requests, apropos hair, from Ajax director Jaap van Praag caused a further storm in the proverbial teacup.

'That's impossible,' van Praag chided. 'Mao Zedong has long hair himself, doesn't he?' His comment was greeted with an icy rebuke from Ajax's hosts; Albania would not tolerate long hair as it was a characteristic of the noxious decadence that emanated from the capitalist West.

Indeed, any signs of Western influence, including foreign music and TV, wearing Western fashions, the importation of religious texts and regalia or having long hair and/or a beard, were categorically banned. Packing a suitcase for a visit to Stalinist Albania could prove a minefield in itself.

But the petty nitpicking continued upon Ajax's arrival in the Hermit Kingdom. The Dutch – like FC Köln before them in 1964 – brought their own provisions to Albania; a perceived display of impropriety and disrespect hastily rebuffed by management at Tirana's Hotel Dajti. Head chef Mihal Kanini baulked at the contraband foodstuffs – sausages chiefly – imported by these petulant, Western bourgeoisie. The club sportingly distributed the contraband goods among Dajti's hotel staff to preserve peace, with Ajax's chief objector, Kanini, receiving nothing.

After an initial settling-in period at Hotel Dajti, the players of Ajax held a meet-and-greet session at Stadiumi Qemal Stafa, which was attended by curious fans and *Tirona* players.

Ajax's entourage, accompanied by their glamorous WAGs, pulled up at the national stadium on the Tuesday afternoon wearing brightly coloured Western outfits; the wives in mini-skirts, a caravan of Western pomp and excess – the natives aghast.

'Who are these people?' scathed the outraged, regime-friendly Albanian press corps. 'Where did they come from? Are they cartoons?'

As the Ajax players indulged in light training, stroking the ball around the seasonally decent playing surface at the Qemal Stafa, Myslym Alla, *Tirona*'s coach and an enjoyer of the finer nuances of the beautiful game, entered into conversation with his staff regarding the youthful Johan Cruyff.

'You see that boy,' Alla is purported to have said, 'very soon you will see how great a football player he will become.' He certainly knew talent when he saw it.

However, the fledgling *Krujfi* would play no part in the first leg, arriving on matchday at the stadium with a heavily bandaged left knee. Alongside fellow *Oranje* legend Arie Haan, the 23-year-old Cruyff would only warm the substitutes' bench in Tirana, much to native disappointment. Ironically, it had been during the team's Tuesday evening cycle ride around the Albanian capital that Cruyff had reportedly sustained his injury.

Matchday observed a packed-to-capacity Qemal Stafa; the pigeons, till rolls and blue and white confetti held in reserve in the event of a *Tirona* goal. Albania was basking in the heat of an unseasonably warm September; men in the *Tribuna* and *njëzet* dressed in short-sleeved shirts and slacks, the women wearing summer blouses and skirts. The sun gazed down on the stadium from above the verdant, overseeing heights of Mount Dajti, small wisps of cloud suspended in an otherwise Alice blue sky; perfect conditions for a football contest of such importance.

Surprisingly, and outside the realms of any reasonable context, the two sides took to the field sporting kits unfamiliar from the trikot we associate them with; *Tirona* donned in Columbia blue V-neck, short-sleeved shirts, white shorts and white socks with a Columbia blue hem, Ajax wearing cherry red, short-sleeved shirts with white V-neck and cuffs, white shorts and white socks with cherry red hem – the consummate Blues versus Reds confrontation.

Despite the absence of Cruyff and Haan, the Ajax side that appeared in Tirana that day was replete with established international talent, ten of their 11 players having represented their countries; goalkeeper Heinz Stuy the only one uncapped in the line-up.

Tirona, as was customary during the Stalinist period, acquired the services of a couple of 'ringers' on short-term loans: Çeço from Dinamo Tirana and Zhega from Vllaznia. Their team was replete with international talent too, albeit derived from less-salubrious means than their illustrious continental rivals.

Chinese footballs employed during *Kampionati* games were traded for a set of Adidas-branded Tango balls, imported for the occasion by UEFA, which Austrian referee Peter Schiller and his officiating team kept safely locked away in their dressing room.

The match was broadcast on screens throughout Albania by the still experimental Radio Televizioni Shqiptar soundtracked by the commentary of Ismet Bellova and journalistic luminary Skifter Këlliçi, who swapped roles at half-time – Këlliçi providing the TV narrative in the first half and radio coverage in the second, Bellova vice-versa. The presence of television cameras meant that football fans from Shkodër to Gjirokastër were united in their support for the team the regime tried to break. And Myslym Alla's *Tirona* were in no mood to disappoint their captive audience.

Captains Fatmir Frasheri and Velibor Vasović exchanged handshakes and wimpels prior to a noon kick-off, *Tirona* opting to kick towards the end to the right of the *Tribuna*. Immediately, the home side strived to maintain possession, going close when a quick passing movement through the centre of the Ajax midfield almost broke for Perikli Dhales in the area only for Stuy to gratefully retrieve the ball.

Despite being tested, Hyka forcing a decent save from Stuy with a speculative long-range drive and Zhega screwing wide a golden opportunity after the Ajax keeper had misdirected a clearance into the forward's path, the Dutch were beginning to show signs of their undoubted quality, Piet Keizer probing the *Tirona* back line down its right.

With 18 minutes gone and the contest even, Ajax stung their Albanian opponents. A *Tirona* corner was cleared as far as Gani Xhafa 40 yards from the Ajax goal. Xhafa's attempted forward prod to Ali Mema failed to reach its intended target, intercepted by Ruud Krol whose first-time pass found Piet Keizer just inside the *Tirona* half. Ahead of him – testament to the tenets of *totaalvoetbal* to which Michels' side were invested – was full-back Wim Suurbier, racing towards the Albanian goal. What Keizer produced wasn't so much a pass, more a moving on of the ball, putting Suurbier one-on-one with opposing keeper Konomi. Taking one touch, Suurbier hammered a low shot past the *Tirona* stopper. Only four touches and seven seconds had elapsed since Krol's intervention; the most speedy and potent of breakaway goals. Ajax led 1-0.

Tirona, stunned by this bolt from the blue, took a while to recover. However, by half-time they had reclaimed some semblance of control, Zhega heading over when handily placed in the box and Stuy clawing an awkward Xhafa cross off the same player's head moments later. But Ajax, a coiled cobra, still looked to exploit their opponents on the break, stretching *Tirona* whenever the Albanians were anything other than totally secure in their passing.

At half-time Myslym Alla rang the changes, replacing the ineffective Niko Xhaçka with the raw, physical presence of Josif Kazanxhi; the substitute immediately making an impression by forcing a fingertip save from Stuy with a towering header, minutes into the second half.

As *Tirona* appeared to be gaining the upper hand, Ajax struck again on 58 minutes, Suurbier collecting a short pass from Keizer before delivering a 25-yard right-footed hammer blow into Konomi's bottom-right corner, the keeper at full stretch. Despite playing exceptionally well, *Tirona* found themselves 2-0 behind against dangerous opposition. Suurbier, who managed only 16 goals in over 400 appearances, had scored two in 40 minutes.

But the nature of the response was admirable. Within minutes, Iljaz Çeço received the ball wide-right and bent a wonderful ball into the Ajax area – inside the 'corridor of uncertainty' – between the edge of the six-yard box and the penalty spot. The ball evaded the ruckus of players scampering towards the near post, finding the late run of Josif Kazanxhi who, unmarked at the far post, spectacularly dive-headed Çeço's bouncing bomb of a cross past Stuy into the Ajax net. The hosts were back in business.

Within a minute of *Tirona*'s goal, their keeper Mihallaq Konomi departed the pitch injured and was replaced by youngster Shpetim Habibi. Aside from some rudimentary goalkeeping basics, it was to prove a quiet 29 minutes for the teenager, with the home side now in the ascendency. Ali Mema had quietly taken a cadenced hold of the middle of the park, providing ammunition for the three-pronged attacking troika of Çeço, Zhega and Kazanxhi.

Despite knocks to defensive partners Fatmir Frasheri and Perikli Dhales, which required medical attention, *bardhë e blutë* pressed hard for an equaliser.

There was little more than five minutes on the clock when Mema's driving run and cross inside the Ajax area created the necessary havoc that enabled Çeço to toe the ball into the path of Zhega, who crashed in a low finish to level the scores at 2-2.

Ajax wore the appearance of a heavyweight boxer who couldn't wait for the final bell to ring. When Schiller finally blew the full-time whistle, it was greeted with a collective sigh of relief by the Dutch champions and wild, joyous applause from the home contingent inside the concrete bowl of the Qemal Stafa. *Tirona* had tested their mettle against the best in Europe – and won. Well, almost.

Sporti Popullor, Albania's football weekly, waxed exultantly over *Tirona*'s display. It had provided a glue with which to unite the country; a metaphor celebrating the collective strength of Albania when confronted by powerful enemies. The journalist wrote, '[When] Ajax – the name of a hero in Greek mythology – came to face 17 Nëntori, they were sure that the victory was in their pocket. Their team came to Tirana with high ideas; coach-general Rinus Michels had brought everyone, the young Cruyff, Hulshoff, Suurbier, Neeskens, etc. But with confidence in their strengths, our footballers can give more.'

For *Tirona*, it was the high point of a disastrous season. They lost the return in Amsterdam; sublime, well-constructed, typically Ajax goals from Piet Keizer and Sjaak Swart giving *De Godenzonen* a 2-0 victory at the Olympisch Stadion.

Domestically, *Tirona* descended into freefall, a seventh-place finish in the *Kampionati* unacceptable for a team with such high standards and so rich in talent. They would have to wait until 1981/82 to win a further title, their next crack at the European Cup in 1982/83 seeing them progress past Northern Ireland's champions, Linfield, in the first round before they were pulled from the competition by The Party after they'd been paired with the champions from the ideologically odious Soviet Union, Dinamo Tbilisi, in the second round.

There would be notable successes in European competition in the future, but 16 September 1970 saw the end of an era for *Tirona*; a five-year window of glory that re-established the club as the best in Albania. But it also hailed the beginning of a new, exciting phase for their victors.

Ajax's 2-2 draw at the Qemal Stafa proved to be the first rung on an upward spiral of success that ssaw *De Godenzonen* win the next three European Cups, taking their deserved place among the royalty of European football, but it was a journey – on a balmy afternoon in the autumn of 1970 – that began in Stalinist Albania.

Chapter Eleven

The North Rises

FOOTBALL, AKIN to history, has a way of repeating itself. As Albanian football languished beneath the malevolent shroud of the 1966/67 season with the nation forced to observe Dinamo's expulsion from European competition (an affair leaving FSHF and The Party oddly contrite) the resumption of the 1967/68 season saw *Tirona* – slighted yet resolute – back at their very best.

Myslym Alla's splendid side blasted their way to a third title in four years (the ill-doings of 1966/67 preventing *bardhë e blutë* from achieving four out of four), their powers of recovery in the aftermath of such appalling bias quite remarkable. Skender Hyka, a hard-working striker, became a reliable source of goals in a season that witnessed *Tirona* plunder 63 goals in 26 league games, conceding only 20, leaving second-placed Partizani in their distant wake.

It was a success they would repeat the following season, romping to a further title, with Partizani again the runners-up.

Partizani put an end to this seam of *Tirona* dominance by winning the 1970/71 championship, a point ahead of a Dinamo side that'd recovered from the embarrassment of 1967, running their city rivals to the wire.

Fittingly, Partizani's triumph came in Panajot Pano's retirement season, an appropriate epithet to a career that had enraptured the Albanian public. Photographs of *Mbreti* in Partizani red, arms laden with bouquets, performing a lap of honour with his young son, Ledio, at Stadiumi Qemal Stafa after his final appearance for *Demat e Kuq* – fans unified in affectionate applause – serve as a poignant and merited testimony to a truly great player.

Partizani's 1970/71 victory signposted 25 years of unbroken Tiranian success, the Kampionati Kombetar trophy apparently finding a permanent home in the capital over the course of the preceding quarter of a century.

However, something was stirring in the mountainous north; a dormant giant of Albanian football slowly awakening from lengthy slumber.

The Gheg city of Shkodër had suffered the worst due to the dark insecurities of the Hoxha regime. The oldest city in the Balkans, inhabited since the Bronze Age, Shkodër isn't merely the birthplace of Albania football, it's also the cradle of the Albanian nation.

It's a dominion which Edith Durham, the British artist, anthropologist, writer and Albanophile, called 'the Land of the Living Past' in her 1908 travelogue, *High Albania*, and it remains easy to see why. Peasants and clanspeople in traditional costume can still be seen pacing the boulevards of modern Shkodër alongside the Mercedes vehicles, the business suits and designer shops.

Its skyline is – was – dominated by the towers of the many mosques and churches encamped there, and it remains a city of religious diversity, freedom and acceptance. It's also a hotbed of intellectual discourse and revolutionary thought, many of the country's finest minds moulded in its surfeit of reputed *shkollat*.

Shkodrans faced a recurrent historical battle for their identity and autonomy, having been occupied by Montenegrin, Austrian-Hungarian, French, Serb and Italian forces in the 19th and early 20th centuries. The people of Shkodër, with the blood of the northern tribes running through their veins and their inexorable fiefdom mindset, weren't opposed to taking to the field to safeguard their heritage – a deeply principled, courageous, battle-hardened people. Hard-won independence set them apart from the rest of Albania, an 'otherworld' – a 'Republic of Shkodër' – and it was a liberty its citizens were, are, determined to protect.

After World War One, Shkodër became the centre of the democratic movements of the 1920s and sought to free the city from its administrative ties to national government in Tirana. Tirana's status riled northern natives; it neither had the history nor the infrastructure of Shkodër. Tirana was a small market town with a population of 12,000 when it was inaugurated as Albania's capital after the end of World War One. The Shkodrans boasted a history dating back centuries; Tirana was a mere infant in comparison. So, despite being an Albanian city in Albania, Shkodër operated under its own steam, pioneering industrialism in the country while peasants in the other districts still tilled the fields.

When the communists ousted the fascists post-World War Two, Shkodrans may have thought themselves impervious to the change. Amid this political and cultural flux, it's understandable why Hoxha identified Shkodër as a city that needed to be broken. Shkodër had observed frequent purges of its brightest minds and spiritual leaders decades before the writing of the 1967 Constitution.

Vllaznia, *Djepi i Futbollit Shqiptar* – the Cradle of Albanian Football as they are regally ordained – suffered hard under Hoxha, meandering in a state of regime-induced stasis since their 1940s heyday, culminating in their disastrous relegation campaign of 1961.

They regrouped fast, achieving immediate promotion to the Kampionati Kombetar by winning the second division ahead of Tomori in 1961/62, but rather than inspire *Kuq e Blutë* – the Red and Blues – to greater things, there unfurled three seasons of epic stagnation. An underwhelming eighth-place finish in 1962/63 predated further melodrama, near-relegation averted via a play-off in 1963/64; a 3-1 aggregate win against Naftëtari of Qyteti Stalin (Stalin City, now Kuçovë) sparing Vllaznia blushes.

However, when repeated close shaves failed to enact change, Skënder Jareci (the same Skënder Jareci who would lead Dinamo to league success in 1966/67) was relieved of his post as team coach in 1965; Xhevdet Shaqiri was implanted into the role in time for the 1965/66 season.

Shaqiri, Shkodran by birth and top scorer when Vllaznia last won the championship in 1946, was a man determined to bring the good times back to the north – from a football perspective, at least.

Alongside the new head coach came his trusted trainer, Xhelal Juka, his old comrade and team-mate during *Kuq e Blutë's* title-winning success of 1946. Juka also represented Ljubiša Broćić's *Shqiponjat* in their Balkan Cup warm-up international versus Montenegro in 1946, scoring twice in the 5-0 thrashing.

Shaqiri not only believed in his team, he also had total faith in the fans, the Stadiumi Vojo Kushi (similar in spirit to Barcelona's Camp Nou) a temple to the epitomes of Shkodran identity. With the football fans of Shkodër inflamed – united behind a side imbuing the innate Shkodran values of spirit, guile and intelligence – they would be virtually unstoppable.

The application of Shaqiri's philosophies marked a period of steady improvement, a fourth-place finish behind the three Tirana teams at the close of 1965/66 signifying progress. A sixth-place finish in the fated 1966/67 season failed to represent how close they'd come to improving on the previous year, a solitary point denying Vllaznia third place. The following year would observe another fourth place prior to further third-place finishes in 1969/70 and 1970/71.

With patience, diligence and intellect, Shaqiri and Juka were constructing a side capable of transforming an awakening Vllaznia into a force to be feared once again.

Vllaznia's prospects of success were further improved by Shaqiri's astute dealings in the dubious minefield that was the Albanian transfer market. Wily in his transactions, Shaqiri managed to lure three former Vllaznia players – all Shkodër born-and-bred and all exceptionally gifted – back into the club fold.

Ramazan Rragami, Sabah Bizi and Medin Zhega returned to their home city following successful spells in Tirana; Rragami and Bizi with Partizani, Zhega at Dinamo. The triumvirate brought with them – in addition to their unquestionable ability – experience and an aptitude to perform at the highest level in pressure situations, their time in Tirana versing them in the art of winning.

The acquisition of Bizi entailed a power struggle that required political intervention. Partizani, averse to releasing Bizi from their staff, were cajoled by the chairman of the Executive Committee of Shkodër, Bilal Parruca – a man with friends in Tirana – who implored Partizani to allow the player to return 'to the people of Shkodër who love him', emoting that a refusal to reunite Bizi 'affects the progress of the city itself' (an allusion – although a carefully worded one – to Shkodran suffering at the hands of the regime). The Tirana giants acquiesced. With Bizi in place, it would prove a creative *troika* integral to 'New Vllaznia' success over the forthcoming years.

With the goalkeeping acuity of Paulin Ndoja, the solidity and *gjak në ballë* – blood on the brow – fighting mentality of Frederik Çapaliku, Rauf Çangë, Hajro Lekaj and Lekë Koçobashi and the attacking thrust of Ismet Hoxha and Česk Ndoja, Shaqiri had assembled a team comprised of both silk and steel.

In spite of a healthy optimism inside Shaqiri's camp, the preparations for the 1971/72 campaign began under a cloud. Vllaznia's volleyball team had embarked on a pre-season tour of Kosovo – then part of the Federal Republic of Yugoslavia

– returning from Pristina with TV sets, radios and other Yugoslavian-made consumer durables superior in quality to poor, homemade Albanian products. On their arrival back in Shkodër, the awaiting *Sigurimi* confiscated the goods and issued life bans to the delegation heads, Qemal Byrazeri and Franc Jakova. Rifat Uruçi, Vllaznia's travelling journalist, was sentenced to a career-ending 'trip to the fields'.

The Party banned Vllaznia teams, across all sports, indefinitely from all international competition, culminating in their withdrawal from the 1971/72 edition of the rebranded UEFA Cup in which they'd been drawn against Rapid Vienna in the first round. The regime switched the blame, claiming it was due to Austrian immigration officials' refusal to issue the necessary visas.

Despite this crushing disappointment, Shaqiri's hard-edged side began the season with gusto and adventure, winning two and drawing three of their opening five fixtures to sit fifth, two points behind early pace-setters 17 Nëntori.

Importantly, the Bizi–Rragami–Zhega trinity was finding itself. The three appeared in the same Vllaznia starting 11 for the first time on 2 October; a return to the capital for the boys, played at a half-full Qemal Stafa against Shkëndija. The game ended in a 0-0 draw, but there were sparks of potential, an announcement that – after 25 years of rigid domestic triopoly – there may be a new challenger in the seasonal title mix.

Vllaznia's next home game at the Vojo Kushi (presently renamed Stadiumi Loro Boriçi), against Luftëtari on 31 October 1971, proved a genuine statement of intent, *Kuq e Blutë* mercilessly tearing into inferior opposition. It ended 4-0, with Medin Zhega netting a superb hat-trick – he'd scored six goals in the opening six games – and their ebullient, home-bred, youth team talent Milan Vaso (aided by the dual force of Rragami and Bizi in central midfield) pulling the strings in a magnificent team performance. Vllaznia were upping their credentials as genuine contenders.

Yet within three days of the Luftëtari game, any whiff of optimism had been expunged by a hybrid of bad luck and Machiavellian intrusion. Zhega, Vllaznia's newly reacquired goal machine, ruptured his cruciate ligament during training, sidelining him for the season and, if that wasn't bad enough, Milan Vaso was called up for the dreaded military service; packed off to Gjirokastër, where he played for KS Luftëtari – the team he had teased days earlier – for two years. The talented utility player, Halil Puka, was also exiled to Durrës-based club Lokomotiva. The regime, once again, crudely sought to take a wrecking ball to Shkodran title aspirations.

Quite where this diminished version of Vllaznia found the resolve to maintain their championship challenge is hard to pinpoint, especially as the decimation of the squad, including the main striker, left Shaqiri with so many difficult tactical questions.

A solution to Shaqiri's goalscoring conundrum was solved by the introduction of converted midfielder Česk Ndoja. Recruited by Shaqiri from Naftëtari in 1970 on the advice of Sabah Bizi (Bizi had played at youth level with Ndoja in the mid-'60s), Ndoja's unselfishness, speed of thought and goal threat filled the Zhega-shaped hole in Vllaznia's formation. Pitched alongside established forward Ismet Hoxha, Shaqiri had found his attacking answer. As Zhega was receiving treatment for his injury in a Bucharest hospital, Ndoja and Hoxha were playing their part in the Vllaznia revival. And they were abundantly fed by Rragami and Bizi.

Bizi had been the beacon in Partizani's title triumph the previous season and now looked to transpose his organisational and creative magic on to a new canvas. Rragami, the captain, added calmness, leadership and superb technique to the blend, contributing – as with Bizi – assists and goals to this heady concoction. They were separate chambers in the beating heart of Shaqiri's Vllaznia.

Yet, heading into late November, *Kuq e Blutë* were suffering a stutter in form; too many draws and not enough wins, exacerbated by a 2-1 defeat in Tirana against a Partizani side vying to get their own Kampionati challenge back on track. Vllaznia resided in their near-customary fourth position – just another typical season up north.

By late December, their plight had worsened, dropping to a season low of sixth. A 3-2 aggregate win in the semi-final of the Kupa e Republikës against Partizani – a 2-1 victory on *Demat e Kuq's* home turf sealing the deal in the second leg – at least offered the opportunity of silverware and a possible place in the 1972/73 edition of the European Cup Winners' Cup. A double date with Besa was Vllaznia's reward in what appeared to be a very winnable final.

By the spring, league form had improved significantly, a run of nine unbeaten games including seven wins elevating Vllaznia above previous leaders 17 Nëntori. *Tirona's* surprise 1-0 defeat at home to Labinoti coupled with Vllaznia's 3-2 win against Traktori of Lushnjë at the Vojo Kushi in early April – Bizi, Česk Ndoja and Esat Rakiqi scoring after the home team had trailed twice – placed them one point ahead of *bardhë e blutë*.

The northerners travelled to Kavajë in a mood of quiet optimism. They'd slain Besa 3-0 at the Vojo Kushi just weeks earlier, a performance suffused with composure and invention.

Besa, having started their league campaign brightly, were now residing in the safety of mid-table, their semi-final victory on penalties against Dinamo Tirana coming as a huge surprise to fans and media alike.

The final, played before wild home support at the grounds that predated Stadiumi Besa on 23 April 1972, was tough and tight, and seemed to be heading for a bland, goalless stalemate until – with three minutes remaining – Shyqri Qerolli plundered a scrappy opener for *Verdhezinjtë*, by no means a disaster, but signifying that repair work would be needed in the home leg. However, Muhamet Vila's side hadn't finished yet, midfielder Zenel Kashami drilling home in the last minute to hand Besa a barely believable 2-0 advantage to defend in the return; Kavaja showgrounds overspilling with joy.

Shaqiri and his players were rattled. They'd controlled the game without ever looking likely winners, Besa's two late bolts from the blue a perceived injustice.

A week later, on the first day in May, Vllaznia and Besa resumed their acquaintance at Stadiumi Vojo Kushi. Vllaznia's Shkodran fortress was a cauldron of noise and emotion, and it would carry the home team to a dramatic and record-making victory.

On a heavy pitch, *Kuq e Blutë* went direct, peppering the Besa box with big-ball; a relentless tide of Wimbledon-esque pressure. How Besa managed to remain unbreached for 31 minutes is difficult to fathom, but a long punt into their area was to prove their undoing; agricultural defending by Osman Kapidani presenting Vllaznia with a penalty. The spot kick was slotted to the keeper's left with consummate ease by captain Ramazan Rragami – Haki Arkaxhiu between the Besa 'sticks' rooted – halving the deficit.

Nine minutes into the second half the tie was level. Another unwieldy foul caused *referia* Ramiz Pregia to point to the spot again, to present Rragami with another penalty opportunity. Again, he dispatched the kick with cool aplomb, high into the right-hand corner – unstoppable; 2-2 on aggregate.

Besa somehow managed to quell the Vllaznia tide, taking the tie to penalties after the remaining minutes of the 90 and extra time failed to produce further goals. With each team designated one solitary taker for all of their kicks, Besa selected forward Nimet Mehori, while Vllaznia stuck with the already twice successful Rragami.

With the score at 3-2 to Vllaznia and all of the preceding kicks converted, Paulin Ndoja in Vllaznia's goal threw himself to his right, clawing away Mehori's third kick. Rragami tucked away his side's remaining two, *Kuq e Blutë* winning the Kupa 5-3 on penalties.

Ramazan Rragami remains the only man to have scored seven penalties in a cup final, domestic or otherwise, a record that seems – in present conditions – unlikely to ever be beaten.

Vllaznia, with Bizi, Rragami and Shaqiri as their guides, had learned how to become winners again, doing so in the most dramatic of circumstances. It was a confidence they carried into the final months of the season.

On 7 May, the weekend after their energy-sapping cup victory, Vllaznia were to call on all of their powers of determination, application and resolve once more, travelling to the Qemal Stafa to face arch-title rivals 17 Nëntori, in a toe-to-toe that would go some way to deciding the destiny of the 1971/72 Kampionati Kombetar.

It has been cited that over 200 Shkodrans cycled the 60 miles that separate Tirana from Shkodër to be present in Tirana that day. What's unarguable is that it was a game – with *Tirona* and Vllaznia level on points with four matches remaining – that both sides could ill-afford to lose.

Despite the recurrent football purges absurdly imposed on both clubs by a regime that didn't want them to succeed, the players who took to the field that day were among the finest in Albanian history. *Tirona*, bolstered by the defensive assurance of Fatmir Frasheri and the creative verve of *Braziliani* Ali Mema, playing at the height of his powers (any rare errors were mopped up with vulpine tenacity by his elder sibling, Osman – *Finoku*) were an outstanding outfit, but Vllaznia, armed with the twin threats of Bizi and Rragami and protected by a near-impenetrable defensive screen that would concede only 15 goals all season, were their equals.

The *stadiumi*, packed with in excess of 20,000 fans, observed the 'old guard' of Albanian football battle out an absorbingly tense 0-0 draw. The players embraced at full time, the small pocket of celebrating Shkodrans duly applauded by the home fans in the *njëzet*. It was a victorious stalemate, Vllaznia departing Tirana the happier, ahead of their rivals on the anorexic margin of goal difference.

It must have been an incredibly convivial atmosphere at the Qemal Stafa on that hot Sunday afternoon; celebratory even. A contest between the two sides that the dictatorship had tried hardest to break, still there; strong, resilient, unbroken, battling it out to decide the destiny of the title in The Party's own backyard. A parable of renewed hope signalling a brighter future, perhaps?

Or perhaps not. In a sad echo of past wrongs, *Tirona* were relieved of the services of the Mema siblings, along with Frasheri and fellow Albanian internationals Josif Kazanxhiu, Niko Xhaçka, Bahri Ishka and talented forward Bujar Tafaj at the season's close, shepherded into ridiculously early retirements by an unspecified power. No reason for their mass exodus was ever given, and none of the *Tirona* players were allowed a farewell ceremony in spite of – or maybe because of – their unfettered loyalty to the *bardhë e blutë*.

The week following the *Tirona* game, Vllaznia played Skënderbeu at Vojo Kushi, home fans packing the *stadiumi* an hour before kick-off. *Kuq e Blutë*, initially inhibited by the vastness of the occasion, eventually found their rhythm, easing to a nervy but deserved 3-2 victory. As the full-time whistle blew, the fans inside the Vojo Kushi tuned in to their transistor radios to check the progress of *Tirona*, still playing in their game – a Tirana derby against Partizani at the Qemal Stafa. And the news was good: goals from Uran Xhafa and Dhori Kalluci propelling reigning champions Partizani to a 2-1 victory. With three games left, Vllaznia were two points clear.

Next up, Vllaznia faced another tussle with Besa in Kavajë on a pudding bowl of a pitch. This time, Shaqiri's side managed to hold out for the full 90 minutes, earning another precious 0-0 draw. With *Tirona* winning 1-0 at home to Lokomotiva, their lead was now cut to a single point.

A now-customary carnival atmosphere at the Vojo Kushi a week later saw another 2-0 win, this time against Flamurtari, *Tirona* beating Tomori 3-1 in Berat and relegating their hosts.

On the final day of the season, Vllaznia were masters of their own destiny. A win would guarantee them the title, a draw might still be enough, but a defeat would leave the gate wide open for *Tirona* to capitalise.

They travelled to Tirana again, to face the lesser lights of KS Studenti Universiteti i Tiranë – their final game in this most dramatic of Kampionati Kombetar seasons. *Tirona* made the trip north of Tirana to Kavajë to face the obstinate obstacle of Besa.

The legion of loyal Shkodrans manned their bicycles once more, in preparation for the long journey south imbued with the rising hope of seeing their heroes make footballing history.

Studenti had found the jump to the top tier troublesome, a paucity of goals scored and an inability to defend effectively condemning them to relegation long before Vllaznia's visit to Tirana.

However, on the day, with the variables swirling in the dust and the heat of the Qemal Stafa, Studenti took an unlikely 1-0 lead, causing perturbation among Vllaznia's travelling support. For ten minutes, nerves were frayed until news filtered from Kavajë that the home team were leading there too.

Besa's goal had a restorative effect on Vllaznia, Česk Ndoja's equaliser bringing parity to the contest and much-needed confidence to *Kuq e Blutë*.

As half-time beckoned, Sabah Bizi found space on the edge of the Studenti area, guiding his shot beyond the keeper and into the net. Vllaznia led 2-1 at the break.

Almost instantly, Shyqri Qerolli added to Kutjim Pagria's earlier strike to put Besa 2-0 ahead in Kavajë. With Vllaznia now totally in control, further goals from Ismet Hoxha and Viktor Plumbini sealed a 4-1 victory as *Tirona* wilted to defeat in Kavajë by the same margin.

When the *referia* blew to bring an end to the Kampionati Kombetar 1971/72, it was the country's oldest club, hailing from the city where the football story in Albania had begun, *Djepi i Futbollit Shqiptar*, who had – for the first time in 26 years – won the title. But not just a title; a league and cup double.

Vllaznia returned to Shkodër as heroes, its people celebrating long into the night. However, their success received only cursory acknowledgement in the regime-controlled, Tirana-centric press. But the weight of their achievement, despite the muted press reaction, uncorked a genie that had been bottled for over a quarter of a century. And it imparted a powerful message that resonated in the smaller backwaters of Albania: if a club from the rebel city could win the league, surely bigger dreams were attainable.

As Vllaznia romped to further successes throughout the 1970s and into the early '80s, their importance and relevance could no longer be ignored, the club's titles in 1973/74, 1977/78 and 1982/83 and the cup wins of 1978/79 and 1980/81 calling time on the long-held notion of Tiranian impregnability.

The press, weighted by the positive national opinion Vllaznia had nurtured, were railroaded into adopting a holistic coverage of the national game, adding to its equality, inclusivity and reach. Vllaznia, via the dual agents of talent and bloody-minded willpower, had enacted progressive change.

As the north rose, so did the belief that anything was possible. It was a time of exciting new opportunities for Albania as a footballing nation.

Chapter Twelve

The Story of the Blues – Dinamo's Golden Era

ON 10 December 1944 an arm of The Party was founded that would become despised by all but those in the regime hierarchy and is still reviled to this day.

Dërêtria e Sigurimit të Shtëtit – the Directorate of State Security – known simply as the *Sigurimi*, was an organisation that exerted physical and psychological control over the Albanian population for 47 years, the mere utterance of its name evoking distrust and dread in the proletariat.

Koçi Xoxe, a communist Partisan who'd fought for the liberation of his country during World War Two, supervised the enacting of a mandate birthing a Party subdivision tasked with the application and maintenance of control over Albanians using any measures necessary.

The *Sigurimi* oversaw all issues pertaining to censorship: the writing, rewriting, addition and annulment of public records, prison management, internal security, physical security, counter espionage and foreign intelligence. Akin in their stylings to the East German *Stasi* and Romanian *Securitate*, the *Sigurimi* – as they evolved – fused the open barbarity of Haitian despot Papa Doc Duvalier's *Ton Ton Macoute* to their appalling arsenal, creating a living, breathing amalgam of George Orwell's fictional Ministries of Truth and Love.

In a dystopian twist resonant of the times, the man who'd assisted with the founding of the *Sigurimi*, Koçi Xoxe, became one of its many victims. Xoxe was arrested, tortured and executed in 1949 for his 'pro-Yugoslav affiliations', links that – prior to Albania's split from Titoist Yugoslavia in 1948 – were written in the constitution.

Appointment to the role of Minister of the Interior – head of the *Sigurimi* – proved a poisoned chalice, with eight of the nine inheritors suffering the same fate as Xoxe. In Stalinist Albania, the things the government encouraged you to support and believe in one day could become the things that got you hung or shot the next.

In the months leading up to the spring of 1950, the new Minister of the Interior, Kadri Hazbiu, oversaw the formation of a football team – adhering to the Soviet model – that would represent the *Sigurimi*. In March 1950, a new club, KS Dinamo Tiranë, were inducted into the Kampionati Kombetar roster, heralding a period of huge success during the early '50s.

Hazbiu remained an active patron of Dinamo; an ever-present in the *Tribuna* at Stadiumi Qemal Stafa and Stadiumi Dinamo whenever *Blutë* played, until his subsequent execution in September 1983.

Hazbiu fell into the role of colonel chief of counterintelligence after the end of World War Two. In 1946, with the nation's *cognoscenti* subject to the first wave of purges (merits and qualifications offering no protective currency for the Albanian academic), intellectual muscle in the Stalinist Albanian political pyramid was scant. Enver Hoxha plugged this shortfall of raw intelligence, implanting trusted, ideologically sound comrades from the military into key governmental positions. Hazbiu, like many of Comrade Enver's cronies, had got lucky – or unlucky – as history would attest.

From inception, Dinamo were afforded preferential treatment to their competitors. *Blutë*'s assemblage of fine footballing talent, sourced from other clubs without recompense, ate three chef-prepared meals a day, travelled by train and built squad morale during pre-match evenings spent together in the comparative luxury of the Hotel Volga. Training sessions were held at the best facilities the country had to offer and were longer and better in structure than those of their opponents with gym work included in the itinerary. In the later years, potential signings were offered cars – totally unheard of in Stalinist Albania – as additional sweeteners to lure them to the club.

This wealth of privilege provided Dinamo with the base from which they would dominate Albanian football in the early to mid-1950s, success that wavered in the 1960s; a decade which yielded just two Kampionati Kombetar titles – the Zyber Konçi-led triumph in 1960 and the deeply contested success of 1966/67 – and a solitary Kupa e Shqipërisë victory, also in 1960.

By the late 1960s the team of the *Sigurimi* were in danger of becoming a spent force.

Ex-player Skënder Jareci was appointed coach at the end of the 1965/66 season, *Dinamovitët* having finished a poor third behind champions 17 Nëntori and runners-up Partizani. Kadri Hazbiu and his friends at the House of Leaves demanded success at any cost; *Tirona*'s dual league triumphs in 1964/65 and 1965/66 observed with a hierarchical disdain that rendered Xhevdet Shaqiri's role as coach untenable.

The incidents surrounding the 1966/67 season have been explored at length within these pages, so we will move beyond them. However, the detritus of that fated season cast Dinamo in the role of perennial villain, with Albanians – aside from a small pocket of *Blutë* diehards – harbouring a mutual hatred for *Bastardet nga Ministria* – the bastards from the Ministry.

The 1970s observed five different Dinamo coaches who enjoyed – and endured – varying degrees of success, but all of whom played a part in creating a team that, although not necessarily loved, were grudgingly respected, even admired, by supporters and peers.

Customarily, Dinamo – divergent to the Marxist–Leninist preachings of the Hoxha regime – were renowned for the superiority of their individuals, not the collectivism of their team play. The talented personalities within their roster were able to conjure moments necessary to win games, but did so in a functional way devoid of the residual joy of victory; *galácticos* before *galácticos* came into wider consciousness.

Jareci's tenure witnessed the beginnings of a new Dinamo, a side displaying an interconnection and fluidity previously unseen in *Blutë*'s short, turbulent history.

Born in the port town of Durrës in 1931, Jareci was a footballer of calibre; skilful, intelligent, powerful. As a 19-year-old, he joined the newly established Dinamo club from Ylli i Kuq Durrës in 1950, winning seven championships and six cups, establishing himself among the finest Albanian strikers of his generation.

In the 1951 and 1952 seasons, Jareci was a component of a Dinamo side that won 25 consecutive Kampionati Kombetar matches, setting an Albanian record (fourth of all time, tied with Scottish club Celtic) in one of Europe's longest domestic winning streaks. Jareci also received the Albanian Player of the Year award three times, in 1952, 1957 and 1958.

Jareci was a club man to his bones, tasked with returning *Blutë* to former heights. His debut year at the helm observed the inglorious *Kampionati i Qymyrit* 'title win', deducting further credibility from Dinamo's store. However, Jareci behaved with integrity in the wake of the scandal, acknowledging that it was *Tirona*'s title in all but name.

From their lowest point, Jareci assembled a squad that would beguile Albanian audiences for the best part of a decade.

Jareci's primary act post-1966/67 was to promote to the first team a 16-year-old forward who would rewrite the record books, topping the domestic league goalscoring charts in six successive seasons between 1971/72 and 1976/77 thus securing his place among the most prolific goalscorers in Albanian history.

This protégé would be part of the 'golden age' of Dinamo between 1971 and 1981, when, under the guidance of Jareci, Sabri Peqini, Durim Shehu and Stavri Lubonja respectively, the club dominated Albanian football, winning five Kampionati Kombetar titles and three Kupa e Republikës.

Ilir Përnaska was born in Tirana in May 1951; his father Jonuz Korça came from the southern city of Korçë, his mother from rural Tirana. The surname Përnaska was added shortly after his birth. Oddly, Përnaska translates to 'I passed out' in English, although there was nothing sedentary or prostrate about Ilir Përnaska.

Built like a tank, the boy from Elbasan Street, within earshot of the roars from the Qemal Stafa, became known to Albanian *tifozët* as *Bombarduesi* (the Bomber) or *Robusti* (the Robust).

Përnaska began his career as a 13-year-old at *Tirona*. Despite being with the club from 1963 to 1966, trainer Xhavit Demneri didn't rate him – he wasn't tall enough, he wasn't fast enough over distance, he lacked flair. Përnaska, slighted by such criticism, moved to Dinamo, keen to wreak *gjakmarrje* – revenge – upon his doubters at *Tirona*. It was ironic that *Tirona*, after suffering decades of having players stolen from them by their city rivals, had allowed one of their greatest ever to slip their grasp into the cradle of the enemy. The short-sighted Demneri – an otherwise capable player and astute coach – was to later rue his lack of judgement.

Possessing confidence and certainty in his own ability, Përnaska joined the excellent Dinamo academy – Leonidha Dashi at the helm – in 1966, Dashi being the defensive foundation stone on which early Dinamo success had been erected during their trophy-caulked years of the 1950s.

A year later, aged 15, Përnaska became an integral performer in the successful Dinamo youth team where coach Skënder Begeja, part of Albania's 1946 Balkan Cup-winning side, recognised his massive potential.

Begeja, interestingly, became the first Albanian to run the 100m in under 11 seconds during a Spartakiad in the mid-1940s. As well as fast feet, he also had a discerning nose for talent; 20 years earlier he had discovered a fledgling Skënder Jareci. And he'd uncovered another precious jewel in Përnaska, a commodity he was delighted to hand over to his former protégé.

Known retrospectively as the 'Albanian Guardiola', Skënder Jareci also knew a player when he saw one, revelling in the dynamism and goalscoring aptitude of the new boy whom *Tirona* had handed Dinamo on a gilt platter.

Përnaska quickly emerged as Dinamo's primary *sulmues qendror*; a fearless and inexorable hunter of goals. Blessed with mobility, invention and bravery, Përnaska would risk going to the hospital in his voracious pursuit of scoring, eyes permanently fixed on goal.

Akin to West Germany's 'Bomber', Gerd Müller, Pernaska didn't care how he scored; left foot, right foot, head or hand, as long as the net rippled.

When quizzed, post-career, on the subject of goalscoring, Përnaska gleefully retorted, 'I liked goals that caused pain' – both to himself and the opposition; a gladiatorial footballer who submitted all of his strength and talent to the service of his team. The most accurate count shows that Përnaska scored 265 goals in the championship, cup and international matches.

In 1967, Skënder Jareci fast-tracked Pernaska to the Dinamo squad, where at the age of just 16 he was promoted to the starting 11. In the closing months of the year, during an away match against Traktori Lushnja, Përnaska – still only 16 – helped his side to a 3-1 win, bagging two goals on his professional debut.

The two seasons succeeding 1966/67 saw a Dinamo side in a consolidatory mood and surfing the peripheries of a title race though never in serious contention of winning it, finishing third in 1967/68 and fourth in 1968/69.

The 1970/71 campaign observed tangible progress. With Përnaska firmly embedded in the Dinamo team and scoring with regularity, *Blutë* returned to silverware-winning ways by beating Besa 2-0 in the cup final at the Qemal Stafa while finishing runners-up – a point behind Partizani – in a hotly contested race for the Kampionati Kombetar. For the media and lay person, it was the first solid inkling that, after four wilderness years, the Blues were, again, a force to be reckoned with, Përnaska winning the league top scorer award for the first time, bagging an impressive 19 goals in 26 games.

In an era when damage to public property resulted in offenders cracking rocks in Spaç or Burrel gulag, a painted slogan eulogising *Robusti's* goal-plundering talents appeared on the outer wall of the *Tribuna* at the Qemal Stafa, daubed there by adoring *tifozët*. It read 'Përnaska Gol'; his name synonymous with the art of goalscoring. That the graffiti remained in place for several years says much about Albanians' relationship – on all societal levels – with *Bombarduesi*.

Another hard-fought Kampionati in 1971/72 concluded in victory for Xhevdet Shaqiri's brilliant Vllaznia team, with Dinamo four points adrift in third and Përnaska the league's top scorer again.

Prior to the 1972/73 season, Jareci promoted another of Dinamo's burgeoning academy starlets to the starting line-up; a 19-year-old striker who'd been causing a huge stir at youth team level.

Shyqyri Ballgjini, tall, slender and elegant, originated from the port town of Durrës. Ballgjini, during this wildly fruitful era at Stadiumi Dinamo, etched his moniker in the Dinamo pantheon, netting a combined 150 goals in league and cup competition during two spells at the club – 1973–78 and 1979–84. In his solitary year of absence, 1978/79, the Blues were abject and he was quickly recalled from his short stop at Vllaznia in time for the 1979/80 season.

The young forward made the transition from youth to first team seamlessly, partnering Përnaska in a season that observed *Dinamovitet* romp to a genuinely thrilling league title victory.

At home, Dinamo were almost perfect, with defending champions Vllaznia the only side to leave Tirana unbeaten following a 0-0 draw in November.

At the season's close, *Blutë* sat at the league summit having lost only once – a 1-0 reverse in Korçë versus Skenderbeu – seven points ahead of city rivals Partizani. A narrow 1-0 Kupa e Republikës Final defeat against Partizani at Stadiumi Qemal Stafa denied *Dinamovitet* the double.

It broke the figurative seal for Dinamo, though the best was yet to come. In the summer of 1973, Jareci – using a large portion of the influence that being the coach of Dinamo afforded – lured a superb prospect from rival Tirana outfit Shkëndija into the club fold.

Shkëndija, founded in 1968, were dubbed in the press as 'the Ajax of Albanian football', sourcing their players from the School of Sports Mastery in Tirana. They were a team with no tradition, no history and no supporters, but for three years in the early 1970s they played stellar football under the tutelage of ex-Dinamo and Albania head coach Zyber Konçi. And Dinamo stole their key protagonist.

Vasillaq Zëri, Tirana-born in August 1952 to Greek parents, Aryan in appearance – blond hair, blue eyes, and a ringer for West German forward Uwe Seeler – had earned a reputation as the Kampionati's next big thing, and his indisputable talent shone through in Shkëndija's meetings with Dinamo during the 1972/73 campaign, the 21-year-old garnering keen interest from Partizani, 17 Nëntori and Jareci's newly crowned champions.

What Zëri lacked in height was compensated by a low centre of gravity, hunger for the ball and range of skills redolent of the greats, Boriçi and Pano. Players of Zëri's template were considered, in 1970s football culture, to be something of a luxury, but this luxury model came with a voracious, relentless engine. Amid a three-way squabble for his signature, Dinamo finally got their man in time for the 1973/74 season.

Zëri would prove to be the third and final piece in an attacking troika that would galvanise the finest team of the Blues' golden era.

Yet, like the best *Kalmet* or *Kavaljon*, it would take time for the partnership of Përnaska, Ballgjini and Zëri to mature. Dinamo's poor fourth-place finish in 1973/74 – nine points adrift of champions Vllaznia – during a season in which Përnaska netted 19 of Dinamo's 24 goals, observed defeats at Flamurtari, Naftëtari, Nentori, Partizani, Shkëndija, Skenderbeu, Traktori and Vllaznia and an embarrassing home loss to Besa. A cup final win against Partizani, 1-0, offered scant consolation. It signalled the end of the road for Jareci.

Jareci was replaced by Belgian-born Sabri Peqini, a studious and intelligent coach, who – after joining from KS Erzeni of Shijak – played for Dinamo between 1950 and 1954, winning four titles and five cups. During his playing days, Peqini, a battering ram of a forward similar in style to Përnaska, earned the nickname *Tarzani* due to his strength and mobility.

Tarzani was part of *Shqiponjat*'s ill-fated tour of eastern Europe in 1950: *Turneu i Zi* – the Black Tournament – as it became known to native Albanians. Preparations for the trip abroad had been shoddy, the players left waiting in Durrës for two days for team passports to arrive. By then, their connecting boat to the Romanian city of Constanta had already sailed. Short of options, the players were forced to travel aboard a goods freighter carrying tar. By the time the group arrived in Romania, two players had literally jumped ship, defecting during a short stay in Istanbul. If the portents were bad, the results were worse; three heavy defeats – with no goals scored – including a humiliating 12-0 pummelling at the hands of the Hungarians.

Peqini, a devout Party man, was thought by Dinamo's masters to be the perfect successor to Jareci; reliable, compliant and informed, prizing work ethic ahead of individuality. In the crop of Dinamo players that Peqini inherited, he found both a team built on the principles of hard work, yet infused with an abundance of skill, playing their own variety of the *futbollit socialist* – 'socialist football' – to which Hungarian coach Gusztáv Sebes had historically alluded; a 'utopian dream of football', absent of ego where the team was all.

Later in his life, Peqini fell out of love with the game, refusing to attend matches, believing that money had ruined football and its demotivated, avaricious practitioners. There are many who would concur with Peqini's blunt appraisal.

Yet during Peqini's one-year tenure, Dinamo shone brighter than ever before, the club stalwart guiding *Blutë* convincingly to the title in 1974/75, five points ahead of second-placed Vllaznia, netting 58 goals in 26 games while conceding just 13. Përnaska top-scored for the fifth consecutive season.

It was the season in which Përnaska's offensive partnership alongside Zëri and Ballgjini bore its richest fruit, all three playing for the adulation of the Dinamo faithful in an era of minimal financial reward. Football for kicks. They are still considered to be the finest offensive trio in Dinamo's history.

In addition to their golden triumvirate, Dinamo boasted the talents of Iljaz Çeço, an all-action, attacking midfielder whose career began in his home city of Lushnja with Traktori. In October of 1964, Çeço became the youngest player to represent *Shqiponjat* in a competitive international, Zyber Konçi blooding the 17-year-old during Albania's 3-0 win against Algeria at the Qemal Stafa. Çeço would enjoy two stays at the club: 1963 to 1970 and 1971 to 1978 (interspersed with a solitary year at *Tirona* during the 1970/71 season), winning five titles and three cups.

After Peqini's wonderfully successful, though short tenure, Durim Shehu became Dinamo coach, leading the Blues to further back-to-back title wins. At the close of the 1975/76 season, Dinamo finished two points ahead of *Tirona*, Pernaska again the league's leading scorer.

However, 1976/77 observed the tightest Kampionati title race for years. The original qualifying stage – 22 games in length – decided the top six sides who contested an additional Championship Round for the trophy (17 Nëntori, Partizani, Vllaznia, Lokomotiva, Dinamo and Skënderbeu), the Korçans mounting their first meaningful challenge since the early 1930s.

Level on points with Skënderbeu going into the Championship Round, with Vllaznia and Partizani in close attendance, *Blutë* showed their class, remaining unbeaten in the ten-game 'round robin', beating Partizani – twice – at a packed Qemal Stafa (1-0 in their designated home game and 2-1 away), triumphing 2-1 at home against *Tirona* while forcing a 1-1 stalemate in the return, and drawing 2-2 in Shkoder against a powerful Vllaznia side before effectively ending *Kuq e Blutë*'s title challenge by beating them 1-0 in Tirana. A double over Lokomotiva (2-1 in Tirana, 4-2 in Durrës) meant that avoidance of defeat in their face-offs with their closest and most vibrant threat, second-placed Skënderbeu, would see the title remain in the capital.

Two tense 0-0 draws, firstly at *Juglindorët*'s Korçan fortress – Stadiumi Skënderbeu – and the subsequent home match at the Qemal Stafa eased Dinamo over the line, four points ahead of the south-easterners.

Blutë hopes of capturing a league and cup double were undone by 17 Nëntori. After destroying Partizani 5-0 over two legs in the quarter-final and edging out Vllaznia 2-1 on aggregate in the semi, it was *Tirona* that won a tense two-legged Kupa e Republikës Final – both ties played out at an animated Qemal Stafa.

Tirona won the first leg 2-1, Petrit Dibra giving them a lead that was equalised by Shyqyri Ballgjini, Arben Cela popping up with a 64th-minute winner.

The second leg witnessed Dinamo in the ascendancy, Vasillaq Zëri putting his side ahead. Sefedin Braho levelled the score from the penalty spot just shy of the hour, Ballgjini bagging a late winner three minutes from time. Extra time saw no further goals with *Tirona* – to the delight of the huge *bardhë e blutë* support inside the Qemal Stafa – eventually taking the trophy 8-7 on penalties.

Irrespective of this minor blot on their copybook, the mid-1970s witnessed a Dinamo side at their peak. Club legend Muhedin Targaj, in an interview with *Gazeta Telegraf* in 2014, attested to this, 'I think that Dinamo of the years 1974–77, [during] which [we] became champions three times in a row, [was] the best of all time.'

Targaj, a stalwart of 13 years' service, captain of the national team and a first-hand observer to the excellence of this particular version of the Blues, was the soul of Stavri Lubonja's Dinamo side during the 1979/80 campaign, his rallying leadership and bornite resolve dragging his team-mates with him on their shared path to glory. The 1979/80 edition of Dinamo Tirana are a team who, too, feature highly in the all-time *Blutë* hall of fame.

In the two years that followed Dinamo's 1976/77 title success, Vllaznia (1977/78) and Partizani (1978/79) won the title, a lean streak for a Blues side acclimated to the glow of success. The barren seasons, led by the tactically flawed Saimir Dauti, earned the coach many enemies. He fashioned early outrage by sacrilegiously breaking up the Zëri–Përnaska–Ballgjini troika, allowing the latter to join Vllaznia in 1978. This, amid a myriad of poor calls, cost Dauti his job, a dreadful fifth-place finish – Dinamo winning only eight of their 26 league matches – further compounded by a cup defeat to Vllaznia proving the final nail in Dauti's coffin.

Dauti's unquestionable commitment to the Blues' cause – he'd spent his entire playing career with the club and coached at academy level until his promotion to coach – had saved him at the end of the 1977/78 season; a disappointing fourth-place finish softened somewhat by the balm of a 1-0 aggregate cup win against Traktori. But there were to be no second chances this time. Dauti was returned to the academy – Stavri Lubonja was drafted in at the close of the 1978/79 season.

Lubonja, like many of his predecessors, was an ex-player who'd spent six years with Dinamo, top-scoring for the club during the 1959 season. His reticence and intelligence were ideally suited to the role of coach, and it was Lubonja who instilled the requisite calmness and veracity that had been amiss during two calamitous campaigns. His first act as manager softened the fury of the *tifozët*, immediately restoring Shyqyri Ballgjini to the squad after his season away at Vllaznia.

It's fitting to say that Dinamo weren't among the favourites for the Kampionati as its 1979/80 edition rolled into life; Partizani and Tirona, the top two the previous year, were considered the main challengers again.

However, Lubonja could now call upon a reunited troika of talents – Zëri, Përnaska and Ballgjini – around whom were assembled a solid group of performers.

A positive start, punctuated with single-goal away triumphs against *Tirona* and Skënderbeu, demonstrated a new-found solidity; an ugliness and determination to grind out results which had been missing during Dauti's tenure.

Ilir Luarasi brought the usual assurance to the goalkeeping role, making important interventions during key moments of games, with Aleko Bregu, Kujtim Cocolli and Muhedin Targaj providing an impermeable rearguard. Andrea Marko and Artur Cobani offered the midfield solidity and structure that allowed Pernaska, Zeri and Ballgjini's natural attacking sensibilities to thrive. Lubonja's Dinamo was a team re-educating itself in the fine art of winning.

Defensively and offensively, Dinamo were the best team during 1979/80, scoring more and conceding fewer than any other side in the league. At the season's close they'd blown away all rivals, finishing a resounding five points ahead of second-place *Tirona*. The Kampionati had returned to the club of the *Sigurimi*.

Yet despite success on the field, there remains a pervading air of tragedy to Dinamo's off-pitch history of the day.

Agron Hazbiu – known as Agron Dautaj (his grandfather's surname) to *tifozët* – was the son of club patron and *Sigurimi* chief Kadri Hazbiu. Agron was introduced to Dinamo by coach Saimir Dauti in the summer of 1977. A talented, left-sided midfielder, *Goni* – as he was known to Dinamo fans – was a champion with Dinamo in 1979/80, but his football career was cut short in 1982 following the arrest and execution of his father. Subsequently banned for life by FSHF, *Goni* was removed from his government apartment in Blloku and sent to work the coalfaces of north-west Albania. He would allegedly take his own life in January 1989, his body retrieved from the shaft at Kurbnesh mine.

Despite resounding domestic success, Dinamo were never able to transpose this dominance to the European arena. Indeed, after winning their titles in 1972/73, 1974/75, 1975/76 and 1976/77 Dinamo, coerced – one can only surmise – by the regime, refused their invitations to the 1973/74, 1975/76, 1976/77 or 1977/78 editions of the European Cup. Whether this was a sullen retort to the ban imposed on Dinamo after the 1966/67 season is unclear. What remains utterly transparent is that The Party's petulance denied *Blutë*'s golden era the opportunities to transpose their outstanding football on to a broader, worldly audience.

It was almost as if The Party and FSHF lacked belief and trust in their football teams to portray an outwardly positive snapshot of the Hermit Kingdom. Yet from a worldly perspective, football was the only window that outsiders had with which to view Albania, and the window had been slammed curtly shut.

In The Party's pyrrhic defence, it was Dinamo players who'd steeped embarrassment on the regime in 1950; as they would in 1990, with their well-documented defections to the West. Perhaps the scepticism was merited.

Dinamo returned to Europe's premier competition in 1980/81, narrowly ousted by Ajax in the first round, but much of the momentum had been lost. Following their title win in 1979/80, it would take another six years for Dinamo to scale such heights.

By then, Kadri Hazbiu was dead and Albania had detached itself from the rest of the global community. Potless, impoverished and bereft of friends, Stalinist Albania was embarking on the most difficult decade in its history.

In the darkest of days, Albanians sought release from their daily existential misery; a small fissure of light to illuminate the unlit path.

And football, in all of its trivial, unimportant importance, was – once more – at hand to oblige.

Iconic Games

Partizani Tirana 1 Celtic 0

European Cup First Round First Leg

3 October 1979

Stadiumi Kombetar Qemal Stafa, Tirana

Attendance: 27,500

Partizani: Perlat Musta, Milan Baci, Kastriot Hysi, Spiro [Curri]*

(Arjen Ahmeti; 77 mins), Safet Berisha (captain/*kapiten*), Ferid Rragami, Satedini [Sefedin Braho]*, Ilir Lame, Feim Breca, Agim Murati, Hajdari [Shyqyri Ballgjini]*

Head coach/*Kryetrajneri*: Bejkush Birçe

Celtic: Peter Latchford, Alan Sneddon, Danny McGrain (captain/*kapiten*), Roy Aitken, McAdam, Mike Conroy, Davie Provan, Vic Davidson, George McCluskey (Johnny Doyle; 54 mins), Murdo MacLeod, Bobby Lennox

Head coach/*Kryetrajneri*: Billy McNeill

Referee/*Arbitri*: Nikolaos Zlatanos (Greece)

The 1979/80 edition of the European Cup heralded Partizani's return to the continent's premier competition for the first time since 1971/72. After an early elimination that year by a very useful CSKA Sofia side – a 3-0 defeat at the Armiyata in Sofia followed by a narrow 1-0 loss at the Qemal Stafa – 1971/72 signalled the beginning of a six-year Albanian absence from the European Cup.

Between 1972 and 1978, FSHF declined UEFA's invitation to the competition. The Vllaznia scandal of the 1971/72 season subjected the Shkodrans to a lengthy punishment from the regime; the champions of Albania deprived of their European Cup berth in both 1972 and 1974.

Dinamo, eligible to compete as champions in the 1973, 1975, 1976 and 1977 European Cups, remained affronted by a historic one-year UEFA ban they'd served in the wake of the dubious title win of 1966/67 – a long-standing grudge that prompted *Blutë* to boycott UEFA competitions of any description until 1980/81. An Albania-shaped hole in the European Cup's roll-call of nations remained uncorked for over half a decade.

The 1978/79 competition witnessed Albania's return to the fray, Vllaznia acquitting themselves excellently against 1978 European Cup Winners' Cup finalists Austria Wien and narrowly exiting the competition 4-3 on aggregate in the first round after an astounding 2-0 opening-leg victory in Shkodër.

Despite burgeoning economic and social problems on the home front following the country's split with China, the footballers of Partizani were in vibrant, optimistic mood. The 1978/79 season saw *Demat e Kuq* win their first Kampionati in eight years – the longest dry spell since their formation in 1946 – finishing one point ahead of 17 Nëntori.

Coach Bejkush Birçe, a former Partizani player who'd managed the youth academy for seven years, took over in 1969, guiding *Demat e Kuq* to their previous title in 1971. Birçe, a pragmatic tactician, assembled a side that was miserly in defence, conceding fewer goals than any other team in the league. But it was a team with a rapier-like point. Agim Murati, a nimble forward from the west-coast town of Shijak whom Loro Boriçi dubbed 'king of the air' due to his enviable heading technique, had proven himself a dangerous and regular source of goals, topping the Albanian scoring charts in 1976/77, 1977/78 and 1978/79.

The 1979/80 edition of the European Cup featured many of the alluring names of 1970s football: BFC Dynamo, Dukla Prague, Hajduk Split, Dinamo Tbilisi and future competition winners Porto and Hamburg, alongside clubs who had already seen their name engraved on the trophy in holders Nottingham Forest, Liverpool, Real Madrid, Milan, and Ajax. And when the draw was made in Switzerland in June 1979, Partizani found themselves pitted against one such European footballing enigma: previous winners Celtic.

The Celtic side of 1979/80 were of a particularly fine vintage. Roy Aitken and captain Danny McGrain provided the defensive granite that permitted fine creative practitioners such as Davie Provan and Murdo MacLeod the freedom to roam, supplying the ammo for twin goal threats Tom McAdam and the newly acquired George McCluskey. In 1978/79 Billy McNeill, during his debut season as coach, hauled the Bhoys to their 31st Scottish Premier League title ahead of perennial Old Firm nemesis Rangers. It served as a worthy retort to the 1977/78 campaign when Celtic's city rivals had dominated domestically. The good times were rolling again in the east of Glasgow.

McNeill captained his beloved Celtic to victory during their greatest triumph of all – the 1967 European Cup Final win versus Internazionale in Lisbon – and was keen to infuse his considerable nous upon this new generation of hooped bucks.

The tournament followed the old European Cup format of 32 clubs, and 16 first-round ties decided over two legs, with Celtic travelling to Tirana in early October to fulfil the first leg of this strangely evocative fixture.

Kilmarnock had visited Albania during their 1965/66 European Cup campaign, a trip beset with difficulties from the off, and Celtic would be confronted by similar snags during their Albanian experience.

Alarm bells threatened to toll immediately after the draw had been finalised, Celtic being denied permission to fly their chartered plane into Albanian air space. The SFA and UEFA vented dual ire towards the Albanian authorities, anger met with obstinacy by the backwards regime.

The situation escalated when Celtic were restricted to 30 entry visas for the trip, meaning that no Scottish journalists or away fans would be able to travel to Albania for the game. UEFA intervened, issuing warnings to the Albanian Sports Committee who, in turn, released two further visas, but no more. Celtic, irritated by the unyielding nature of their Albanian 'hosts', issued a further complaint to UEFA coupled with a threat to withdraw from the competition if they were denied access to more visas. When SFA secretary Ernie Walker fought the Celtic corner, declaring that he would not accept the game being played 'in secret' with no Scottish media present, he was snottily rebuffed by the Albanian News Agency, who chided his 'arrogant and arbitrary ultimatums'.

When the Albanian authorities failed to meet further UEFA deadlines demanding permission for Celtic fans to travel to Tirana, the club decided to play the game 'under protest'. Once again, an ineffectual UEFA – in negotiations with the Albanian Sports Committee – had summarily failed to broker acceptable concessions for a team visiting the Hermit Kingdom.

Celtic flew to Tirana from Glasgow Airport unsure of which hotel they would be staying in and indeed whether they would have any accommodation at all, and there were the usual vagaries regarding what food they would be permitted to bring into the country.

Also, there was the small matter of hair. It remained uncertain whether Davie Provan and Johnny Doyle's perms or Danny McGrain's facial hair would survive the customs lane at Rinas Airport; the Albanian regime was still diligent in its outlawing of anything deemed 'of Western influence'.

In alignment with Albania's constitutional rewrite of 1967, beards were banned to discourage Westernism and Islamic expression, leaving McGrain, disproportionately hirsute, in danger of becoming the centrepiece in a diplomatic incident. It was much to McGrain's reluctance – and to the hilarity of the Scottish press and his team-mates – that the beard was removed, courtesy of his wife Laraine, prior to boarding their flight at Glasgow Airport.

The two sides approached their face-off in Tirana in very different veins of form – Celtic in glorious fettle, top of the league, unbeaten, travelling to Albania off the back of a 5-1 destruction of St Mirren at Parkhead; Partizani in an early season rut and already conceding ground in the Kampionati to Stavri Lubonja's rejuvenated Dinamo.

As the wheels of Celtic's chartered jet hit the pocked tarmac at Rinas, one would have forgiven them for feeling the collective dread that had inhibited so many other sides who'd ventured upon this road less travelled.

A feeling of disquiet was reinforced within the Celtic camp during their short drive from the airport to Tirana. McGrain noted, 'The countryside [was] dotted with these pillboxes that gave us the uneasy feeling that they might be expecting unwelcome visitors at any time.'

Yet despite their reservations, Celtic were greeted with warmth and enthusiasm by the Albanian public; a stark contrast to the aloofness of their hostile regime.

The day prior to the game, 8,000 excited natives turned up at Stadiumi Qemal Stafa to watch Celtic train. The game had already been confirmed as a sell-out with ticket prices ranging between 7p and 21p.

The Celtic players would later share their observations on life and football in Albania. There was a reason for the mass popularity of the sport as there seemed little else to do by way of entertainment.

McGrain, in reflection, said, 'The streets of Tirana [were] full of people walking with seemingly nowhere to go. Imagine Argyle Street on a Saturday afternoon, but with no shops. There were very few women about. I reckon the ratio [was] about 50 men to one woman and it [was] a common sight to see men walking down the road arm in arm.'

Yet when the Celtic players embarked on an afternoon stroll in Skanderbeg Square, they were mobbed by fans buoyed by the excitement that the arrival of foreigners to their door-bolted republic incited. Bobby Lennox commented favourably regarding the 'enthusiasm of the Albanian fans who watched Celtic train', but observed a noticeable difference in their mood when an agent of the state police – the despised *Sigurimi* – appeared on the scene, intent on exerting all of the terrifying authority his blue uniform granted.

The pre-match team sheet caused mild disquiet, with Partizani fielding three players with negligible affiliations, to the club. A tactic regularly adopted by Albanian clubs during the 1960s and '70s was to offer 'ringers' on short-term loans to other teams who were competing in Europe. After UEFA attempted to clamp down on the subterfuge, the Albanians devised new means with which to include guest players in their line-up; namely listing players by their Christian names (or, indeed, different names entirely) on match documentation while omitting their surnames, causing administrational confusion among UEFA officials. A feature of the Partizani–Celtic team sheet for the fixture in 1979 is that three players are listed with the partial omission of their names. Spiro Curri, Sefedin Braho and Shyqyri Ballgjini – asterisked in the list and all starters against Celtic – were sourced from Flamurtari, Luftëtari and Dinamo respectively.

Celtic started with 21-year-old George McCluskey, the new goal-plundering starlet in a potent team, despite the talented marksman carrying a knock. Celtic had intended to work on McCluskey's injury using a portable treatment machine they planned to take to Albania, but feared that local authorities would refuse to allow this mystery of Western technology through their innately suspicious customs control, so it was struck off the pre-flight inventory.

When the sides took the field just prior to 5pm on 3 October 1979 – a kick-off time that allowed local Albanians to complete their prescribed shifts in the city environs and converge upon the *stadiumi* in good time for the game – they received a rowdy and exuberant welcome from the near-30,000 supporters crammed into an over-subscribed Qemal Stafa.

The Celtic players were surprised to be presented with individual bouquets of flowers during the line-up, with captain McGrain doubly perplexed when – during the exchange of handshakes and pennants – Partizani's *kapiten*, Safet Berisha, in returning the gift of a Celtic wimpel, handed him a book on the history of Albanian architecture.

Celtic's players were advised, pre-match, that the home crowd would be quietly reticent. Any misconceptions they harboured regarding the degree of influence the fans in the stadium would have on proceedings were blown away within minutes of the start. Raucous and emotionally charged, Partizani's *tifozët* provided the necessary wall of sound on which the home team could daub their authority.

Roy Aitken recalled the reaction of the Partizani support upon earning an early corner, 'The ground erupted. The Albanians went off their rockers. They made the Parkhead jungle sound quiet.'

Sustained by this channelling of communal fervour, Partizani grew into the game and showed themselves to be more than capable opponents. With Celtic ruffled, it was Partizani who took the lead in the 35th minute, charitable defending allowing the ever-alert Agim Murati to get his head on the end of a loose, bouncing ball in the visitors' box and elevate it over the advancing Peter Latchford. It was a splendid opportunist strike, indicative of the poacher that Murati had matured into since his move from Erzeni in 1970.

It was to prove Murati's only sniff of a chance during a cagey, tight battle. After the break, Celtic's fitness and paid professionalism threatened to overwhelm the home side, but a combination of partisan support, resilient play, solid goalkeeping and some questionable refereeing by Greek official Nikolaos Zlatanos – twice pulling play back on dubious offside calls when Celtic seemed certain to score – saw Partizani survive until the full-time whistle, recording a notable win that fully announced Albanian club football's return to the international forum. It was a voice that would grow louder over the forthcoming years.

As a footnote, Celtic would win the return at Parkhead 4-1 and progress on aggregate, despite Partizani leading early on via a preposterous headed own goal by the hapless Alan Sneddon.

A resonant feature of the fixture in Tirana – a detail foretelling of hopeful times ahead – was the disparity between the ugliness of the regime and the playfulness and enduring spirit of the Albanian people, *joie de vivre* recognised by the Celtic players who had made the trip.

In the early 1990s, shortly after the fall of communism in Albania, Celtic would dabble in the eastern European transfer market when signing native Albanian Rudi Vata from Dinamo Tirana. Vata would win the Scottish Cup with the club in 1995, ending a trophyless period spanning six years.

One of the great ironies of the piece is that Celtic's players – upon their visit to Tirana during the dire, ramshackle days of the late 1970s – were privy to observe a failing city that was grim, penurious and devoid of hope; a place of limited prospects.

In an act verging upon satire, Vata – the first Albanian footballer to ever play in Scotland – made the reverse journey to his Celt predecessors 13 years later, keen to see what the new world outside of Albanian borders had to offer. He now continues, by choice, to live in Hamilton.

Perhaps human aspiration, when you have been used to having nothing, ceases to be a particularly broad church; small improvements suffice. And one perk of living in this grey South Lanarkshire enclave is that – unlike Tirana – Hamilton has a McDonald's. Maybe that was the lure. And that has to signify a progress of sorts, doesn't it?

Chapter Thirteen

Futboll Lagjesh (Neighbourhood Football): the Birth of Albanian Calcetto

AS THE 1970s ended and the 1980s began, Albania found itself in a state of stagnation, desperation and disarray.

In contrast, barely a decade earlier, the late 1960s saw a firming of relations with China; Enver Hoxha's constitutional re-write of 1967 echoing the ideas and imitating the deeds enacted by the Chinese communists during their own cultural revolution of 1966.

Albania's value to China had never been greater; a Western state copying Chinese social edicts? It was a glorious win for the Chinese press to feed its subjects back in the homeland, and it was a propaganda stream for which Mao paid well. The fact that Albania provided the Asian superpower with a strategic naval facility in southern Europe was another notable plus.

Bolstered by Chinese technical and monetary aid, Albania grew economically. Between 1960 and 1970, Albania's national income was 56 per cent higher than the European average. The Sino-Albanian partnership was bearing glorious fruit.

Observing film coverage of Albania's European Championship qualification match against West Germany in Tirana in 1967, the sight of Chinese diplomats at the Qemal Stafa carousing openly with their Albanian hosts provides stark evidence of a kinship that was at its height.

From a footballing perspective, the merger offered Albanian coaches and players the opportunity to test their mettle in another country with, most notably, Loro Boriçi becoming the technical director of the Chinese national team from 1972 to 1975.

But cracks were already showing in the friendship. Henry Kissinger's and Richard Nixon's reconciliatory trips to China in 1971 genuinely infuriated Enver Hoxha.

'When the Americans were killing and bombing in Vietnam, China held secret talks with America?' Hoxha queried. The mere notion was 'anti-Marxist ... a betrayal of the Chinese towards the Vietnamese', both 'scandalous' and 'revolting'. On this issue at least, one could confidently debate that Hoxha probably had a point.

The following year, when China reduced annual funding to Albania to a mere £112m, Hoxha commented that the 'initial ardour [between Albania and China] has died', that Albania was no longer China's 'faithful, special friend'.

1977 hailed Yugoslavian president Tito's visit to China – *Broz* greeted warmly by the leadership of the Chinese Communist Party. In 1978, China stopped sending money to Albania on the order of Deng Xiaoping. The Sino–Albanian love affair was over, the nations retaining minimal diplomatic ties, and only then at ambassadorial level.

With the boom years of the 1960s over, China stripped Albania of much of its natural resource as part-payment on massive investment over the previous 17 years, and – post-split – the Chinese handed their former ally a loan repayment bill that would make an oligarch wince.

The termination of Chinese funding to Albania rang like a death knell for Hoxha, and its chimes would echo resonantly over the forthcoming decades.

For the first time in Hoxha's reign, Albania was utterly alone; without a monied sponsor to absorb its mounting debts. The economy – dependent on gifts to survive – was in tatters.

Albania was left with few remaining assets to broker and even fewer goods to export.

Resultantly, all aspects of life in the Hermit Kingdom suffered. A stark decrease in the number of items your money bought – don't call it inflation, there was no inflation in Hoxha's Albania – left Albanians counting their lek more vigilantly than they'd done in the previous 35 years. And the quality of the goods worsened, cheaper materials inevitably being used in their manufacture; recessionary haemorrhaging that continued untreated until Albanian communism's dramatic fall in 1992.

Football suffered too, with fewer fans willing to part with the admission fee, preserving their limited capital for more worthy familial causes. Attendances, for the first time in Kampionati history, decreased. Fans still attended the big games and fixtures that featured the national team, but home games for the big three in Tirana, against the league's lesser lights, failed to draw the same volume of crowds they had just a few years earlier; the Qemal Stafa and Stadiumi Dinamo meagrely sprinkled with the privileged functionaries of the regime for the minor games.

In desperate times, Albanians cut their cloth appropriately. Yet, instead of signalling the demise of competitive football in Tirana, the recessionary years observed its reinvention, and the birthing of a new type of football in the city: a football with different rules played at modest, improvised stadia throughout the suburban sprawls of the capital. It was a variant of the beautiful game that featured new heroes and, inversely, new villains. A football born of the streets and played on the streets. Its name – in Albanian parlance – was *futboll lagjesh*, translating to neighbourhood football, but to the natives in the east of the city it was known, simply, as *Calcetto*.

From humble beginnings

Kongresi Lushnjës is a school in the east of Tirana sandwiched between *rrugët* – streets – bearing the monikers of Albanian icons who lived through, yet transcended, the Stalinist era; namely Odhise Paskall and Xhanfise Keko.

Paskalli, born in 1903, became Albania's principal sculptor, completing in excess of 600 pieces; patriotic in content, including *Luftëtari Kombëtar* – the National Fighter – in Korçë and *Ushtari i panjohur* (the Unknown Soldier) and the Skanderbeg Monument, both in central Tirana.

Keko was Albania's first female filmmaker; a woman whose originality and sensitivity earned plaudits beyond Albanian shores, directing 25 films between 1952 and 1984 that remain well-regarded to this day.

It's notable, in a Tirana that's grown beyond recognition since 1992, that the street names of the *bulevardeve* that straddle Kongresi Lushnjës remain unchanged. Despite the nation's dark past, there exist a revered few who – in a modern context – retain both their status and their social relevance.

The same could be said of Kongresi Lushnjës itself. Named after the historic conference of 1920 in which Albanian politicians vied to wrestle the country from foreign occupancy, it has kept its original name since it opened in 1946.

Despite modern renovations, the school is pretty much the same as it looked in the summer of 1980 – when the *shkolla*, unexpectedly, became the hub of a new footballing craze that was taking hold in East Tirana; a high-speed variant of the game, called *Calcetto*.

At the rear of the Kongresi Lushnjës school building stood a patch of concrete ground – a ramshackle tennis court – surrounded by a 5ft high perimeter brick wall bound by 10ft mesh fencing. At each end, goalposts were painted on the wall, the bricks inside the goalposts inexpertly removed to leave an open space through which a ball could pass thus creating a serviceable 'goal'. At each end, the two corners to the right of the 'posts' were set back five yards by three yards, creating a 'tricky little oblong' from which players often struggled to extricate themselves when in possession of the ball. These rectangular crooks of 'dead space' were built into the structure as storage for sports equipment, their incongruent presence impeding the transit of smooth, free-flowing football. The oblongs were an anomaly that, in time, became an inherent, accepted part of the *Calcetto* experience at Kongresi Lushnjës.

Overshadowing the pitch were four five-storey apartment blocks; new-builds erected by political prisoners to house the influx of migrants who'd relocated to east Tirana from the country's north-west, tasked with manning – and womaning – the factories in Hoxha's newly industrialised Albania. Their proximity to the court made these prefab behemoths the perfect vantage point from which to spectate over *Calcetto* battles.

The encircling perimeter wall also provided a seating option for voyeurs who enjoyed their *Calcetto* up close and personal, individual bricks later removed from other parts of the wall to provide peepholes through which the action could be safely observed.

Lore dictates that during the summer of 1980, three modest footballers – who would ascend to the status of legend within the narrow clique of the *Calcetto* community – were looking for a permanent venue to host a variant of football they had happened across while illegally tuned in to Italian state TV.

The game – *Calcetto*, derived from the Italian word *calcio* meaning to kick – had ignited their imagination, and the boys tasked themselves with locating a regular setting in which to fulfil their collective vision. It didn't take them long.

The three friends – Di Jashari, Gimi Dires and Tole Cungu – befriended the school janitor, a portly, balding man named Fiqo, in the glass-fronted *Lokal* in Xhomlliku after his shift had ended at the *shkolla*. Plying him with Fernet as a sweetener, they convinced Fiqo to leave the court gates unlocked at weekends. The caretaker, loosened by booze, duly agreed.

This trio of protagonists hailed from the districts approximate to the school; all friends, although their life paths diverged greatly.

Di was the cool one; the leader, a confidence siphoned down from educated, capable parents who worked as medics at the hospital in Tirana. Adversely, young Di opted for a polar opposite career choice to his folks, working as a film stuntman at Kinostudio Shqiperia e Re – the New Albania Film Studio – on the outskirts of town. Over the course of four decades, Di regularly put his body on the line in the service of the Albanian film industry, breaking many bones along the way. Even now, nestled in his mid-60s, his is still the first name on the list when an upstart director needs some local lunatic to buck a wild stallion or crash a motorbike into the sea.

Gimi Dires – 'Son of Gimi' – portered at the Hotel Dajti. His regular dealings with dignitaries from transnational communist states, and the stories these exchanges unpacked, afforded him a fair degree of kudos in Xhomlliku. On one shift, he'd walked in on a married member of The Party in a state of advanced undress carousing with a female Chinese delegate. Rather than causing Gimi trouble (and the subsequent forfeits that being on the wrong side of The Party ushered) his 'discretion' bought him a small pay rise and a promotion – although he was less discreet when sharing his droll tales among friends.

As a footballer, he was a liability; slow, bereft of any discernible skill. It was joked among the *Calcetto* crowd that Gim would struggle to trap a bag of Elbasan cement. But he did possess a trick which made him a useful addition to any *Calcetto* team. With a penchant for playing bare-footed (shoes in Stalinist Albania were notoriously abject in quality), Gimi possessed a shot of incredible velocity, requiring almost zero backlift, earning him another pseudonym, *Gim Gishti* – Gim the Toe-Man.

Tole Cungu worked in one of the many factories that sprung up on the peripheries of Tirana during the cultural revolution. *Cungu* in Albanian parlance literally means 'the deformed', Tole's missing fingers and scars lasting souvenirs of his shifts working the heavy machinery that Comrade Enver promised would enable Albania to take the great leap forward. Cungu had been deformed by communism in the same way that it had deformed many Albanians, though never complained of his injuries. In Stalinist Albania, there was always some eavesdropping nark willing to report your voiced gripes to the local *Sigurimi* office.

Tole's girlfriend, Lëndina – pretty, young, affable, with a keen sense of the absurd – was an avid *Calcetto* fan, propping herself on the wall to get as close to the action as was feasibly possible. She worked at the local state-run canteen as a dishwasher despite her undoubted savvy.

'Why work in an office doing The Party's dirty laundry?' she would opine. 'Those kinds of jobs can get you killed. At least if I'm washing dishes, I'm out of their range of sight.'

In Hoxha's Albania, there was solace to be taken in performing a simple task like cleaning a pot and a pan; to know your role absolutely with no recourse for doubt or error – two plus two equals four.

Lëndina made *outré* noise whenever she turned up; whispers of contumacy uttered with wry, genial caution. Until, one day, she stopped turning up. Tole never told anyone where she'd gone, and nobody ever asked.

The rules of *Calcetto* were a trimmed version of the full-size game: five-a-side, no offsides, no breaks in play, first team to score five goals declared the winner. When a goal was scored, play was restarted with a goalkeeper roll-out. The surface, ball and rules favoured good close control, skill and passing in small spaces; a game centred around improvisation, creativity and technique. Quite where Gimi fitted into this equation was subject to constant, humorous debate.

It was bewildering how quickly this new footballing craze took hold. Within weeks, crowds numbering in excess of 300 arrived at the gates of Kongresi Lushnjës to watch and participate, with supporters turning up hours in advance to gain prime vantage. Adversely, as popularity mushroomed it became clear that the only hope for *Calcetto*, if it intended to remain underground, was to branch out.

In a country where capitalism was the devil – though, in the world's only atheist state, he didn't exist either – the word 'franchise' had no definable meaning. Yet the *Calcetto* set of east Tirana brokered a kind of moneyless franchise, with friends from adjoining neighbourhoods finding new venues in which to host their own weekly tournaments, thus driving the concept forwards. *Calcetto* was an inclusive, democratic idea set against an autocratic backdrop; an arcane act of defiance hiding within plain sight.

Makeshift *stadiumi* popped up at Fusha Ushtarve (Soldiers' Field) next to the army barracks by the Vorri Bommit (Tomb of Bomi) beneath Mount Dajti's lengthy panorama; a five-minute walk from Xhomlliku.

There was another pitch – Fusha Dibronsve (the Dibra Pitch) – in an area of Tirana that lay between the Lana River and the low-cost, concrete-panelled, aesthetically dead Khrushchevska estate spawned from Soviet roubles during the rebuilding of east Tirana in the 1950s.

Further sites sprung up at Fusha Gaberle (Gaberle Field) – the 'Gypsy Pitch' as it was unofficially christened, which sat at the southern tip of Dëshmorët e Kombit Boulevard (Boulevard of the Martyrs of the Nation) and also at the 23 Nëntori Shkolla (23 November School), a short walk from *Fusha Dibronsve.*

Each pitch spawned a team of coordinators – akin to Di, Gimi and Tole – who oversaw it; drawing up fixture lists, keeping records of scores and ensuring some small semblance of fair play was adhered to. In a short time window, these separate yet connected hubs of *Calcetto* created their own league system with teams travelling a short distance to away pitches to challenge rival *lagjeve* outside of their territory.

But the initial familial feel of Tirana *Calcetto* was changing. From humble beginnings, borne of fraternity and friendly collaboration, the sport was mutating into something different.

Calcetto teams were quickly becoming brands with their own identities – often affiliated to the pro teams of the capital or supportive of governmental bodies – featuring their own batch of star players with singular, loyal and vocal fan bases. This, in turn, birthed a culture of banter and braggadocio from which several intensely felt local rivalries were born.

With increased popularity came increased scrutiny. On a few occasions, known *Sigurimi* narks would turn up at Kongresi Lushnjës on matchday. Their questions were always the same, with the answers tailored to fit.

'What are you doing?'

'Playing football.'

'Who said you could play here?'

'Nobody.'

Try making a story out of that in your report to the local chief officer, you *Sigurimi* scum.

As *Calcetto* grew, new heroes were unearthed enhancing the standard of play and augmenting the game's growing audience. Stars like Bruno Hoxha – *I Madh* (simply 'the Best') – a player of abundant skill with innate, hardwired awareness that bordered on telepathy. A *bad bio*, a defector in the family during the 1950s, robbed him of any chance of going pro.

'Ben' Kamarieri – *Të Famshmit* ('the Famous') – waited on tables in Xhomlliku despite his self-confessed hatred of customers. Yet on the *Calcetto* court, with the ball at his feet, his disdain for restaurant patrons ceased to matter.

Xhelal – *Cigani* ('the Gypsy') – heralded from the poorest enclave of the city, yet his ability between the posts was the stuff of local legend. Allegedly, he'd been a trialist for Partizani, who were ready to recruit the swarthy stopper until some scurrilous fink pointed out his Romani roots.

Many of the crossover tournaments brought with them animosity that manifested itself in on-court dispute, enmity with a combustive hybrid of history and caste at its core.

One such altercation took place on Fusha Gaberle at Parku Rinia (Rinia Park); a tennis court reappropriated for *futboll lagjesh*, frequented, chiefly, by teams of Romani heritage. After the fall of communism in 1991, this corner of the park became a hotbed for the activities of Tirana's *mafioso*, but in the 1980s it was where the *romët* (Romani) hung out.

The significance of a small pocket of *Cigani* turf, within earshot of the prime minister's office and a stone's throw away from the nefarious, incestuous trappings of Blloku, cannot be overstated. In an era when gypsy ethnicity was subject to relentless persecution from the regime, the Gypsy Pitch was a place where cultural identity could be expressed and perpetuated outside of public view.

Sunday, as always, observed the usual procession of wannabe footballers funnelling their way down the tree-lined boulevards that fringed Rinia Park, onwards into Fusha Gaberle. Among their number on this particular Sunday were a team from inside Blloku; sons of the cruel bureaucrats who determined the bleak fate of the Albanian *tzigane*, enamoured – one can only presume – by the dormant need of the socially advantaged to gravitate among those less fortunate than themselves.

The arrival of the boys from the Blloku at Fusha Gaberle was greeted without any modicum or pretence of warmth. The enemy stood at the gate – literally – to the hub of Romani recreational life in Stalinist Tirana. Replete with their dark blue matching tracksuits, Adidas-branded trainers and sports holdalls, their reek of privilege must have spiked a primal anger in the bellies of *ciganët*.

The Blloku team were allowed to play. Despite the pervading mood of antipathy, *ciganët* of Rinia Park were canny enough to understand that denying the offspring of the government sufficient court time would be an unwise move.

When Blloku eventually took to the court against a team garbed in the dismal, mass-produced rags and shit, plastic shoes that symbolised Albanian penury in the 1980s, there could be little confusion among those present that what was happening in Fusha Gaberle that afternoon was – in Albania's egalitarian utopia – an enacting of class war.

When the *arbitri* blew the opening whistle, the gypsy team of Rinia Park hit *armiku* – the enemy – hard and fast, tackles flying in with the dual agenda of ball recovery and infliction of maximum hurt upon their opponents. It was open season, *ciganët* distilling decades of retribution into minutes of game time.

When one of the Blloku boys finally took the bait, using words that criticised his antagonists' ethnicity, sexuality and cleanliness, a fight ensued which saw two of the Blloku team hospitalised. The *Sigurimi* hastily intervened and Fusha Gaberle was shut down, with the perpetrators thrown in the back of a GAZ 66 and ghosted away for a private word.

For the boys from the Blloku, the wounds would heal. For the gypsies, eight-year stretches in the labour camps of Qafë Bar and Burrel awaited.

Elsewhere in Tirana, the games went on with the new *heronj dhe kampionë* – heroes and champions – of *futboll lagjesh* coming and going. The games would continue until communism's death in 1992. Indeed, a game similar to *Calcetto*, but closer to futsal, is still played in the suburbs of New Tirana, but there are stark differences between this modern variant and old *Calcetto*.

The virtuous, upstanding members of *The Party* watch the game from the Tribuna at the Stadiumi Qemal Stafa in May 1986.

Riza Lushta – *La Bombardiere* – sports Juventus colours after his move from Bari in 1940. He would establish himself as a favourite amongst the Bianconeri *tifosi*.

AS Roma – *Campioni D'Italia* 1941/42 – Naim Kryeziu – *La Freccia* – is seated on the front row, fourth right.

Enver Hoxha – 'Dear Leader' to his Albanian subjects from 1946 until his death in 1985.

Ljubiša Broćić; the Yugoslav coach who led Albania to Balkan Cup glory in 1946 pictured during his tenure at PSV Eindhoven in 1959/60.

Stadiumi Dinamo – Built in 1956 to a Soviet architectural template by political prisoners; a new home for the '*Sigurimi*' team, Dinamo Tirana.

KS Partizani Tirana – League & Cup Winners 1957; the side (managed by Rexhep Spahiu) that advanced to the Spartakiad Final in Leipzig where they lost 1-0 to CSKA Sofia of Bulgaria.

Two giants of Albanian football; Loro Boriçi (far right) in his role as coach and Panajot Pano (next to him) on national team duty for *Shqiponjat* in 1967 – a year of seismic change in Stalinist Albania.

Stadiumi Selman Stërmasi in 2009. Built by the regime in 1956, Stadiumi Dinamo was renamed in 1992 in honour of SK Tirana's anti-communist coach and benefactor, an irony the *Tirona* legend would've enjoyed.

中阿两国人民永恒的、牢不可破的战斗友谊万岁！

Enver Hoxha's and Mao Tse-Tung's *Albanian-Kino Alliance* (1961–1978) observed the 1967 Cultural Revolution in Albania where religion was banned and its figureheads liquidated.

Shqiponjat cause a huge shock, drawing 0-0 with West Germany at Stadiumi Qemal Stafa in December 1967 thus eliminating *DFB Team* from the 1968 European Championships.

Robert 'Bert' Jashari pictured on duty for Albania in the Netherlands, 1964. Jashari quit playing in 1968 after the regime refused him permission to join his Partizani team-mates for a European tie in Turin.

Panajot Pano – *Mbreti* (The King) – bearing an uncanny physical resemblance to Ferenc Puskas, Pano's gladiatorial, offensive style of play was also redolent of the brilliant Hungarian.

17 Nentori – *Kampionë* 1965/66 – the season prior to *Kampionati i Qymyrit*.

17 Nentori arrive in Amsterdam for their 1970/71 European Cup tie against champions-elect, Ajax.

Myslym 'Lym' Alla; the architect of the great *Tirona* sides of the late 1960s pictured in 1968.

The House of Leaves - *Shtëpia me Gjethe* – HQ to the Albanian Secret Police – *Sigurimi* – from 1946–1991.

Ali Mema – *Braziliani* – and nephew, Sulejman share tactical ideas at *Tirona*'s City of Students training ground; now the Skënder Ahmet Halili facility (circa 1975).

Osman Mema – *Finoku* – pictured during his second spell at 17 Nentori – Tirona – part of Lym Alla's dominant *Bardhë dhe Blutë* team of the mid-to-late 1960s.

Tirona substitutes and management take their place in the dug-out prior to a Kampionati fixture against Besa at Stadiumi Besa in the early 80s.

Celtic presented with bouquets – and a book on Albanian architecture – prior to their European Cup, first leg tie against Partizani Tirana at the Stadiumi Qemal Stafa in September 1979.

The master tactician, Shyqyri Rreli briefs Arben Minga, Skender Hodja, Anesti Stoja, Mirel Josa and Agustin Kola (left to right) prior to a Kampionati Kombetar game during *Tirona*'s successful 1987/88 season.

Arben 'Ben' Minga celebrates his opening goal in 17 Nentori's European Cup Winners' Cup 2-1 win away at Dinamo Bucharest in 1986/87.

In the days immediately after communism's fall, fans converge on the Stadiumi Qemal Stafa waving national flags removed of the communist, five-pointed star. Freedom had arrived in Albania, but at what cost?

Post-communism and entrepreneurism and a market economy – of sorts – comes to downtown Tirana, 1993.

The new game takes place in smart, custom-built indoor arenas with level astroturfed playing surfaces that boast metal goalposts and real nets. There are no tricky little oblongs that hinder smooth passage of play, no peepholes in the brickwork and no neighbours screaming their support and ire from overlooking tenements.

And the people who play the game look different too, dressed in a vivid medley of fashion-branded attire – alien to the dull colour palate of the Stalinist era – as mindless, modern pop music is piped into the building through a network of hidden speakers.

There are no Dis, Gimis or Toles any more in this sanitised environment. Albanians are just no longer made this way; an anomaly of different and harder times.

Calcetto, when it arrived – exported to Albania via the crackle of TV images illegally sourced from across the Adriatic – was a diversion from the mundanity and evils of prescribed Stalinist Albanian life. Yet on these small, heavily pocked, often dilapidated courts the football dreams of an enslaved proletariat were transposed into a kind of reality; a reality that, in spite of societal restrictions, could be shared and enjoyed with others. Is this what real freedom felt like?

In the years to come Albanians would come to know all too well what it meant to be free. But for a short time period, in a dark corner of their nation's history, where servitude reigned, they had *Calcetto*.

Chapter Fourteen

1984: Small Revolutions and the Birth of the *Shpresa*

WHEN VLLAZNIA reaffirmed themselves as a serious provincial threat to the three Tirana clubs by winning the Albanian title at the close of the 1982/83 season, narrowly edging out Partizani on goal difference, there was tacit acceptance that a power-shift within the domestic game was continuing to run a course. Success at *Djepi i Futbollit Shqiptar* echoed the question that Vllaznia's title victory ten years earlier had saliently voiced: if a club from the rebel city could win the league – again – surely bigger dreams were attainable?

As previously explored, Albania's split from the Soviet Union in 1961 saw them allied with Maoist China, a courtship that supplied The Party with a continuance of the money stream previously provided by Yugoslavia and the USSR. In return, Albania allowed China to use their military and naval base.

By 1979, Sino-Albanian relations were in their death throes, the Chinese leaving Albania for good, taking with them their essential funding. Stalinist Albania was on its knees. By the mid-'80s it was the third-poorest nation in the world, unthinkable for a country tucked into the rich, agricultural furrow of southern Europe.

Throughout the years of his dictatorship, Enver Hoxha aligned himself to countries willing to finance his failing socialist experiment. All of Hoxha's major accomplishments were achieved by harnessing 'collaborative' Yugoslavian, Soviet and Chinese aid. The drip-drip of foreign funding had now run dry, any allies Hoxha had, gone, tired of his obstinance and duplicity.

The years prior to his death in April 1985 espied a perennial scramble to retain power, using the negligible threat of external enemies to justify a repressive internal policy. Comrade Enver's greatest strength as a politician – his wily ability to use international turbulence as a bargaining chip to guarantee Albanian economic survival – had now become his greatest weakness. Europe was entering an era of progressive flux; times were changing while Albania watched from afar.

Within this picture, Hoxha cut a forlorn figure; a high-stakes gambler who'd run out of creditors reduced to scraping around in the gutter for loose change. Investment in sport was sizeably cut, the savings utilised in more practical societal areas.

Meanwhile, up north, under the tutelage of club old boy Ramazan Rragami, *Kuq e Blutë* were playing football with a guile, fluidity and skill that was an extension of their coach. Rragami sought to instil the same principles into the new Vllaznia that his old hero and mentor, Xhevdet Shaqiri, had imbued little over a decade before; a team that was brave, committed and good to watch, a success story in which Rragami had played a huge part.

In his attempts to duplicate Shaqiri's success, Rragami assembled a Vllaznia side upon the firmest of foundations, boasting a defensive shield which included Hysen Zmijani, regarded by many as Vllaznia's greatest right-back of all time, Fatbardh Jera – a centre-half of ominous presence and staggering consistency – and the solid and dependable Hysen Dedja, whose elder brother was a component of Shaqiri's '70s Vllaznia; all Shkodran born and bred and all willing to spill blood for the *Kuq e Blutë* cause.

The midfield was manned by the brilliant Viktor Briza, a player widely lauded by Vllaznia fans as one of the best ever seen. Briza was discounted from national team selection due to a rebellious streak and the fact that he – and his parents – weren't members of The Party.

Alongside Briza were Roland Luçi and Luan Vukatana, a pairing who played the game for fun, emphasised by their 'penalty-pass' goal against Ylli I Kuq in 1981, redolent of Johan Cruyff and Jesper Olsen's collaboration for Ajax against Helmond Sport, which it predated by a year. In 2009, Vukatana was immortalised, taking his place in the greatest Vllaznia XI of all time as voted by club supporters.

Another stalwart of Rragami's talented side was namesake Ferid, whose career was culled five years later for his part in the defection scandal involving team-mates Lulëzim Bërshemi and Arvid Hoxha. The pair absconded in Athens during a stopover on Vllaznia's return journey from a European Cup Winners' Cup tie against Finnish side Rovaniemi in November 1987. The younger Rragami was, among others, banned from football for life and sent to work in a brick factory.

The 1982/83 triumph observed a potent Vllaznia score more goals than any other side in the division – 39 in 26 games – conceding only 19, their +20 goal difference superior to Partizani who finished on the same points total of 34 but with an inferior goal difference of +15.

Since 1938, the National Championship had been the dual property of two footballing cities: Tirana and Shkodër. As 1983/84 beckoned, there appeared scant likelihood of a break in the hegemony; Partizani, Dinamo, 17 Nëntori and Vllaznia all lauded as pre-season favourites for the forthcoming campaign.

However, apropos of no previous realistic title credentials, 1983/84 heralded the rise of a club who, for 34 years, bore the name of a town that failed to host a single Kampionati fixture.

In Elbasan County – the midpoint of Albania – beyond the river valleys of the Shkumbini and smashed greenhouses that once heated the old metallurgical plant, above the ancient Roman trading post of Scampi stands the bijou rural settlement of Labinot-Mal. Home to 5,000 people, Labinot is an agricultural village; a drive-through on a journey to better places. A triviality like football has no place amid the impoverished daily struggles of Labinot-Mal.

Yet between 1957 and 1991, KS Labinoti – who played their football in Elbasan, an important centre for Albanian soccer development four miles south of Labinot-Mal – took the name of this remote outpost, rechristened to celebrate Labinot's communist-era import. During The Party's Stalinist rewrite of history, Labinot was earmarked as a historical landmark town; a meeting place for the Party of Labour of Albania during World War Two – an assembly that witnessed the formation of a united National Liberation Army.

Founded in 1913 as Klubi Futbollit Urani Elbasan, Elbasani endured many name changes until they assumed the regime-imposed moniker of 1957.

Elbasan is positioned north of the Shkumbini River – Gheg territory – unfavoured by the Tosk-friendly regime in Tirana. Stationed between the Malet e Skënderbeut – Skanderbeg Mountains – and the Myzeqe Plain (an expanse of malarial marshland where political prisoners were banished to drain the bogs), the fortress city was at the centre of Albania's concrete manufacturing industry, supplying much of the cement that would forge its plethora of bunkers.

Seventy-one years of existence brought smatterings of success for the team from Elbasan; two Kategoria e Pare (second division) titles in 1933 and 1958 and a solitary cup win in 1975, beating Lokomotiva Durrës 1-0 both home and away to secure a 2-0 aggregate triumph.

After a typical ninth-place finish in 1983, Labinoti recruited ex-Albanian international Frederik Jorgaqi and

Dashamir Stringa as joint coaches; both men pragmatic and cautious in their footballing approach.

In December 1967, Jorgaqi was the defensive rock in the Albanian side that forced a spirited 0-0 draw against West Germany in a European Championship qualifier in Tirana, eliminating *Die Mannschaft* from the competition. It was a pragmatism, solidarity and spirt he conveyed to the footballers of KS Labinoti.

Their opening managerial gambit was to install Ferdinand Lleshi, a former Albania international, as captain. Lleshi's footballing career had lost momentum since his final cap in 1981, but driven by a hunger to prove his detractors wrong, he embraced the captaincy role with a renewed pride, energy and application.

Jorgaqi's Labinoti boasted the considerable talents of Roland Agalliu, recently acquired from Dinamo, predominantly a forward but gifted with the tactical and technical nous to perform acts of creative magic to the mutual benefit of Labinoti's front two.

Agalliu would become the first foreigner to play in post-revolution Romania, helping Universitatea Craiova to the Divizia A and Cupa Romaniei double at the close of the 1991/92 season.

On 28 August 1983, Labinoti embarked on a season etched in collective memory as one of the greatest in Albanian footballing history.

Their opening game was a home fixture against Traktori of Lushnja, the compact, atmospheric Stadiumi Ruzhdi Bizhuta roused by an encouraging 3-0 victory courtesy of goals by Dashamir Luniku, Ardian Popa and an own goal by Traktori's Muzaka.

The convincing win placed Labinoti top of the table one game in, a symbolic lead lauded in *Sporti Popullor* as a 'happy moment' while expressing an oddly telling prophecy; that 'a moment' had the potential to become a 'continuum'.

Within a week such haughty aspirations seemed ill-founded; Labinoti soundly thrashed 3-0 in Vlora by Leonidha Curi's rampant Flamurtari.

Two 1-0 victories, away at 31 Korriku Burrel and home to Lokomotiva, courtesy of Stavri Mitrollari winners, were followed by a further chastening defeat – 2-0 – to 17 Nëntori at Stadiumi Dinamo.

Another Mitrollari strike inspired a 2-0 home triumph over Skënderbeu before Labinoti embarked upon a further trip to the capital on 16 October 1983 – the 75th anniversary of the birth of Enver Hoxha – their opponents, the Ministry of the Interior club, Dinamo.

The Stadiumi Qemal Stafa, full to bursting and in celebratory mood pre-kick-off, readied itself for a routine home win to commemorate Comrade Enver's birthday. Floral tributes were rested pitchside and paeans of praise expounding vows of eternal love towards Albania's 'Dear Leader' rang through the loudspeakers.

Amid the displays of organised sycophancy, the small pocket of Labinoti fans present – who'd travelled to Tirana aboard rickety trains from Elbasan more in hope than expectation – were witness to a performance and a result that changed the trajectory of their season.

An early forage out of defence by the away side resulted in Popa's cross-shot being scythed beyond Dinamo keeper Ilir Luarasi, by his own centre-half Arben Ndreu; a sobering, shock deficit for the home fans to absorb.

By half-time the natives were truly restless, frustrated by the near-impenetrable Labinoti back line of Zamir Arapi, Luan Deliu, Edmond Mustafaraj and Konstandin Rama serving as the protective screen to their flamboyant and legendary goalkeeper, Buljar Gogunja. More of him shortly.

A brief, post-break rally nearly summoned a Dinamo equaliser – but didn't. When Dashamir Luniku plundered a second Labinoti goal shortly beyond the hour, Dinamo wore the demeanour of a team short on ideas and devoid of belief. Labinoti, alternatively, were steadfast in their determination to become unlikely party-poopers at Comrade Enver's commemorative shindig.

A late Sulejman Demollari drive offered the home side brief hope, but Labinoti held firm for a historic, season-defining victory.

Sporti Popullor hailed Labinoti's win as a triumph centred on 'tactical calmness' and a determination to win 'the war for the first ball', strongly identifying the Elbasani defence as its 'strongest point'.

Post-match, coach Jorgaqi claimed that the 'main objective [was] a place in the top six', quickly gainsaying this by adding, 'It would be a very nice thing if the champion this season is a team that has never won the title.'

A week later, a 1-0 home win against 31 Korriku Burrel, courtesy of teenage forward Vladimir Tafani's second-half goal, took Labinoti to the top of the table.

Wins against direct rivals Partizani, Flamurtari and Vllaznia saw Labinoti crowned Autumn Champions in mid-December – the mid-campaign trophy awarded to half-season leaders – prompting sports journalist Teodor Laco to write, 'Now they [Labinoti] have a cup, why not win a championship? Appetite comes from eating.'

Labinoti emerged from their winter break in January by comfortably winning 2-0 away at Traktori, goals from Stavri Mitrollari and Zyber Bega rekindling their momentum.

On 12 February 1984, Labinoti beat Flamurtari 1-0 at home in a tightly contested game decided by a moment of sublime opportunism from Bega. The win served as the catalyst to a record-making run in which Bujar Gogunja would remain unbeaten for 11 league games – 1,037 unbreached minutes – in total.

The run took in crucial victories: the return against Dinamo at Ruzhdi Bizhuta, Mitrollari and Bega, again, providing the goals in a 2-0 victory and an equally key 1-0 win at Qyteti Stalin achieved while all of the chasing pack were dropping points elsewhere.

For three months, Gogunja – and the Labinoti defence – were impassable, Albanian sportswriters and football fans nicknaming them the 'Concrete Net'.

On the penultimate day of the season, Labinoti's closest rival for the title, 17 Nëntori, visited Elbasan in need of a victory that would take the race to the final day of the season. Despite controlling possession for protracted spells, *Tirona* failed to unlock the solid home defence. Upon the final whistle, Labinoti had successfully contained *Tirona*, a 0-0 draw securing the club's first Kampionati. In 26 games they had kept 17 clean sheets and conceded only 14 goals. It was the first time a club outside of Tirana and Shkodër had won the title in 46 years.

Scenes of delight enveloped the Ruzhdi Bizhuta, grown men shedding tears of unfettered joy as players embraced and celebrated with a zeal uncommon in a country where emotions, friendships and revelry were annulled, traded for the mercenary pursuits of self-preservation and the consolidation of power.

As The Party led its people into the abyss, egalitarianism, democracy and humanity found giving ground within the seldom monitored vacuum of sport. Shorn of the meddling of the regime, who in their desperation to preserve rule had lost sight of all else, football was now given the oxygen to blossom organically.

Alongside Labinoti's unique success, a renaissance was taking place at national team level too.

Shpresa buron e përjetshme – Hope springs eternal

Shyqyri Rreli was, in the opinion of those who witnessed him play, an outstanding footballer. Former *Shqiponjat* international, veteran of the pre-World War Two *Tirona* side and the creative engine in the all-conquering Dinamo team of the early to mid-1950s, Rreli was entrusted with the job of overseeing the national under-18 and under-21 squads in 1972.

It was a role that would increase in scope, Rreli eventually overseeing all non-senior international levels by 1981.

During a tenure with the national team setup spanning 18 years in total, Rreli brought about a qualitative change transforming Albania into a credible, winning side and inspiring the nation to dream of international honours and possible qualification for the 1986 World Cup in Mexico.

Previous to Rreli's reign, a paucity of international competition had deprived *Shqiponjat* of an arena in which to hone collective talent. Yet by the late 1970s, Rreli had instilled in his young Albanians a style of play that was bearing considerable fruit.

In his first assignment as under-21 coach, Rreli took the team to İzmir, Turkey, in August 1972 to compete in the Turneu Ballkanik i të Rinjve – Balkan Youth Tournament – where they finished a credible fourth, beating Romania 2-0 in the group stage.

Two years later they were finalists, beating Greece 2-1 and drawing with Turkey 1-1 before losing narrowly, 1-0, in the final to hosts Romania in Bucharest.

When Rreli's charges visited Salonika, Greece, in 1976, they beat a strong Bulgarian side 5-3 in the third-place play-off. Signs of improvement were clear to see, Rreli cultivating a composed and expressive unit who weren't afraid to take the game to their opponents.

The 1978 edition of the Balkan Youth Tournament was played between 1977 and 1978, initially in a group format; Albania facing Yugoslavia and Greece with the group winners contesting a two-legged final against the victors of a second group that included Romania, Bulgaria and Turkey.

First up for Albania were Yugoslavia, though this was no experimental, state-of-flux Yugoslavian side. Managed by Ivan Toplak, who would later coach the senior Yugoslav national team, Yugoslavia would use the Balkan Youth Tournament as a conduit providing competitive preparation for the Under-21 European Championship, also in 1978, for which they were serious contenders.

The opener in Skopje, in June 1977, pitted Rreli's team against an array of lavish talents that included Nenad Stojković of Partizan Belgrade, already a title-winner with the club; Vladimir Petrović, remembered by Arsenal fans for his brief stint in London during the early 1980s; and Vahid Halilhodžić, a brilliant, predatory goalscorer from Velež Mostar who would later ply his trade in France for Nantes and Paris Saint-Germain.

Halilhodžić would capture the UEFA European Under-21 Championship Golden Player award when Yugoslavia eventually won the title in May 1978, defeating Hungary, England and East Germany along the way.

Against considerable odds, *Shqiponjat* escaped Skopje with an almost unbelievable 1-1 draw, gazumping that result with a 2-1 victory in Tirana in October 1977.

When Albania faced Greece in a double-header in the March and April of 1978, Yugoslavia had already thrashed the Greeks both home and away. It meant that two points from two games against their Hellenic neighbours would take Albania to the final, where the Romanians lay in wait.

They needed only one, a gritty 1-0 away win in Salonika; the 0-0 return in Tirana mere gloss.

On 6 December 1978, Rreli's young Albanians embarked on the short trip north-east to Bucharest, facing off against a physical Romanian side. In a rough game marred by a poor pitch and some partial refereeing, Albania lost 3-1.

Ten days later at Stadiumi Dinamo, Romania faced an Albanian side with an appetite for *gjakmarrje* (revenge). In one of the great undocumented performances in the country's footballing archive, *Shqiponjat* tore their bewildered opponents apart and won 7-1, thus securing a second international honour – their first since 1946. The goals were spread among three players who would become key names in the history of the Kampionati Kombetar, 19-year-old Arben 'Ben' Minga of *Tirona* scoring twice with the two overage players, Shyqyri Ballgjini (Dinamo Tirana, 24) and Dashnor Bajaziti (Besa Kavaje, 23), weighing in with the other five; the latter bagging a hat-trick.

Unbelievably, in June 1981, Rreli's side did it again, beating Romania 4-1 before edging past Bulgaria 2-1 in the final at Volos Municipal Stadium, Greece.

Sandwiched between the successes was a runners-up placing in the under-18 variant of the 1979 Balkan Youth Tournament in Sofia, Bulgaria. After beating Romania 3-1 and drawing with the host nation 1-1, Rreli's side yielded to a tight 1-0 loss against Yugoslavia in the final.

Rreli took control of the senior national side after Loro Boriçi's unsuccessful 1982 World Cup qualification campaign. Finishing with a mere two points from eight games and enduring heavy away losses to West Germany (8-0) and Austria (5-0), FSHF called time on Boriçi's managerial reign. It would prove to be his final stint as national team coach. Boriçi died in April 1984.

Rreli bestowed the under-21 role on Ramazan Rragami – fresh from his title win with Vllaznia – and assistants, Petraq Ikonomi and Aurel Verria, in 1983.

The immediate target was qualification for the 1984 European Championship at both senior and under-21 level. It would be the first time an Albanian under-21 side had entered a qualifying tournament for a major championship. In time, the players who represented Albania during this historic campaign formed the core of what became known to natives as the *Shpresa* – hope – team.

The senior side, despite finishing bottom of Group 6, showed a steep improvement in performance during the 1984 campaign.

Drawn in a strong group featuring three sides who'd performed excellently at the 1982 World Cup, Rreli's new Albania achieved creditable draws against Northern Ireland and Turkey, suffering narrow one-goal defeats in all but one of their other qualifiers – West Germany (twice), Austria, Northern Ireland and Turkey. But it was the football they played that sparked genuine excitement, stretching very good sides with their imaginative and expansive brand of possession-based play. The portents appeared to be good for the 1986 World Cup qualification campaign.

But the real gold lay in the progress made by Albania's under-21s. Their group mirrored that of the senior side, minus Northern Ireland, who abstained from entering.

On 29 September 1982, Albania faced an Austrian side coached by former Rapid Vienna forward Karl Ritter in Klagenfurt. Playing without a recognised striker and using a 5-5-0 formation, the young Albanians appeared to be set up for containment. However, the presence of creative midfield livewires Mirel Josa and Skënder Hodja, both from *Tirona*, and Dinamo's Sulejman Demollari created an interchangeable trident of attacking intent that caused havoc in the *Burschen* defence. Albania's collective verve was capitalised upon by first-half goals from Dinamo's rugged centre-half, Agim Canaj, and *Tirona*'s tricky winger, Arben Vila. Despite a consolation by Rapid Vienna's Peter Hrstic, Rragami, Ikonomi and Verria's side hung on for a deserved 2-1 victory.

A 1-0 win in İzmir against Turkey in October preceded a 1-1 draw against group dreadnoughts West Germany the following March.

The game in Shkodër played before 12,000 passionate Albanians gave a true measure of the capabilities of Rragami's group of players. In a robust contest, Demollari fired *Shqiponjat* into a 20th-minute lead before Bayern Munich's Reinhold Mathy equalised 15 minutes later.

Albania had performed well. More pointedly, they headed the group having played the same number of games as the West Germans, a position they solidified by beating Turkey 1-0 at Stadiumi Dinamo in April 1983, Agim Canaj heading the decisive second-half winner.

In July, a beleaguered Austria visited Shkodër. With just one point on the board and any chance of qualification out of reach, the Austrians proved easy prey for an Albanian side playing with energy and panache. The 3-0 victory, played out before now-customary fervent home support, was facilitated by two fine goals in each half from Albert Topçiu, added to by an Arben Vila penalty late on.

With a game left, Albania stood a point ahead of West Germany; qualification for the 1984 European Championship quarter-finals in their own hands. On a sourer note, that remaining match was against the West Germans away.

On 19 November 1983, 16,000 confident home fans converged on the Moselstadion in Trier, deep in the Rhineland, with the expectation that West Germany would brush aside an Albanian team that had performed beyond themselves, but were now punching well above their regulated weight.

The West Germans, coached by Berti Vogts and containing *Deutscher* footballing heavyweights such as Matthias Herget, the Bayer Uerdingen sweeper who would earn 39 senior caps for *Die Mannschaft*; Ralf Falkenmayer, another full international who would win the UEFA Cup with Bayer Leverkusen in 1988; Thomas von Heesen, European Cup winner with Hamburg months earlier; Stefan Kuntz, a future German Footballer of the Year and Euro winner with a unified Germany in 1996; and the jewel in the crown, Michael Rummenigge, the younger brother of Karl-Heinz and a Bayern Munich regular gifted with wonderful vision and technique.

Albania, cautious of their opponents' excess of riches, played a 4-5-1 formation with Mersini guarding the gate, Canaj, Ocelli, Jera and Zmijani at the back, Josa, Liti, Vila,

Hodja and Demollari attempting to flood the midfield and an overage Sefedin Braho – who was winning titles with Partizani when many of his team-mates were still in kindergarten – the lone wolf up top.

For almost 40 minutes, Albania negated any German threat, but in a moment of rare freedom, Michael Rummenigge escaped his marker and crashed a rapier-like drive past Halim Mersini into the Albanian net.

As the Germans huddled in mutual congratulation, Albania reset. A minute later, Hysen Zmijani whipped in a cross that was asking to be headed home. The call was answered by Mirel Josa, arriving late at the far post to thump the ball emphatically beyond a prayer-less Uwe Zimmermann in the West German goal; 1-1.

Level at the break, Albania sat deep in the second half, depending on the physicality of Braho to offer an out-ball in their direst moments of defensive need. It almost culminated in a winning goal, Braho screwing wide when well placed.

In the end it didn't matter. As the final whistle blew, the young Albanian side and their coaches who'd masterminded their improbable and significant success – Rragami, Ikonomi and Verria – celebrated wildly.

Their endeavours would earn them a berth in the Euro '84 quarter-finals against Italy. They were also invited for a conference at the Albanian parliament with Enver Hoxha; a poor return for such an outstanding achievement.

The triumph registered globally, Albania's under-21s ranking joint eighth with France in the World Soccer World Team of the Year poll behind Hamburg, Aberdeen, Roma, Liverpool, Denmark, Anderlecht and Grêmio.

Drawn against Adriatic neighbours Italy (managed by Azeglio Vicini who would nurture the *Azzurri* back to health between 1986 and 1991, guiding them to within touching distance of home World Cup glory in 1990), both legs of the quarter-final were incredibly tight affairs.

Vincini's *Gli Azzurrini* – Little Blues – contained superb competitors such as Michelangelo Rampulla in goal, Milan's Filippo Galli and Andrea Icardi, Massimo Mauro of Udinese and not just one but two creative tours de force, Juventus's Beniamino Vignola and Sampdoria's Roberto Mancini.

The first leg, played before a packed Qemal Stafa in March 1984, was ebbing towards a mutually satisfactory scoreless draw when, in injury time, Fiorentina's Paolo Monelli stole a late, barely deserved winner.

Victory buoyed Vicini's side, the return at Stadia Mario Rigamonti in Brescia in early April a more comfortable proposition due to the Italians' away goal.

Albania fielded a 4-6-0 formation, playing without a recognised forward and, although Italy regularly probed, it took a moment of set-piece magic by Vignola in the 33rd minute to win it 1-0.

The excellence of Vignola's goal – a left-footed bullet from the right apex of the 18-yard box that arced into the top-right corner of a static Halim Mersini's net – was symbiotic of the *Bianconeri*'s young playmaker. Vignola would win the Serie A title with Juventus at the season's end and score a magnificent opener in their 2-1 European Cup Winners' Cup Final triumph over Porto at the St Jakob Stadium in Basel a month later.

The heroics of Rragami, Ikonomi and Verria's youthful Albania augured well for the future of the national side. Indeed, six of the starting 11 from the second leg in Brescia took their place in the senior side's opening World Cup qualifier against Guy Thys's Belgium at the Heysel Stadium, Brussels, in October of 1984.

In a performance full of spirit and potential, the plucky Albanians fell to late goals by Enzo Scifo and Eddy Voordeckers in a 3-1 loss. However, the quality of the Albanian goal was unquestionable; the trickery of Sulejman Demollari releasing *Tirona*'s whip-sharp forward Bedri

Omuri, who finished extravagantly – high into the net of Anderlecht stopper Jacky Munaron – to make it 1-1 on 71 minutes, cancelling out Nico Claesen's opener.

Shyqyri Rreli kept faith with the youngsters, fielding six under-21s in the team who faced Poland in Mielec two weeks later; the Poles having recently achieved a third-place finish at the 1982 World Cup in Spain.

Poland led at half-time via a bouncing bomb of a header from the great Włodzimierz Smolarek 23 minutes in.

Chasing the game, Albania manufactured two well-constructed goals after the break; Bedri Omuri scoring, again, with a wonderful back-heeled lob on 55 minutes, a triumph of improvisation, and his 17 Nëntori club-mate Agustin Kola capitalising on brilliant wing play by right-back Hysen Zmijani to fire *Shqiponjat* into a 2-1 lead with 15 minutes left. Only a late header by Andrzej Pałasz rescued an undeserved point for Antoni Piechniczek's shell-shocked side.

In two games, Rreli's *Shpresa* team had fashioned moments of quality and ingenuity to unpick sides that were among the finest in Europe, so it was with a muted optimism that Albania welcomed the Belgians to Tirana for the return Group 1 fixture in December 1984.

Albanians would often joke that the Qemal Stafa could either hold 20,000 or 30,000 depending on how close together 'bottoms were placed'. On 22 December 1984, the fanatical band of *tifozët* were definitely seated cheek-to-cheek, the *stadiumi* – distended beyond its prescribed capacity – serving as a wonderfully animated platform for a pulsating contest.

Rreli fielded eight of the under-21 squad against a Belgium side containing Jean-Marie Pfaff, Georges Grün, Franky Van der Elst, Michel Renquin, Enzo Scifo, Franky Vercauteren, Nico Claesen and Jan Ceulemans; campaigners from the 1982 World Cup and a fulcrum that would guide *Les Diables Rouges* (the Red Devils) to a fourth-place finish at Mexico '86.

On the day, Albania outfought the Belgians; determination and skill affixed, in a near-perfect performance that subdued and, eventually, overran their lofty opponents.

The goals came late, Mirel Josa bundling in a close-range finish after an Arben Minga knock-down from Zmijani's cross in the 69th minute. *Tirona*'s Minga completed the 2-0 victory with three minutes remaining, firing a right-footed, near-post shot past Jean-Marie Pfaff, prompting scenes of joyous pandemonium within the stadium.

In a year of miracles, observing Labinoti crowned champions and the country's under-21 side inaugurated among the top eight in Europe, 1984 closed with the Albanian seniors occupying one of the qualification berths for the 1986 World Cup in Mexico.

Small revolutions and bigger dreams were in play, prompted by the footballers of Albania rather than the flawed rhetoric of a crumbling regime.

The sadder reality was that Enver Hoxha had created an Albania that was the mirror-opposite to the revolutionary, socialist dream; iniquitous, dependent, destitute. But for a few short months, the small Balkan nation had reached out to the modern world, talking in a language that was universally understandable.

It would take a further seven years for the nation to free itself from the shackles of five decades of isolation and oppression, but in 1984 – the year of Orwellian prophecy – in an act of accidental rebellion, Albania and its beleaguered people, via the wonderful, all-encapsulating medium of football, were looking outwards with a renewed optimism, into a bigger world of infinite possibility.

Iconic Games
Albania 2 Belgium 0
World Cup Qualifying Group 1

Stadiumi Qemal Stafa, Tirana

Saturday, 22 December 1984

Attendance: 19,802

Albania: Perlat Musta (Partizani Tirana), Hysen Zmijani (Vllaznia Shkoder), Skënder Hodja (17 Nëntori Tirana), Muhedin Targaj (captain/*kapiten*; Dinamo Tirana), Adnan Oçelli (Partizani Tirana), Ferid Rragami (Vllaznia Shkoder), Sulejman Demollari (Dinamo Tirana), Shkëlqim Muça (17 Nëntori Tirana), Mirel Josa (17 Nëntori Tirana), Arben Minga (17 Nëntori Tirana), Agustin Kola (17 Nëntori Tirana)

Substitute/*Zëvendësues*: Arben Vila (Dinamo Tirana; not used)

Coach/*Trajneri*: Shyqyri Rreli

Belgium: Jean-Marie Pfaff (Bayern München), Georges Grün (Anderlecht), Franky Van der Elst (Club Brugge), Michel De Groote (Anderlecht), Eddy Jaspers (Beveren), Michel Renquin (Servette Geneva), Enzo Scifo (Anderlecht – Lei Clijsters (Waterschei); half-time), Franky Vercauteren (Anderlecht), Jan Ceulemans (captain/*kapiten*; Club Brugge), Nico Claesen (VfB Stuttgart), Alex Czerniatynski (Anderlecht – Eddy Voordeckers (Waterschei); 62 mins)

Coach/*Trajneri*: Guy Thys

Referee/*Arbitri*: Victoriano Sánchez Arminio (Spain)

'I was an excited child; my curiosity awakened.
After school, I would spend hours at the library
reading about this mythical place; an oasis in a
world that operated outside of Albanian borders.
It was then I knew it was all over for the regime;
Hoxha, communism, The Party – all dead –
replaced by a word I would repeat over and over
again. A new mantra: Mexico! Mexico! Mexico!'

Kurt, Tirana

In the early 1980s, a shift was taking place within Albania. Bankrupt, with Chinese ties cut, The Party was forced to strengthen relations with its European neighbours, Yugoslavia replacing China as Albania's primary trade partner.

For Hoxha, who'd spent the last three decades espousing the evils of Titoism and Yugoslav 'Eurocommunism', this must've been a thorn in his craw; Albania forced to break bread with its perennial and hated enemy. Ghosts were returning to haunt the beleaguered Comrade Enver.

The thaw, however, didn't last, Yugoslavia's ill treatment of ethnic Albanians in the Yugoslavian state of Kosovo leading to a further fissure in Albanian–Yugoslav relations. Two million Albanians lived in Kosovo, and Hoxha supported Kosovan demands for independence. It gave Hoxha occasion to cast himself as a national hero once more, spitting poisonous – yet ultimately pointless – vitriol in the direction of Belgrade. Hoxha's well-documented delight in the wake of Tito's death in May 1980 poured further petrol on the embers of discontent. Yugoslavia accused Albania of interfering in its national affairs, prompting a significant reduction in cultural, diplomatic and trade links between the nations.

But Albanian acquiescence to its detested foe had broken a hitherto impenetrable seal and prompted further alliances with Italy, Greece, and Turkey. With Hoxha, ill and bed-bound, steadily receding from public view, his heir apparent Ramiz Alia made a very pointed speech.

'Albania,' Alia opined, 'is a European country and as such it is vitally interested in what is occurring on that continent.'

The message couldn't have been clearer: Albania was ready to reconnect with the West.

Trade deals with Italy and Greece were forged in the early 1980s and – in 1983 – Albania signed an agreement with Italy creating a sea link between the port cities of Durrës and Trieste. The two countries also sanctioned a long-term trade agreement.

It was amid this wave of hopeful transition that the qualifying groups for the 1986 World Cup in Mexico were drawn in Zurich on 7 December 1983, placing Albania in a tough-looking quartet composed of Poland, Belgium and neighbours Greece.

The tournament was initially awarded to Colombia. With massacre, assassination, guerrilla warfare and drug trafficking subjects of Colombian daily national and international news – coupled with failures to comply with FIFA requirements – the offer was rescinded and a replacement chosen. Mexico received the nod in May 1983. They would become the first nation to host the tournament twice.

The excitement generated by the success of the under-21 team during their qualification for the quarter-finals of the European Championship earlier that year left its mark on the Albanian people and the national football team. Six of the side that ran *Gli Azzurrini* so close would feature in the vital World Cup qualification match versus Belgium in Tirana three days shy of Christmas Day 1984.

The team to face Belgium reflected how the 1984/85 edition of the Kampionati Kombetar was shaping up, with 17 Nëntori in imperious form, already threatening to run away with the title by the time *Shqiponjat* locked horns with Guy Thys's Belgium in late December.

Adhering to a recurring theme common to Albanian football history, *Tirona* – akin to all of the great champions of the Stalinist era – were led by a creative trio around whom much of the magic happened.

Arben Minga, Agustin Kola and Shkëlqim Muça – Ben, Gust and Çim (Gjim) as they were known to the club's supporters – were very different players cast within a mould set by coach and former *bardhë e blutë*, Enver Shehu.

Shehu wore the *Tirona* shirt for eight years between 1955 and 1963, a time when the club from the east of Tirana had suffered hardest at the hands of the regime. As a coach, Shehu saw his team's recent success as payback for the crimes that had been committed against his beloved *Tirona*. *Tirona*'s *Trekëndësh i artë* – golden triangle – were steering Shehu in his pursuit of suitable vengeance.

Minga and Kola provided the physical stature to the triumvirate: both measuring over six feet in height, Minga being an out-and-out striker with the galloping stride of a prize racehorse paired with phenomenal heading ability, Kola a left-sided forward with great feet and wonderful technique who was also pretty decent in the air. Yet it was Muça who dominated the tempo of this team; organiser, creator and scorer of spectacular goals. The trio were the catalysts behind *Tirona*'s first title in 12 years at the close of the 1981/82 season and were providing the performances and the goals that would see them land another Kampionati in 1984/85 with Minga winning the Albanian Golden Boot.

All three players were part of the Shyqyri Rreli team that faced the Belgians alongside two other *Tirona* club-mates, the free-scoring Mirel Josa and the tungsten-tough centre-half Skënder Hodja.

But it wasn't a one-club national team. The early 1980s brought with it a period of refreshing parity within the game, five different clubs winning the title since 1980 – Dinamo, Partizani, *Tirona*, Vllaznia and Labinoti – and four of these *kampionë* were represented among the 12 men who would take the field for Rreli's youthful side.

Three players were drawn from the police club, Dinamo: captain and leader Muhedin Targaj, the splendidly gifted midfield general Sulejman Demollari and livewire forward Arben Vila, so vital during the under-21s' campaign of 1983/84.

From Partizani, Perlat Musta guarded the Albanian *gate*, solid and spectacular, and Adnan Oçelli worked the right channel as a stylish and adventurous overlapping full-back.

Vllaznia added the brilliant and legendary right-back Hysen Zmijani plus the gritty midfield anchor Ferid Rragami to what was a very accomplished mix of players.

With an average age of just 23, many Albanians refer to this side as *Brezi i Artë* – the Golden Generation – high praise indeed considering what has gone before and since. But the game against Belgium would garner a more formidable accolade. It would become known to many, in hindsight, as *Rilindja e Kombit* – the Rebirth of the Nation.

Facing *Shpresa* at Stadiumi Qemal Stafa were a Belgian side with their own reserves of fabulous talent.

In goal stood Jean-Marie Pfaff from West German club Bayern Munich – a *Stern des Südens* side who were well on their way to winning a seventh Bundesliga title in 1984/85. Pfaff set the template for the immaculate lineage of Belgian keepers that carries into the modern era.

The Red Devils boasted a quintet of players from RSC Anderlecht: Georges Grün, Michel de Groote, Enzo Scifo, Franky Vercauteren and Alex Czerniatynski, a new generation of *Les Mauve et Blancs* who were threatening to recapture the essence of their great 1970s side, reaching the 1983/84 UEFA Cup Final and sealing their 18th Belgian title at the end of 1984/85.

Additional home-spun ballast was added by national team mainstays Jan Ceulemans – their rugged, yet creative captain – and Franky Van der Elst (both of Club Brugge), with the youthful Waterschei pair Lei Clijsters and Freddy Voordeckers complementing the mix.

Further Germanic influence was provided by the excellent Nico Claesen of VfB Stuttgart, whose determined performances at the Mexico World Cup in 1986 would earn him a lucrative move to the English First Division with Tottenham Hotspur.

At the centre of the Belgian side was cultured defender Michel Renquin of Swiss champions Servette Geneva.

Renquin, Ceulemans, Van der Elst, Pfaff, Vercauteren and De Groote were the skeleton of the 1980 European Championship side that pushed West Germany so close in the final at Rome's Stadio Olimpico, and remarkably defeated Diego Maradona-led reigning world champions Argentina in Barcelona's Camp Nou at the 1982 World Cup. They would show their mettle again in the heat of Mexico two years later. There was no doubting the pedigree of Guy Thys's side.

In the end days of 1984, the footballers of Belgium flew into Rinas Airport from Athens, descending into an Albania that found itself locked in the midst of a bitter, unforgiving winter. Dark, malevolent skies loomed high above the Skanderbeg Mountains and icy winds tore through the tree-lined boulevards of Tirana.

Despite unfavourable portents, the Belgians were overwhelming favourites to secure the two points. Their opening brace of fixtures had observed a late, and somewhat fortunate, victory against their hosts in the reverse fixture at the Heysel Stadium in Brussels, two goals in the final six minutes securing a flattering 3-1 win in a game in which Albania had caused numerous problems. Three days prior to the Albania game, *Les Diables Rouges* escaped a hostile Olympic Stadium in Athens with a share of the points after a cagy scoreless draw.

Belgium v Albania had been subject to protests from Albanian anti-Hoxha royalist expats who'd attended in number to voice their disapproval of the country's regime, the Belgian Police Fédérale's inertia causing ire among the visitors and their small travelling enclave. It was ill-will that would add texture to the return in Tirana.

Albania's exciting 2-2 draw versus the Poles in Stadion Stali Mielec in late October positioned Poland at the head of Group 1 with three points and five goals scored, with three conceded. Belgium were second with three points having scored three and conceded one with Albania third on one point, ahead of Greece – also with one point – on goals scored.

The Saturday noon kick-off prompted The Party to permit its workers the rare luxury of a half-day holiday – Saturday being a work day in Hoxha's Albania – with jubilant comrades, already in keen party mood, heading straight to the stadium from the factory floors and administrational offices of Stalinist Tirana.

Although tempered by the ominous overhang of muddied heavens, the surrounds of the Qemal Stafa were a well of pre-match goodwill, anticipation and noise, as fans with and without tickets gravitated toward the hub of the action. Those who'd arrived at the small ticket portholes at the bottom of the stadium staircase too late, or couldn't squeeze their way into the swarming arena, sat in huddled groups on its concourse listening to the action play out on the silver, oblong transistor radios mass-produced by the regime. The heaving *Lokal* on Rruga Elbasanit, the only *tavernë* in proximity to the Qemal Stafa that boasted a TV screen – a small black-and-white portable propped on a plinth above the bar – was a mess of drunken expectancy, weary Albanians determined to enjoy their rare, allegorical day in the sun. Saturday, 22 December 1984 was the day when the whole of Albania had its ears on the radio and its eyes on the TV screen.

Minutes prior to noon, the teams took to the field on a dull, bitterly cold afternoon, the eight *flamujt* – banners of the Socialist Republic that stood like sentinels above the *stadiumi* – rapping angrily in the wind around their tall flagpoles.

Upon conclusion of the national anthems, 'De Brabançonne' sung with drab, muted disinterest by a Belgian side who already appeared to be winding down for the Christmas holidays, and 'Himni i Flamurit' – 'Hymn to the Flag' – bellowed out with moist-eyed, patriotic zeal by the Albanian players and their 'up-for-it' *tifozët*, it became apparent, even to the casual onlooker, that there was a momentum shift taking place prior to a ball even being kicked. When the captains met at the halfway line for the customary exchange of wimpels and handshakes, the mood was succinctly captured by an eight-year-old boy present in the *njëzet* (the '20' – the cheap seats at the Qemal Stafa) that day, 'Their captain; the great warrior Ceulemans, had shrunk in stature. Muhedin Targaj was a giant in comparison. We could all see it! The *njëzetat*, the *Tribuna*, we all witnessed the change happening. There was no fear in the stadium; fans and footballers united in battle.'

This lack of fear displayed itself in a crackerjack of a performance, *Shqiponjat* starting fast and maintaining pace throughout an opening period in which they hit Jean-Marie Pfaff's bar and saw a goal-bound header cleared off the line in a fretful flurry of Belgian attrition. Admittedly, the surface at the national stadium had a bit of a bobble to it, but it was a snag that both sides were at duty to unpick.

Despite the incoming Albanian storm, Thys's team weathered the *tornado e kuqe* – red tornado – arriving, upon the knell of Spanish official Victoriano Sánchez Arminio's half-time whistle, in a state of undeserved parity; 0-0.

To many observers, a lack of product – the tangible currency of goals – in light of the excellence of the display rang the usual alarm bells; it wouldn't be the first time that a promising national team performance had devolved into heart-breaking defeat.

But in Hoxha's godless dystopia, it seemed that any sway the gods might exert was working in favour of the Albanians when Enzo Scifo, influential playmaker, Belgian Golden Shoe winner and Ballon d'Or nominee for 1984, failed to re-emerge from the tunnel after half-time, replaced by the lesser threat of Waterschei's Lei Clijsters.

If the Belgians were expecting a more pliable, compliant opposition to appear after the break, they were to be sorely disappointed, *Shqiponjat* resuming the contest with plenty of crunch to their tackles, displaying an insatiable appetite in the winning of every second ball.

But there was more to their play than mere perspiration. In the game-altering chambers of midfield stood fabulous technicians Shkëlqim Muça and the 20-year-old Dinamo dynamo, Sul Demollari, whose creative élan and goalscoring verve would propel Dinamo Bucureşti to the Romanian Divizia A title in 1991/92. He was also the artist in Ramazan Rragami's overachieving under-21 side.

After the break, Demollari and Muça wove neat patterns around a moribund, static Belgian defence. Yet despite their artistry, it was a sequence of scrappy, but importantly won 'second balls' inside Belgium's final third that provided Albania with a vital opener with little over 20 minutes remaining.

From a half-cleared Albanian corner, Demollari's lobbed pass found touchline-hogging right-back Zmijani, who instinctively whipped a useful first-time cross into the penalty area. The cross was met on the penalty spot by Michel Renquin, who headed it towards the right-hand corner of the box where Demollari bullied Vercauteren off the ball before delivering a shot which hit the shins of De Groote, deflecting it into the path of Arben Minga. Minga's quick shot was blocked by the left boot of De Groote again; the ball now loose 12 yards out. A further attempt by Minga – now prostrate – to get another shot away span off a melee of bodies to Mirel Josa on the edge of the box who outjumped Jan Ceulemans, directing a header to the right-hand side of the area where Zmijani won a further aerial battle, this time with Georges Grün, leaving the Belgian full-back on the ground and the ball spinning to the touchline. Zmijani retrieved the ball before it ran out of play for a goal kick, digging out a cross to the far post. It was met by the now-upright Minga, whose target-bound header went back across the goal and had Pfaff beaten, but was cleared off the line by Eddy Jaspers. The ball hung in the air, barely a yard from goal, waiting to be won. It was Josa who got there first; the johnny-on-the-spot again, as he had been for the under-21s in West Germany a year earlier, nodding in from close range, unleashing an explosion of noise inside the *stadiumi* rarely heard before or since. Unbelievably, with 70 minutes on the clock, the hosts had taken the lead.

In the *Lokal* on Rruga Elbasanit, well-oiled patrons showered the bar staff with a tsunami of Fernet and Cognac, while on the concourse of the Qemal Stafa fans danced in wild delight.

But there remained 20 minutes for the Belgians to save themselves from unlikely defeat, and although initially stunned, the Albanian goal sparked the previously flaccid Red Devils into a late flurry of life.

Eddy Voordeckers saw his close-range effort bravely blocked by Perlat Musta and when the same player directed a goal-bound header past the *Shqiponjat* gatekeeper with eight minutes left, it was only a last-ditch clearance by Zmijani, on sentry duty at the right-hand post, that preserved his side's narrow advantage.

With the game increasingly stretched, Belgium continued to probe. In the 86th minute, an agricultural punt into the Albanian area was won by Muhedin Targaj, a header which found Muça in a pocket of rare space. His instinctive pass released Mirel Josa, to his left, on the breakaway. Josa's first-time crossfield pass wrong-footed De Groote, enabling the supporting Minga to push the ball past the defender just inside the Belgian half and, more importantly, put him one-on-one with Pfaff.

Georges Grün tried to recover lost ground in pursuit of Minga, but with the *Tirona* man ahead by a couple of yards – his galloping stride carrying him ever closer to the edge of the Belgian box – it was never a chase Grün was liable to win. As Minga approached the right-hand side of the area, he arrowed in a powerful shot that tore low into the Belgian net.

Again, the Qemal Stafa and its environs erupted, but this time it was celebration suffused with relief. There would be no way back for the Belgians. Minutes later, on the peal of the referee's final whistle, victory was confirmed. Albania had won 2-0.

Jubilant scenes immersed Albania's national stadium, an adrenalin-fuelled cortege of humanity that carried itself, en masse, into central Tirana via Rruga Elbasanit, the tiny *Lokal* en route dried of anything alcoholic and drinkable.

Ecstatic natives congregated in Skanderbeg Square where strangers hugged, more *raki* was imbibed and an oddly configured word fell, recurrently, from the whispering lips of the collective: *Meksika* – Mexico.

Nobody really knew where Mexico was, what it looked like or whether they would even be allowed to travel there if the miracle were to happen. They certainly wouldn't be able to afford it. But it was the mood that the Belgium result ignited, the promise of an oasis in an unrelenting wilderness of sterility; the dream of something better beyond Albanian borders. *Një rilindje* – a rebirth.

In hindsight, the dream failed to be realised. In February 1985, the national team visited neighbouring Greece for what appeared an ostensibly winnable qualifier against Miltos Papapostolou's *Galanolefki* in Athens, fielding the same starting 11 that had held a nation rapt against Belgium.

But this Albanian side, garbed in an uncommon all-white strip *a la* Real Madrid, failed to show. Panathinaikos legend Dimitris Saravakos benefitted from poor goalkeeping by Perlat Musta; the Partizani stopper allowing Saravakos's cross-shot – from the tightest of angles – to squeeze between his legs at the near post, inside the first ten minutes.

It was a strike from which Shyqyri Rreli's *Shqiponjat* never recovered, Saravakos's Panathinaikos club-mate Kostas Antoniou heading home a rebound after the former's close-range volley had been brilliantly saved by the Albanian keeper on 37 minutes.

The second half ebbed away from an Albanian side who'd failed to reach the heights of the previous December. Indeed, it could've been worse, but a goalpost and Greek profligacy spared Albania further damage at a cavernous and sparsely populated Spyros Louis.

The damage was sizeable, though not terminal, the forthcoming fixture against Poland in Tirana shaping up as a winner-takes-all decider that would see the victors of the contest almost certain of their place on the plane to Mexico. As the people revelled in the excitement, they were unaware that *Faraoni i Kuq* – the Red Pharoah – Enver Hoxha, was teetering on a deathly tightrope.

By the time Poland arrived in Tirana in late May, the Albanian leader was dead; a protracted period of compulsory, regime-enforced mourning still in observance. Against this morbid backdrop, the scene was set for the completion of what had been a 13-year journey for Shyqyri Rreli – with more still to come – in which, under a stewardship that began with his appointment as under-21 coach in 1972, the national team had ascended from international football primitivity to within touching distance of their first major world tournament.

The fixture was, again, hosted by a full-to-bursting Qemal Stafa, but this time something didn't feel right; the air of positivity that pervaded the stadium during the previous home game replaced by an aura of nervy trepidation.

In a tight game defined by key moments, Minga squandered a seemingly unmissable early chance, blasting wide from inside the six-yard box after two minutes. It was lack of composure that set the tone, *Shqiponjat* dominating possession yet unable to convert their pressure into clear-cut chances.

The one moment of real quality during a tense, tough game was provided by Polish superstar Zbigniew Boniek.

Boniek was integral to a Juventus team that won its first European Cup against Liverpool in the ill-fated final at the Heysel Stadium the evening prior to this crucial game. By minor miracle – and via a tricky matrix of connecting flights and ambassadorial negotiation – Boniek managed to make it to Albania in time for the 5pm kick-off to wear the captain's armband in Tirana.

On 24 minutes, Jan Urban caressed a short pass into the path of the oncoming forward on the edge of Albania's 18-yard box. Boniek's speed of thought outfoxed goalkeeper Musta, whipping an instant drive low into the bottom-left corner of the net. It was a glint of brilliance that decided the contest.

Retrospectively, a home win, coupled with the 1-1 draw earned in the final home game against Greece, would've taken Albania to Mexico. Yet despite falling short, the 1986 World Cup qualification campaign – a clutch of six games that, by and large, witnessed *Shqiponjat* playing marvellous, expansive football – did much more than merely enhance the country's profile on the world stage. It planted a seed. And it was a seed that bore roots that would serve as the foundation for what was to come.

For better or for worse.

Chapter Fifteen

The Great Unsung –
E Madhe e Pakënduar

1956 WAS *viti i ndryshimit* – a year of change – for Albania. At home, Enver Hoxha's rejection of the USSR's de-Stalinisation programme caused ructions with Khrushchev, leaving the Hermit Kingdom in a state of political limbo.

Khrushchev, in turn, was scathingly critical of the Hoxha-sanctioned execution of Liri Gega – the only female co-founder of the Communist Party of Albania, a woman with Titoist and Khrushevite tendencies. Gega and her husband were shot dead trying to leave the country in 1956. Khrushchev claimed that Gega was pregnant at the time of her death.

Away from home, whispers of revolution were gaining volume in Hungary. They would reach full voice later in the year but were ruthlessly silenced by Soviet military intervention. The brutality of the Soviet culling of Hungarian disscent contributed to Hoxha's desperation to cut ties with the USSR: if Khrushchev could wield the axe in Budapest, he wouldn't shy from doing so in Tirana.

And it was amid this era of uncertainty and paranoia that a child was born into an impoverished family in the central-Albanian city of Berat; a boy whose personality, strength of character and rejection of social norms would earmark him as both an irritation to authorities and a cult hero among *tifozët*.

Përparim Kovaçi – Rim – arrived in the world at Thimi Nika (Berat Hospital) on 8 January 1956. Born with a liver condition that blighted him throughout his life and, at one point, threatened to kill him, his mother surrendered her child to a father later deemed an unfit parent. Orphaned aged three, he was released into the care of his sibling, Fatmir, the eldest brother of seven Kovaçis, who instilled in Rim a keen work ethic, teaching him carpentry as a supplement to his formal education. It was hardly an ideal start to life, but from inauspicious beginnings good things began to happen for Rim.

Although there was no tradition of sporting aptitude in the Kovaçi clan, Rim began to show ability on the athletics field, running the 100m in 12 seconds and 30m in less than four. Blessed with natural pace, Kovaçi adapted this unteachable gift to the game of football, spending the lion's share of his spare time honing skills on the scorched fields neighbouring the old Stadiumi Tomori. Rim, now eight, played with boys much older than himself, learning the more rugged aspects of the game.

It was during one such kick-about that Rim was spotted by Tomori youth scouts Zogi Konomi and Filip Leci. Kovaçi's strength and prowess in front of goal earmarked him as an exciting new talent. He was immediately referred to the *Shtëpia e Pionierit* – Pioneer House of Tomori Football Club – where his talent was given the necessary nurture with which to succeed.

Under the tutelage of youth coaches Guxim Mukli and Agim Matrapazi, Kovaçi quickly garnered a reputation as a free-scoring *sulmues qendror*, breaking local schoolboy records. But, aside from the quantity of goals scored, it was the variety and quality of his haul that made him special, his diminutive stature defying the red-blooded predator that lay hidden therein.

Standing 5ft 6in in his stockinged, size-six feet, Rim bore little resemblance to the archetypal marksman. Physically, he was thickset with short legs, similar in physique to Diego Maradona. But he was incredibly fit and fast; a brilliant box-player with two great feet who could – to the shock and regular embarrassment of those who attempted to thwart him – easily outjump towering centre-halves and deliver a decisive bullet header. He was also uncommonly brave, throwing his body in among a hail of boots to get the job done. Prodigiously hard-working with values imparted by his elder brother, Rim regularly stayed behind after training to work on the improvement of his technique. But there was also needle in his DNA – the product, possibly, of a fractious, unparented upbringing. He would be red-carded seven times in his career and receive a plethora of yellows – this in an Albania where sending-offs and cautions were virtually unheard of and ruthlessly punished by FSHF.

Aged 13, Kovaçi left the academy, taking his place in the Tomori youth team where the goals continued to flow. For three years, under the watchful instruction of Mukli and Matrapazi, Rim was modelled to fit Tomori's senior team. When head coach Mon Xhamo included him in his squad for the 1973/74 pre-season, Rim was already primed to apply himself to the rigours of first-team football.

The Kampionati, however, had to wait, as Second Division (*Divizioni i Dytë*, now the *Kategoria e Parë*) Tomori would need to earn promotion before Rim could grace the top tier and stake a claim to a place among the pantheon of the Albanian footballing greats.

Mired by overwhelming odds, but armed with ability, determination, self-belief and the right mentors, Rim became a living paradigm to the maxim that hard work bears fruit; that greatness via toil is attainable. To paraphrase not one, but two Albanian proverbs, each person builds his own destiny, but, as in every journey, a good start is half the battle.

On the opening day of the 1973/74 season, the Tomori players boarded their rattletrap bus and travelled to the deep south of the country; the frontier city of Delvinë, where they faced newly promoted Bistrica.

On arrival, the players embarked on a pre-match stroll through the mosaic-filled streets of the old Ottoman city, and it was there where Xhamo delivered the inevitable news: the 17-year-old Kovaçi would be starting.

For *Mistrecët* – the Captious – it provided an opportunity to get the season off to winning ways. And so it proved, with Tomori returning to Berat happy after securing a 4-2 victory in which Rim scored twice.

Week two of the season provided a sterner test, with perennial promotion contenders KS Dajti visiting Stadiumi Tomori. In an even contest, it was Kovaçi who provided the deciding moment in a 1-0 win.

As the season progressed, Tomori were a reoccurring voice in the promotion argument, entering a three-way tussle with Dajti and Punëtori Patos, a slugfest ultimately won by the club from the oil-rich plains of Patos-Marinza. Punëtori finished a solitary point ahead of Tomori and despite *Mistrecët* outscoring them, it was they who qualified for the promotion play-off final against Apolonia Fier; a game they duly won 1-0. Despite the disappointment of missing out, Kovaçi had announced his arrival with a continual stream of important goals.

The 1974/75 season witnessed a further tightly fought scrap for ascendency, Tomori falling short again behind promoted Luftëtari of Gjirokastër. By 1975/76, Tomori fans began to speak of a *mallkimi* – a promotion curse – as the perennial bridesmaids fell at the final hurdle again, losing 1-0 in the play-off final to Skënderbeu Korçë.

Teenager Kovaci's goalscoring form alerted the attention of national team coach Loro Boriçi who, it's said, liked what he saw. However, the pragmatic Boriçi decided against including the youngster, contesting that Kovaçi had yet to prove his mettle at the highest level.

The 1976/77 season observed a Tomori side hardened by failure. In the league, they breezed to qualification for the new-format, two-legged play-off final, finishing top of their regional division unbeaten, hugely outscoring their local rivals, the very distant second-placed Naftëtari from Qyteti Stalin – Stalin City, now Kuçovë.

The final pitched Tomori against Second Division Group B winners Besëlidhja from the north-western city of Lezhë, close to the Montenegrin/Yugoslavian border. Besëlidhja had proven equally dominant in their qualification, conceding just eight goals during their own impressive campaign.

The first leg in Lezhë was hard-fought with Tomori surrendering their unbeaten record, yielding to a narrow yet repairable 1-0 loss.

The return at the Stadiumi Tomori a week later is a game entered into *Mistrecët* folklore. Ninety minutes of nip-and-tuck football saw Tomori lead 1-0; the scores level on aggregate, taking the contest into extra time.

After three years of heartbreaking near misses and laden by an encumbering frustration that held the whole city in its grip, Tomori were in no mood to be denied this time around. It was amid scenes of unrestrained joy, at a bouncing Stadiumi Tomori, that Kovaçi etched his signature into the historic tomes of the Captious. Rim provided the two dead-eyed finishes – deep into extra time – that killed off stubborn, attritional opponents, elevating the club to a 3-0 success and the holy grail of Albanian football once more. The *mallkimi* had been broken.

Shortly prior to the beginning of the 1977/78 season, and in a significant tangent to his story, Kovaçi's work duties as a mechanic in the Berati waterworks were rescinded. He was enlisted in the army as liaison duty officer in the town of Uznovë, a key military base two miles from Berat, his working hours shorn from eight to five per day with Fridays free for training and conditioning. Inadvertently, his subscription as a full-time soldier rendered Kovaçi exempt from national service and the subsequent regime-implemented manipulations this could unfurl for a player of his significant ability.

Tomori's return to the Kampionati Kombetar proved to be a season assailed by relegation doubts, *Mistrecët* treading perilously close to the relegation line on several occasions. In honesty, it was a season of slim margins all round, with a svelte 11 points separating bottom-placed Skënderbeu and league champions Vllaznia. Tomori eventually finished seventh – three points shy of the relegation zone.

One positive constant, aside from the campaign's many misgivings, was the input of Kovaçi. Despite shipping more goals than any other team in the division, Tomori scored the same amount as fourth-placed Dinamo. Ironically, it was their captious nature in front of goal that had been their saviour – with Rim a key contributor.

A more defensive-minded Tomori approached the 1978/79 season. Indeed, it was a campaign that observed six 0-0 draws, six 1-0 scorelines and included 11 clean sheets with fewer goals conceded and, consequently, fewer scored than the previous year. An eighth-place finish yielded four more points than 1977/78 and, although Tomori's football suffered due to their new, pragmatic style of play, they comfortably side-stepped relegation, Kovaçi top-scoring.

The year of 1979 heralded the beginning of the end for Stalinist Albania. Ties with existing allies were cut and all avenues of communication with the outside world closed. Propaganda, oppression, authoritarianism and xenophobic nationalism were the tools Hoxha wielded to preserve power as the country shambled towards third world economic status.

The Party hid Albania's abject 'reality' from its people; hollow soundbites bragging of Albanian resistance in the face of alleged enemies the emollient used to grease the wheels of national obeyance, while Comrade Enver – himself in a state of advanced ill health – presided over a nation that was slowly starving to death.

With the situation on the home front dire, Tomori began to feel the pinch on a sporting front too. News of Rim's progression to the status of fully realised player ignited the interest of the superclubs, with both Partizani and Dinamo eager to secure his services. Kovaçi, Berati to the marrow, was unwilling to bow to their overtures, adamant to remain in the place of his birth with the club that he loved.

Partizani chairman Patriot Alia was particularly active in his pursuit of Kovaçi with offers of plush accommodation in the big city cited. When Rim refused his advances, Alia – an acquaintance of national coach Loro Boriçi – was alleged to have remarked to Tomori chairman and local Party commissioner Bardhyl Dardha, 'At Partizani, we have long memories. Just tell the boy that I hope his decision doesn't come back to haunt him.'

In Kovaçi's reasoning, leaving Berat to move to the big city would rob him of any ounce of freedom he had left. In Tirana, watchful eyes were everywhere, harsh in their scrutiny. It was where The Party's flame burned brightest, and those who stood too close to its flicker were the ones devoured in its pyre.

Football as escapism brought sustenance of a sort to the impoverished masses with Rim's goals a spiritual comestible to the Berati people. In the 1979/80 season, the diminutive forward would feed them well.

During the early months of 1979/80, *Gazeta Shqtiptar* used an epithet to describe Kovaçi – and it was a name that stuck. *Pantera e Beratit* – The Panther of Berat – was fully unleashed on the Kampionati Kombetar stage, and it was a campaign that added lavish detail to Kovaçi's already florid story. What had gone before was merely a titillating foreword.

Blessed with the enhanced confidence and knowhow that two educational seasons in the Albanian top tier imparted upon him, Rim – still only 23 – was approaching his prime. When newly instated first team coach Guxim Mukli's *Mistrecët* embarked on their league campaign, they did so with their key asset hungry for goals.

The fixture list pitted Tomori against local rivals Naftëtari – the Oilmen – from Stalin City in the crude-rich, central lowlands of Albania, in an early season derby at the Stadiumi Tomori. The Tomori–Naftëtari rivalry has always been the most keenly contested of small derbies. In Stalinist Albania, it was also one of the most incestuous, with fans not only sharing the same strip of provincial territory but in many cases the same workplace.

For those not working in the oilfields that scarred and poisoned the landscapes on the outskirts of Stalin City and Berat, where many Tomori and Naftëtari supporters toiled, there were limited avenues of employment. One employer in need of continuous man and womanpower was the textile industry, in which the region of Berat lay at its heart.

In the early 1970s, Tomori and Naftëtari fans stood united on the factory floor of the Mao Zedong Textile Factory, equidistant between the cities of Berat and Stalin. When the Chinese left Albania in 1978, Mao's name was erased, but the workforce remained. It was on the floors of the textile factory that the hot rivalry between *Mistrecët* and the Oilmen was augmented and perpetuated.

On matchday in Berat, fans from rival factions – but the same factory – met on the public thoroughfare of Rruga Skrapari, adjacent to Stadiumi Tomori, for pre-match drinks, laughs and light-hearted banter; a model of good-natured revelry from which the ultras of modern Albania would do well to take heed.

The match hinged on two moments of opportunism from the story's protagonist, Kovaçi sweeping home a couple of efficiently dispatched finishes, easing *Mistrecët* to a narrow 3-2 win.

Derby-day goals make heroes and villains of players, and it wouldn't be the last time the Panther would return to spook the Oilmen, a cultured free kick in the corresponding fixture in Stalin City cementing his status among opposing and fans for different reasons.

It also prefigured a goalscoring run that witnessed Rim net against all of the top clubs in the Kampionati, finishing the season as the Albanian Golden Boot winner, contributing 18 of Tomori's 31 goals.

During the season, Kovaçi – never shy to voice an opinion – earned a reputation as the dissenting voice in the Tomori dressing room. Prior to a home fixture against Lokomotiva, Tomori players were ordered to attend a 'tactical conversation' at the stadium in the morning. As coach Mukli presented his analysis, Rim interrupted, saying, 'The stadium will be full. What need is there for analysis? The players on the pitch will do the analysing ourselves.'

In the wake of Rim's caustic and concise logic, Mukli – whom, it must be said, Kovaçi respected deeply; it was he who'd mapped the Panther's path to success – was reported to have thrown his chalk to the floor, dismissing his players, requesting they return 30 minutes before kick-off.

It wouldn't be the last time Mukli would experience chagrin in dealings with Kovaçi. After recovering from a minor injury, Mukli chose to omit Rim from the line-up for a forthcoming game as a precaution.

Jani Semani (an influential Tomori patron) in his day duties as Berat's cinema director, often took the Kino Studio truck on the road, delivering government-financed propaganda movies to comrades in the region's remotest outposts. While playing a film to villagers in the hilltop settlement of Mbrakull, a native informed him of Mukli's intentions. Semani, incensed, drove directly to the Kovaçi home in the 13 Shtator district of uptown Berat. It was the early hours of the morning when Semani knocked Kovaçi's door. It was answered by his young wife, Bukuroshja, with Rim in close attendance. Semani demanded to know why he wasn't included in the team. Kovaçi spoke of his injury, adding that it had cleared up and, although he considered himself fully fit, 'It depends on the coach whether I play or not.' The content of Semani's conversation with the Tomori coach is lost in time's vacuum. However, after Semani paid Mukli a visit the next morning, Rim was miraculously reinstated to the team.

Upon his return to the starting 11, the stream of goals continued to flow. But when further suitors came knocking in their close season, Rim refused their advances. His only concessions were that Tomori repay his loyalty with a promise of better accommodation and the provision of an Obodin refrigerator – the bespoke brand of the era – for his wife, Bukuroshja.

Both were provided by club president Bardhyl Dardha, who pulled the necessary strings with his friends at the local Party Commission to seal the deal.

In late 1980, a short-term loan between Tomori and Flamurtari was agreed so Kovaçi could feature in *Flota Kuq e Zi's* – the Red and Black Fleet's – 1980/81 Balkan Cup campaign. Rim performed with distinction, scoring against both AEK Athens (twice) and Velež Mostar in the group stage, Flamurtari denied progression to the final on the slim metric of goal difference.

Despite Rim's continued excellence, Loro Boriçi refused to pick him for the national team, answering calls from the Albanian press corps to play Kovaçi with the benighted aside, 'He's too short.' In earlier years, Boriçi cited Kovaçi's second-tier status as his reason for non-selection. Now the striker was bagging goals in the top flight and against quality European opponents, so why the continued reticence? Considering Boriçi's long affiliation with Partizani adjoined with Rim's recent snub, it isn't beyond the realms of imagination to conceive that the Panther was denied his berth in the *Shqiponjat* squad simply because he refused to play for Partizani. In Stalinist Albania, memories were long and resentments ran deep.

The story of Rim Kovaçi is interesting as it serves as an inverse parable; an antidote to a morally squalid dictatorship where loyalty and integrity could be brokered. The fiscal amount earned from his football career equates to the house he was given by the Party Commission of Berat during communist times – a home in which he and Bukuroshja, his wife of over 30 years, still reside – and the Obodin fridge, which one can only presume has long-since chilled its final *legume*.

Yet it was the joy he brought to the people of Berat, the devoted *tifozët* who sang his name and celebrated his goals, and the spiritual currency contained within that joy that resonates. It's also the legacy he left behind, inspiring a new generation of Berati footballers to achieve greater things. It was no surprise when, in 1990/91, Kliton Bozgo top-scored for Tomori in the Kampionati and Klodian Arbri did so, again, in 2000/01, that they were both lauded as *Kovaçi i Ri* – the New Kovaçi.

Kovaçi's story was emblematic of what was happening all over Hoxhaist Albania during the late 1970s and early 1980s with a small but growing incidence of muted dissent taking place. Via sheer weight of personality and a refusal, for motives all his own, to join a club that were, at the time, an extension of The Party, the Panther played a support role in the hushed revolt. And he did it, in part, for the price of a serviceable fridge.

Chapter Sixteen

Albanian Club Sides in Europe

WITHOUT RECOURSE to exaggeration, it's reasonable to declare that no nation has endured a more ill-tempered relationship with Europe's footballing community than Albania and, during the three decades they participated in UEFA club competition under the umbrella of Stalinist rule, chaos reigned.

Post-World War Two, as the Hoxha regime bedded itself in for the long haul, The Party remained unswervingly peevish in its interactions with the outside world, and this innate narrow-mindedness transposed itself on to sport.

Partizani's escapades in the Spartakiads of the late 1950s and early 1960s have been covered in Chapter 6, the 1958 edition of the tournament observing the first participation in legitimate competition football, on foreign soil, by an Albanian club.

Previous to Partizani, 17 Nëntori were guests at the first World Festival of Youth and Students football tournament, held in Prague in 1947 – an event organised for socialist countries – where they faced hosts Bohemians and Yugoslavians Crvena Zvezda of Belgrade. Against excellent opposition, *Tirona* acquitted themselves well, losing 2-1 to Bohemians after they'd led via guest player Loro Boriçi's early goal.

They scored late – twice – in their second game versus Crvena Zvezda, trailing 3-1 before securing a 3-3 draw.

Trailing to Aristidh Parapani's goal, the Yugoslavs cruised into their lead with Zlatko Čajkovski, the match-winner in Yugoslavia's 3-2 Balkan Cup win against Albania a year earlier, netting twice and Branko Stanković adding a third.

Fatally, *Crveno-beli* removed their foot from the gas, Boriçi scoring again on 74 minutes to reduce the deficit before Skënder Begeja levelled a minute from time.

It had been a successful tournament for *Tirona*, but it wasn't recognised by UEFA or other affiliated footballing bodies.

Also, Partizani beat Partizan Belgrade home (1-0) and away (4-2) in 1947 in two prestige friendlies marking the Albanian–Yugoslavian alliance. *Demat e Kuq* then appeared in the 1961/62 version of the Balkans Cup – *Kupa e Ballkanit* – another non-UEFA-affiliated competition.

Drawn in a tough group including Turkish champions Fenerbahçe, Levski Sofia, AEK Athens and elaborately monikered Steagul Roşu Braşov – *Red Flag* – from Romania's second city, Braşov (a city that, for a short period post-World War Two, was named Staline), Partizani did well on home turf, achieving 0-0 draws against Fenerbahçe and Steagul Roşu alongside 2-0 victories against both Levski and AEK. However, in what would become a recurrent theme for Albanian club sides, away from home they disappointed, losing – without scoring – in Turkey, Romania and Bulgaria, with a 2-0 win awarded to them against AEK when the Greek side failed to fulfil the fixture in Athens.

The Balkans Cup offered a realistic gateway to continental success to competing Albanian teams, with Dinamo in 1969, Besa in 1971 and 17 Nëntori in 1982/83 all losing finalists.

For Dinamo, their 1969 final defeat to Beroe Stara Zagora was a dark portent of campaigns to come, a 1-0 win for the Blues at Stadiumi Dinamo via Ishka's strike negated in Stara Zagora when, already 1-0 down, their players walked off after a penalty was awarded to the Bulgarians, who were subsequently handed a 3-0 win and the trophy.

It would fall to city rivals Partizani to eventually win the Balkans Cup in 1970, beating Universitatea Craiova 1-0 home and away, results instrumental in setting up a final against Beroe, the four-time winners and reigning champions. A first-leg 1-1 draw in Stara Zagora served as the predecessor to one of the Balkans Cup's stranger occurrences when – in the return leg at the packed Stadiumi Dinamo in August 1970 – the Bulgarian side failed to show. *Demat e Kuq* were awarded a 3-0 victory.

Among other notable performances in the tournament by Albanian sides were Dinamo's 3-2 win away at Dinamo București in March 1962, Partizani's troika of 2-0 home wins at a heaving Qemal Stafa versus Cherno More Varna, UTA Arad and Fenerbahçe during the doomed season of 1966/67, Labinoti's near-miss campaign of 1973 that observed home wins at Stadiumi Ruzhdi Bizhuta against Yugoslavs Sutjeska Nikšić (1-0) and ASA Târgu Mureș of Romania (2-0) – Labinoti denied a final berth on goal difference – and *Tirona*'s 6-0 destruction of Panionios of Athens at Stadiumi Dinamo; Ilir Përnaska scoring four times.

The Balkans Cup had proven a good test of mettle for its *Shqiptare* participants, but it was the 1962/63 season when the UEFA-recognised European adventure began for Albanian clubs. And it was during this debut campaign that the fun and games really started.

It was Partizani who entered the fray first, in 1962/63, embarking on their inaugural European Cup campaign. Partizani's draw pitted them against Swedish champions IFK Norrköping in the preliminary round, a first-leg reverse in the Idrottsparken courtesy of second-half goals from *Blågult* internationals Harry Bild and Hans Rosander giving *VitaBlå* a decent margin of victory to defend in the return.

The second leg didn't start well, a section of the 18,000 crowd inside the partisan Stadiumi Qemal Stafa greeting Ove Kindvall's sixth-minute opener – a goal extending the visiting

Swedes' advantage to a virtually unassailable 3-0 aggregate lead – with an avalanche of stones, a display of ill courtesy repeated when Czechoslovakian referee Václav Korelus's full-time whistle heralded a 3-1 aggregate loss and Partizani's early exit from the competition.

Stonings would almost certainly incur huge fines and exemptions in the modern era. In this instance, the corridors of UEFA merely echoed to whispers of mild annoyance. One can only guess that an act of blind-eyed Swiss *laissez-faire* had occurred, designed to appease UEFA's recently inaugurated and highly volatile member.

The following season, Partizani fell in the preliminary round again, a 1-0 lead in Tirana courtesy of Kolec Kraja's neatly converted winner against Spartak Plovdiv overturned by a 3-1 loss in Bulgaria despite Panajot Pano's strike.

German champions FC Köln incurred Albanian wrath when, previous to Ajax in 1970, they arrived in Tirana prior to their European Cup tie in September 1964 – again against Partizani – with their own food and chef. After much toing and froing regarding the tenets of mutual host/guest respect, a compromise was reached: the food stayed, the chef went home.

A sterling performance and a useful 0-0 draw against *Die Geißböcke* at the Qemal Stafa preceded a 2-0 loss in the Müngersdorfer Stadion; a game in which *Demat e Kuq* squandered opportunities before succumbing to two very late goals from Hans Sturm and Wolfgang Overath.

Kilmarnock's experience of Albania, ahead of their 1965/66 European Cup tie against 17 Nëntori, was flawed. Killie boss Malky MacDonald planned to take 16 members of staff to the away leg, but only 15 visas arrived. The Scottish champions then travelled by coach from Ayrshire to London to catch a plane to Tirana via a stop-off in Rome.

On arrival at their hotel in the Albanian capital, players eager to phone home to announce their safe passage discovered that the antiquated phone lines were available for only one hour in the morning and two hours in the evening.

Anomalies continued to occur when the team sheet was released prior to the game. MacDonald, uneducated in the nuances of Albanian football, approached a journalist to identify his opponents' 'danger men'. The list included the name of Panajot Pano, the previous season's Albanian league top scorer. This immediately narked Killie staff, the problem being that Pano – arguably the finest Albanian footballer of that decade – was registered with Partizani Tirana. Other players representing 17 Nëntori that day also played for different clubs. Kilmarnock were, effectively, up against the Albanian national team.

Killie escaped Tirana with a 0-0 draw, narrowly winning 1-0 on aggregate. Good job too. If the game had required a play-off, the 1960s method of deciding drawn ties, the Albanians had already suggested to UEFA that it be played in the land of their country's key political ally, Maoist China. Nice commute.

Indeed, Northern Irish club Linfield endured a virtual facsimile of Kilmarnock's experience when they faced the same opposition in the same competition almost two decades later. Time, in Albania, appeared to have stood still.

17 Nëntori withdrew from the 1966/67 edition of the European Cup on the eve of their away tie against Norwegian champions Vålerenga. Their extraction was initially attributed to the regime's purported reluctance to send an Albanian representative to play in a country that welcomed a Nazi invasion in the 1940s. It was a strange decision timing-wise, as the draw had been made weeks earlier without any snicker of opposition. Yet, as explored in greater depth in Chapter 8, there may have been darker forces abroad in this instance.

In 1967/68, Dinamo had their European Cup invitation revoked, arcane goings-on during the 1966/67 Kampionati Kombetar campaign rendering their success illegitimate in the eyes of UEFA; another story afforded detailed inspection in Chapter 9.

With champions 17 Nëntori withdrawn from the European Cup in 1968/69 and 1969/70 by the regime in the dual wake of Dinamo's UEFA ban and the Skënder Halili scandal of 1966, attention turned to the 1968/69 European Cup Winners' Cup where Partizani were paired with Italian behemoths Torino in the first round.

During their stay in Tirana, the Italians were rudely awakened in the early hours of the morning by staff at the Hotel Dajti, The Party enacting one of their regular and mandatory evacuations; a preparatory exercise in anticipation of Soviet invasion. *La Granata* players were hastily ushered – in a state of bewilderment and fear – into a pitch-black Skanderbeg Square before they were permitted to return to their rooms 30 minutes later. Hardly the best preparation for the rigours of top-end European competition football.

Torino, riding high in Serie A when they arrived in Tirana in September 1968, were outplayed by Partizani – *Demat e Kuq* wearing an uncommon all-white strip – who were good value for the 1-0 lead provided to them by Shevdet Shaqiri's winner in the 46th minute, but equally inspired by excellent performances from Sabah Bizi, Ramazan Rragami, Panajot Pano, Lin Shllaku and the sublime Robert Jashari.

Yet controversy preluded the return, the regime refusing Jashari permission to travel to Turin; his Italian roots earmarking him as a possible defector. It was an affront that prompted Jashari's immediate retirement from football, although he would later return to the sport in a managerial capacity.

Partizani's trip to Turin was arduous: a coach ride from Tirana to Dubrovnik followed by a flight from Yugoslavia to Rome, then a further energy-sapping train ride from the Italian capital in the deep south to the heights of northern Italy.

Despite the difficulties of their journey, the game, at a half-empty Stadio Communale, crackled and effervesced, with Partizani missing a glorious early chance to seize control of the tie; Pano uncharacteristically snatching at the opportunity. By half-time, however, *La Granata* were in control, Alberto Carelli and Carlo Facchin giving the home side a 2-0 advantage. When Emiliano Mondonico added a third a minute shy of the hour, Partizani looked dead and buried, but they drew upon all their reserves of spirit and determination to fashion a response, Neptun Bajko grabbing a reply on 85 minutes.

However, when the final whistle blew, bedlam unfurled. Partizani officials, still evidently unclear of the vagaries of the away goals rule, refused to return to the dressing room, arguing that Bajko's late strike counted as double thus levelling the tie 3-3 on aggregate. It prompted Czechoslovakian referee Josef Krnávek to consult UEFA officials present on the matter, before declaring Torino 3-2 aggregate winners.

17 Nëntori's return to European Cup football in 1969/70 shuddered to an abrupt halt, a 3-0 loss at Stade Maurice Dufrasne to Belgian champions Standard Liège with midfielder Henri Depireux netting a hat-trick a dire prequel to a creditable draw in the return at the Qemal Stafa, beefcake striker Josif Kazanxhi heading a last-gasp leveller.

Tirona's exhilarating 2-2 draw with Ajax in the 1970/71 version of the European Cup – documented in the recurring Iconic Games sections of the book – stole the limelight from the notable achievements of Partizani in the European Cup Winners' Cup of the same year.

Partizani's qualification for the 1970/71 competition came after a convincing two-legged Albanian Cup triumph against a newly emerging Vllaznia; a 4-0 win in the first leg at the Qemal Stafa – Sabah Bizi (two), Ramazan Rragami and Lin Shllaku adding goals to a dominant performance – rendering the away leg a formality.

In the draw for the Cup Winners' Cup preliminary round, they were paired with Swedes Åtvidabergs FF. In the first leg at the Koppavalen, Partizani quickly established control, an early own goal by Orjan Johansson levelled after the break by Leif Franzen.

The return at the Stadiumi Qemal Stafa observed Partizani in majestic form, delighting their adoring support with sublime football, Pano and Rragami scoring well-constructed strikes before half-time to win the game 2-0. It could've – should've – been many more.

At last, an Albanian side had – despite many creditable performances – advanced beyond an opening round of a European tournament. It had taken eight years.

Their prize was a trip to Austria to face Wacker Innsbruck. At the lactose-tolerant Tirol Milch Stadion in an open contest, the Albanians stunned their unwary opponents, Pano and Agim Janku scoring twice in a minute at the first half's midpoint to lead 2-0. A Hans Ettmayer penalty, harshly awarded by Yugoslav referee Milivoje Gugalovic just before the break, altered the momentum of the first leg, Wacker recovering with two goals in the second half by Jozef Obert and Josip Francesin, presenting the Austrians with a narrow 3-2 advantage.

Despite trailing marginally, the stage was set for another afternoon of celebration at Albania's national *stadiumi,* and everything appeared to be going to plan when Rragami's 24th-minute net-tearer of a drive raised the roof on the *Tribuna.* But, thereon, Partizani failed to sustain the intensity of their performance in the previous round, allowing Branko Elsner's men back into the game, nippy forward Leopold Grausam scoring twice to win the tie for the visitors, 2-1 on the day and 5-3 on aggregate. Disappointment was exacerbated when the draw for the second round was made; a tie versus Spanish giants Real Madrid the reward for their victors.

In 1971/72, UEFA added a third competition to its portfolio, the UEFA Cup, serving as a worthy consolation prize for teams finishing second or third (and occasionally fourth and fifth) in their national leagues. The resultant competition proved itself to be incredibly difficult to win due to its greater quality in depth.

However, Vllaznia, Albania's first UEFA Cup qualifier – drawn to play Austrian opposition in the shape of Rapid Vienna – were denied the chance due to the Vllaznia basketball scandal detailed in Chapter 11. The Albanian Sports Committee snottily exonerated Albania of any culpability, blaming Vllaznia's withdrawal on Austrian bureaucratic tardiness due to their provision of insufficient visas. Albanian clubs, due to a shortfall in sports expenditure, would not return to the UEFA Cup fold until 1981/82.

The 1971/72 versions of the European Cup and European Cup Winners' Cup saw both Partizani and Dinamo exit early; Partizani losing 4-0 on aggregate to Bulgarian champions CSKA Sofia, Dinamo ousted by the odd goal in three to a decent Austria Vienna side.

Besa Kavajë, purveyors of a brand of football since dubbed 'Albanian tika-taka', were Albania's sole participant in Europe in 1972/73 (league champions Vllaznia forcibly withdrawn by the regime, again) and the debutants from Kavaja, playing a style of football based on ball retention and favouring a high defensive line, successfully navigated their way past Danish amateurs Fremad Amager on away goals in the first round, a 1-1 draw at the Sundby Idrætspark in Copenhagen preceding a 0-0 draw in Kavaja.

Verdhezinjtë – the Yellow and Blacks – found themselves paired against an attack-orientated Hibernian in the second round, the Edinburgh club battering Sporting Lisbon 7-3 on aggregate with a 6-1 home thumping of the Portuguese one of the highlights of the opening round.

The first leg at Easter Road witnessed Hibernian, a potent force who would later win the Scottish League Cup and finish a creditable third in the title race behind the usual suspects, revert to the rampant form that had destroyed Sporting in the previous round. Leading 2-0 at the break, the Scots blitzed Besa with a five-goal salvo in 12 short second-half minutes, a late Kariqi consolation drawing derisory cheers from the home faithful.

With the tie dead, Hibs struggled at a packed Stadiumi Lokomotiva in Durrës, the home side – playing 80km (50 miles) away from their home city – leading 1-0 through Kujtim Pagria's 54th-minute opener before Alan Gordon restored parity on the hour; 1-1 at full time and Besa out, embarrassingly, 8-2 on aggregate.

In the wake of the Besa debacle, Albanian clubs disappeared from the European competition radar, reappearing a full six years later.

The elapsing years had been unkind to Albania, a split with China leaving the country in a burgeoning state of destitution. With the nation staring into the void, football, as is common in times of existential despair, was there to transpose a ray of rare gilt upon an otherwise dark vista.

With the FSHF rejecting UEFA's offer of a place in the European Cup Winners' Cup prior to the 1978/79 draw, it was left to Shyqyri Rreli's Vllaznia to fly the Albanian flag in Europe's premier club competition, the European Cup. Vllaznia's progress, however, would be hindered by a tough-looking pairing with Austrian champions – and the previous season's beaten European Cup Winners' Cup finalists – Austria Vienna, a side boasting key players from *Burschen*'s (the Boys') impressive 1978 World Cup campaign in Argentina including Robert Sara, Herbert Prohaska and Walter Schachner.

At the Stadiumi Vojo Kushi – named after a communist partisan, now renamed the Stadiumi Loro Boriçi – the whole of Shkodër came to watch, as did Televizioni Shqiptar, in anticipation of Vllaznia's first crusade into the previously uncharted frontiers of European football.

As the clock ticked round to the 4.30pm kick-off, the stadium almost buckling under the weight of the fervent *Kuq e Blutë tifozët*, anything seemed possible in the rebel city.

By the time Romanian referee Otto Anderco had blown the full-time whistle, the home support's appetite had been fully sated by a wonderful Vllaznia showing, goals by Medin Zhega and Haxhi Ballgjini early in each half giving the Shkodrans a very useful 2-0 advantage to defend in *Die Österreicher*'s City of Dreams.

But, as with most Albanian stories, it came with a bitter twist. At the Praterstadion the Viennese, resurgent, were level on aggregate by the break, eventually winning 4-1 (4-3 on aggregate) although Astrit Hafizi's late consolation ten minutes from time saw Hermann Stessl's side endure a few uncomfortable moments late on. Vllaznia's victors would make it to the semis where their progress would eventually be stalled by Malmö of Sweden.

With Albania accepting UEFA's invitation of two European berths in 1979/80 – one in the European Cup, one in the Cup Winners' Cup – it appeared that the post-China split had prompted a thawing in Albania's transactions with their European neighbours. Any scintilla of brittle optimism was silenced immediately after the Cup Winners' Cup draw was made, Vllaznia delegated a two-legged rendezvous with the USSR's Dynamo Moscow, the first leg to be played at the Dynamo Stadium in Moscow, deep in the administrative heart of enemy territory. The Albanian regime protested noisily, but when UEFA refused to compromise, FSHF withdrew their representatives and Vllaznia were, once more, denied their shot at European football.

But Vllaznia's extraction didn't alter Partizani's status as Albanian representatives in the 1979/80 edition of the European Cup. Despite the regime's purported ire at Vllaznia's situation, they didn't retract all of their club sides from UEFA competition, Partizani being allowed to proceed upon their European journey unimpeded. Clearly, the FSHF weren't as affronted by the Vllaznia affair as they purported to be. In the Orwellian vortex of Stalinist Albania, all clubs were equal, but some were more equal than others.

Partizani faced Scottish champions Celtic, who arrived in Albania on an enviable seam of good form; unbeaten in all competitions. As detailed in Chapter 12, *Demat e Kuq*, courtesy of a Murati goal and a spirited performance, won the first leg in Tirana 1-0.

The Albanians were greeted by a deluge at Parkhead, incessant rain threatening to spoil the contest as a spectacle. The match had been under threat of not taking place at all, when Celtic officials learned, on the Saturday prior to the game, that Partizani had yet to apply to the Home Office for visas for their party.

But Partizani did turn up and, early on, threatened to create a major shock in the Bhoys' own backyard, Alan Sneddon heading an absurd own goal past Peter Latchford, directing a sky-catching defensive punt by Partizani centre-half Starova into Celtic's net.

Alarm bells were ringing around Celtic Park, but, aided by the creative magic of Davie Provan – involved in all four Hoops goals – and some truly abysmal goalkeeping by Perlat Musta, Celtic won the night 4-1 and the tie 4-2 on aggregate.

With Vllaznia's refusal to travel to Moscow fresh in the mind (earning the club a further year UEFA ban), sighs were exhaled when both 1980/81 participants – Dinamo in the European Cup and Partizani in the Cup Winners' Cup – avoided opposition objectionable to Albania's moral code.

Dinamo, playing in UEFA-branded competition for the first time, acquitted themselves pretty well, losing late to Ajax 2-0 in Tirana, *De Godenzonen* captain Frank Arnesen netting twice, with *Blutë* succumbing 1-0 in the return to Søren Lerby's late penalty at the Olympisch Stadion. Ajax head coach Leo Beenhakker was so taken with Dinamo's midfield pocket-Merlin, Vasillaq Zëri, that he tried to sign him shortly afterwards, an attempt that wasn't welcomed warmly by FSHF or the regime.

Partizani were eliminated by the narrowest of margins against Swedish club Malmö – European Cup finalists in 1979 – a 1-0 aggregate win decided by a Paul McKinnon winner in the first leg at the Malmö Stadion; McKinnon arriving in Sweden via the unlikely conduits of Woking and Sutton United.

An Albanian return to the UEFA Cup in 1981/82 – substituted for their usual Cup Winners' Cup berth – observed Dinamo defeat East Germany's Carl Zeiss Jena (a team fresh from their own Cup Winners' Cup adventure in 1981, losing in the final to Soviet side Dinamo Tbilisi) with Vasillaq Zëri's goal, a fine finish after some controlled, probing Dinamo football, winning the first leg at Stadiumi Dinamo.

Two weeks later, at the Ernst-Abbe Sportfeld, Carl Zeiss Jena were in no mood for charity, goals from Jürgen Raab, Rüdiger Schnuphase (two) and Martin Trocha, without reply, culminating in a 4-1 aggregate triumph for the team from the German Democratic Republic.

In the European Cup, Partizani led, briefly, away from home in the Praterstadion via a Genc Tomorri goal before yielding to a 3-1 defeat to Austria Vienna.

Demat e Kuq stretched *Die Veilchen* to their limits at a seething Qemal Stafa in the return leg, a first-half strike from Haxhi Ballgjini setting up an exciting climax in which Partizani huffed and puffed, but couldn't quite blow the Austrian house down. They exited the competition, heads held high, losing 3-2 on aggregate.

In the 1982/83 season, Albanian football's reputation suffered further embarrassment on the continent. 17 Nëntori, European Cup first round winners against Northern Irish champions Linfield, were poised to engage in a second round of competitive coitus until they were paired with 'Soviet revisionists' Dynamo Kiev, at which point the Albanians hastily pulled out.

In the Cup Winners' Cup, Dinamo faced an Aberdeen side who'd thrashed Sion of Switzerland 11-1 on aggregate in the preliminary round, and they played well in both games, losing to the only goal of the tie scored by John Hewitt early in the first leg at Pittodrie. *Blutë's* achievement would prove doubly commendable, their opponents progressing to the final where they would beat Spanish colossi Real Madrid in Gothenburg – Hewitt again supplying the winner, this time in a 2-1 extra-time triumph.

Despite winning the title in 1982/83, Vllaznia were, again, withdrawn from the 1983/84 European Cup by the regime, adding additional evidence to the notion that *Kuq e Blutë* were a side Hoxha and his cronies actively wanted to fail.

17 Nëntori were allowed their European Cup Winners' Cup soiree in Sweden, a sound 4-0 thrashing to Hammarby in Stockholm seeing them virtually eliminated prior to the second leg in Tirana. A 2-1 home victory in the return saw a gutsy performance and goals from Arben Vila and Ali Mema's 19-year-old son, Sulejman – a further component in the *Tirona*/Mema dynasty.

After their heroics of 1983/84, the newly crowned champions Labinoti were Albania's sole participants in 1984/85. There would be no repeat of the previous season's promise, a 3-0 reverse at the Ruzhdi Bizhuta in Elbasan against modest Danish opponents in Lyngby putting an immediate end to Frederik Jorgaqi's side's European Cup aspirations. A further 3-0 loss at Lyngby Stadion added symmetry to a heavy 6-0 aggregate defeat.

By the time the 1985/86 European competitions commenced, Enver Hoxha was dead, replaced at the helm of The Party by Ramiz Alia, but in the era of Soviet-induced *glasnost* and *perestroika* there would be no such thaw in Stalinist Albania. This will be explored in Chapter 17.

With champions 17 Nëntori robbed of their European Cup place by Alia's regime, it fell to Dinamo in the UEFA Cup and Flamurtari in the Cup Winners' Cup to blaze the European trail, with differing degrees of success.

Dinamo, drawn in the first round against Maltese minnows Hamrun Spartans, laboured to a 1-0 home victory at the Qemal Stafa, an opportunist strike by Eduard Abazi on 57 minutes winning a scruffy game. The second leg at the Victor Tedesco Stadium wasn't pretty either, although *Blutë* prevailed courtesy of an untidy 0-0 draw.

For Fatmir Frasheri's side, there was a decent reward for their first-round success, a tie against Portuguese giants Sporting Lisbon. At the Qemal Stafa, Dinamo showed little respect for their illustrious Mediterranean opponents, a battling 0-0 draw infused with moments of controlled, quality football keeping the tie well and truly alive. At Estádio José Alvalade in Lisbon, as *Verde e brancos* (Green and whites) struggled to find any semblance of fluency against a grittily attritional Dinamo, it seemed that there might be a shock on the cards. It took a goal via the head of Portuguese international centre-half Pedro Venâncio after 53 minutes to settle home nerves. They would hold out for a 1-0 win.

Flamurtari, appearing in Europe for the first time, faced HJK Helsinki. A narrow 3-2 first-leg loss at the Helsinki Olympic Stadium, with two away goals in the bag via Shkëlqim Muça and Agim Bubeqi, offered realistic hope of progression, but poor defending and wasteful finishing allowed the Finns to escape a packed Stadiumi Flamurtari with a barely deserved 2-1 win; 5-3 on aggregate. *Kuq e Zinjtë* – the Red and Blacks – would return, hardened and sharpened by their disappointment.

The 1986/87 season was particularly tough for Albania, food shortages bringing malnutrition and near-starvation to all but the privileged elite of the country. Attendances at football stadiums throughout the 26 districts dwindled domestically, yet in Europe something of an Albanian renaissance was in the offing.

Three clubs – Dinamo in the European Cup, 17 Nëntori in the Cup Winners' Cup and Flamurtari in the UEFA Cup – populated the European berths. It was the first time Albania had fielded a team in all three European club competitions. And it would prove an exciting and fruitful ride.

Dinamo fell early. Defeats to Turkish champions Beşiktaş – 2-0 away, 1-0 at home – confirmed their exit amid angry, petulant behaviour directed, chiefly, towards Hungarian referee Lajos Hartmann during a bad-tempered second leg in Tirana. The clubs representing the twin powers of the army and the *Sigurimi* would steep further shame on The Party prior to communism's fall. But while Partizani and Dinamo misbehaved, 17 Nëntori and Flamurtari revelled in European club football's ebullient glow.

When 17 Nëntori were pitched against Mircea Lucescu's Dinamo București in the European Cup Winners' Cup first round, few anticipated anything other than a comfortable Romanian victory. Romanian football was experiencing a *belle époque* of its own, Steaua crowned European champions in 1986, with Dinamo losing narrowly to Liverpool in the semi-final of Europe's premier club competition two years earlier. Indeed, many of the 1984 Dinamo semi-final team remained; *Tirona* appeared to be in for a rough ride.

At Stadiumi Qemal Stafa, the Romanians were the better side, Dacian goal-machine Rodion Cămătaru's expert finish adjudged to be narrowly – and harshly – offside in the first half, with the livewire forward forcing a more-than-useful save from Halim Mersini after the break. Cămătaru would score 44 times during the course of the 1986/87 Romanian Divizia A season, a remarkable 22 goals ahead of second-placed Victor Pițurcă of Steaua.

But the tide changed as the game reached its dying embers. *Tirona* began to create chances, Arben Minga forcing an excellent, flying stop from Dumitru Moraru in the Dinamo goal.

With four minutes left, *Tirona* built a move down their right, Bedri Omuri receiving a Shkëlqim Muça pass on the wing, deep in Romanian territory. As the ball reached Omuri, already winding himself up for a first-time cross, it bobbled on the uneven turf to alter the trajectory of his delivery, spinning through the air towards the near post where Moraru appeared to be readied for a comfortable catch. However, he appeared to lose its flight, allowing the ball to squirm between his legs and directly into the path of the disbelieving Agustin Kola, who stroked it into an unguarded net from five yards. When Polish referee Tadeusz Diakonowicz blew for full time, the Qemal Stafa exploded in wild celebration, although it was delight tempered with caution; a difficult second leg in Bucharest lay in wait.

Two weeks later at Stadionul Dinamo, the coven of Romania's very own Secret Police club, *Tirona* played neat football from the off, eliciting glares of muted horror from the home support when Arben Minga bundled the visitors into a surprise second-minute lead. The shock of conceding early brought a state of communal paralysis upon a Dinamo team used to winning – and winning big – on their own patch.

After the break, with Dinamo's demanding *supoteri* growing increasingly impatient, *Tirona* sat deep and continued to frustrate the *Alb-roşii*'s (White and reds') increasingly desperate attack. With nine minutes left Cămătaru eventually plundered an equaliser, but as his team-mates pushed to retrieve the tie dangerous gaps were appearing in their stretched rearguard. With a minute to go, Mirel Josa sprung the Dinamo offside trap to slot home a *Tirona* winner.

A heavy 3-0 home defeat to Malmö in the first leg of the second round somewhat spoiled things, the Swedes taking control after a scoreless first period. A decent performance in the second leg – a 0-0 draw – proved too little, too late.

It was in the southern, naval base city of Vlora – on the barbed-wired, bunker-fortified coastline where the Adriatic and Ionian Sea met –that the biggest upsets took place. In both 1986/87 and 1987/88, Flamurtari imposed themselves upon the European scene in the UEFA Cup with explosive intent.

Flamurtari qualified for the 1986/87 UEFA Cup off the back of their finest league campaign for years, finishing a close second to Dinamo Tirana on goal difference. They would suffer the same misfortune in 1986/87: a three-point penalty imposed by FSHF for accruing more than 20 red and yellow cards saw Partizani pinch the title from them – by an implausibly ironic three-point margin.

The 1986/87 UEFA Cup saw Leonidha Çuri's humble team drawn against the might of Catalan giants Barcelona, the first leg played at a splendidly exuberant Stadiumi Flamurtari.

Terry Venables' expensively assembled side, featuring British duo Mark Hughes and Gary Lineker, arrived in Vlora with hopes of consigning the previous season's heartbreaking European Cup Final defeat against Steaua Bucureşti to history's dustbin. However, their unfancied but hugely committed opponents harried, hassled and ultimately outfought them, taking a deserved lead on 65 minutes when Vasil Ruci's rising half-volley almost tore a new hole in the back of the *Blaugrana* net. In the 90th minute, as the hosts and their rowdy *tifozët* willed Maltese referee Charles Scerri to blow the full-time whistle, Barça pieced together their most fluid attack of the match, a neat build-up freeing Esteban Vigo in the box, who cooly stabbed the ball beyond Artur Lekbello into the Flamurtari net.

Barcelona had undoubtedly dodged an Albanian bullet, but if the Camp Nou – barely a quarter full – anticipated easy passage to the second round, Çuri's hungry Flamurtari side hadn't read the script, giving the hosts a few hairy moments before a scratchy 0-0 deadlock took the Catalans through on the away goals rule.

Flamurtari thoroughly enjoyed their adventure, and it readied *Kuq e Zinjtë* for a further stab at European glory the following year. However, a tough draw seemed to portend another early exit, neighbouring Yugoslavia providing opponents in the shape of Partizan Belgrade.

A history of shared animosity (stories of Yugoslavian-Serb persecution of ethnic Albanians in the state of Kosovo were rife) meant that this fixture – in the Stalinist-friendly Tosk south of Albania – had added needle.

With nearly 20,000 fans squeezed into Stadiumi Flamurtari, the home side 'went long', testing their technically superior opponents with plenty of high, direct ball. It was from one of these aerial drops that Flamurtari took the lead on the half-hour, home keeper Anesti Arapi launching an agrarian punt in the direction of forwards Vasil Ruci and Sokol Kushta. As Ruci and marker Alexsandar Đorđević wrestled for possession of Arapi's bouncing bomb, the hapless Slav scythed the bobbling ball past Fahrudin Omerović in the Partizan goal.

Flamurtari, buoyed by passionate support, kept pace and continued to test a brittle Belgrade back line from dead-ball situations. With seven minutes to go, a Flamurtari corner on the left wasn't properly cleared by Partizan, allowing defender Roland Iljadhi to crash home an unstoppable second through a ruck of players. Upon the final whistle, with local pride abundant, many of the Flamurtari players were chaired from the pitch by their joyous fans.

With a useful 2-0 advantage to protect at Stadion JNA in the Yugoslavian capital, Flamurtari defended deep. The tactic appeared to be working until a minute before the break when a careless foul inside their box saw Polish referee Andrzej Libich point to the spot. Goran Stevanović accepted the gift to give *Crno-beli* an apparently crucial half-time lead.

After the break, Partizan laid siege on the Flamurtari goal with a bullet header from Yugoslavian-Kosovan Fadil Vokrri, a fixture in the *Plavi* national team, levelling on aggregate just past the hour.

With the Albanians on the ropes, Vokrri almost added to the home lead minutes later, an identical header saved by the legs of Anesti Arapi. It proved to be the turning point in the match and tie.

Flamurtari, unable to assert any impact upon the game, reverted to the direct football that had yielded such glorious rewards in Vlora and, on 76 minutes – apropos of nothing – they spawned a goal from out of nowhere.

Arapi's long clearance was met by centre-forward Alfred Zijaj, whose header reached Flamurtari's new signing from Partizani Tirana, Sokol Kushta (who'd recently been ranked 30th in the 1987 European Footballer of the Year placings), wide on the left. With two Belgrade defenders for company, Kushta's options seemed limited until he spun right, inside both of his markers and drilled a brilliant and unstoppable angled right-footed shot into the top-left corner of Omerović's net via the underside of the crossbar, giving the Albanian side an invaluable away goal and complete control of a contest that appeared to have passed them by. When the final whistle blew, silence descended on the Stadion JNA as Flamurtari's players rejoiced in the Belgrade mud.

Flamurtari's heroics were rewarded with another tie against Eastern Bloc opposition, their adventures taking them to the Saxony mining town of Aue and a rendezvous with four-time East German champions Wismut.

A tough, well-organised outfit, Hans Speth's *Veilchen* (Violets) had taken the DDR Oberliga by storm the previous season, their efficient brand of football earning a fourth-place finish marginally behind the recognised powerhouses of East German football, the Dynamos – Berlin and Dresden – and Lokomotive Leipzig. At the Otto-Grotewohl Stadion, amid the dark forests and eclipsing shadows of the Ore Mountains, Wismut showed their teeth, Flamurtari dealt a 1-0 defeat courtesy of Steffen Krauss's goal – a loss that could've been far worse for the Vlorans had their hosts not spurned a glut of chances.

In early November 1987, the players of Wismut arrived in an Albania striving to be on its best behaviour after enduring two crushing PR disasters in the earlier rounds of the other European competitions.

Champions Partizani, drawn against the mighty Benfica in the European Cup first round, played only one leg of the tie, away at the Estádio da Luz. With four players red-carded – Perlat Musta and Niko Frasheri (51 minutes), Arjan Ahmetaj (72 minutes) and Ilir Lame (82 minutes) – during their 4-0 away tanking, Partizani were disqualified by UEFA for the conduct of their players and officials prior to the second leg in Tirana taking place.

In the European Cup Winners' Cup, Astrit Hafizi's Vllaznia – having comfortably navigated the first round by beating Hamrun Spartans of Malta 6-0 on aggregate – were drawn against Finnish outfit Rovaniemen Palloseura.

After a chastening 1-0 home defeat in Shkodër, *Kuq e Blutë* travelled to the Arctic Circle hoping to unpick the damage caused by Birmingham-born Stephen Polack's strike at the Stadiumi Vojo Kushi. On return from their chilly away day – another Polack goal giving the Finns a second 1-0 win – two Vllaznia players, Arvid Hoxha and Lulzim Bërshemi, separated themselves from the travelling entourage during a short stop in Athens, defecting from the Hermit Kingdom for good.

Security was tight at Stadiumi Flamurtari, the *Sigurimi* desperate to present unto the peripheral world a favourable account of a country whose subjects were becoming increasingly errant.

The East Germans were greeted by a wall of noise, the Flamurtari faithful inspiring their heroes to produce a dominant performance on the field. Immediately on the front foot, the home side had already tested the Wismut keeper Jörg Weißflog when, three minutes in, defender Rrapo Taho – unaccountably high up the pitch – seized on a long ball, bringing it under his spell with his left boot before executing a perfect right-footed lob over the advancing Weißflog. The *stadiumi* erupted – the East Germans never recovered.

After 72 minutes, Ruci scored a goal that was almost a carbon copy of the Sokol Kushta strike that dumped Partizan Belgrade out of the competition in the previous round, cutting inside from the left before curling an exquisite right-footed finish into the keeper's bottom-left corner.

The shrill toot of Hungarian *arbitri* László Molnár's final whistle saw Flamurtari's jubilant *tifozët* flood the pitch to celebrate another improbable but hugely deserved success. Unbelievably, the club from the south were through to the third round of a European competition; the first Albanian side to ascend to such heights.

The draw saw *Kuq e Zinjtë* pitted, once more, against Barcelona, the first leg taking place at an eerily under-populated Camp Nou; only 16,000 fans choosing to pay the admission fee. The Catalans that did show observed the *Blaugrana* put in a decent shift with Urbano breaking the deadlock after 43 minutes before two Lineker strikes either side of a Lobo Carrasco goal propelled the hosts into a 4-0 lead before the hour. But Flamurtari continued to fight, winning a penalty in the 68th minute which Ruci duly converted to give the scoreline a veneer of respectability.

Back in Vlora, the whole of the city converged upon the *stadiumi* for the second leg, and they were rewarded with a fabulous team performance with Viktor Daulija, outstanding in midfield, pulling the strings. With Flamurtari in the ascendency, Kushta headed home a neat opener to give the hosts the lead. It was an advantage they would retain until the final whistle, beating the mighty Barcelona 1-0 on the day.

Despite exiting the competition, Flamurtari had provided a yardstick showcasing just how good the standard of Albanian football could be during the Stalinist era. On home turf, they played with determination and no shortage of style; away they were compact and competitive. The future looked bright for Flamurtari.

A further second-place finish for the Vlorans kept the momentum going, with their Albanian Cup win – a 1-0 victory against Partizani via the boot of Agim Bubeqi – qualifying them for the 1988/89 edition of the European Cup Winners' Cup. In spite of two good performances, they exited in the first round, narrowly, to Polish club Lech Poznań – 3-2 in Vlora, Ruci bagging twice prior to a last-ditch Lech winner, and 1-0 at the Stadion Miejski.

Champions 17 Nëntori were favourably drawn against Maltese club Hamrun Spartans in the European Cup first round. At the Ta' Qali in Valletta, *Tirona* sped into an early lead through midfielder Anesti Stoja, but made hard work of it thereon, allowing Lolly Aquilana's team back into the tie, a Leo Refalo brace – the second coming with virtually the last kick of the game – giving the hosts a 2-1 win.

Tirona coach Shyqyri Rreli, angered by his side's complacency, demanded greater focus in the return leg at the Stadiumi Qemal Stafa. Again, *Tirona* struggled to break down resilient opposition.

It took two goals in three second-half minutes from Skënder Hodja and Mirel Josa to vanquish the stubborn Maltese outfit; Refalo, Hamrun's hero in Valletta, receiving his marching orders after a spiteful foul shortly after *Tirona*'s second goal.

A second-round pairing with 1987 UEFA Cup winners IFK Göteborg signalled the end of the road for *Tirona*'s European ambitions, the Swedes ruthlessly dominant in the first leg at the Qemal Stafa and winning 3-0 before completing the job with a 1-0 victory at the Ullevi.

17 Nëntori returned to Malta – and the Ta' Qali – in the 1989/90 European Cup. Their opponents this time were the newly crowned champions of the island nation, Sliema Wanderers. *Tirona* stuttered to another chastening defeat in Valletta, ex-Bolton and Gillingham winger Roger Walker's solitary strike on the hour giving the home side a slim advantage to take to Tirana.

The second leg at the Qemal Stafa proved an entirely different contest, a fluid and potent *Tirona* racing into a 3-0 half-time lead, Agustin Kola bagging twice with Sinan Bardhi adding a third. Further goals from Skënder Hodja and Florian Biza completed a 5-0 rout – 5-1 on aggregate – safely transporting *bardhë e blutë* into the second round. It remains the biggest win by an Albanian club side in a UEFA-affiliated competition.

Awaiting *Tirona* were European royalty in West Germany's Bayern Munich. At the Olympiastadion, the visitors acquitted themselves well, losing while plundering a useful away goal in a 3-1 defeat. Ludwig Kögl and Radmilo Mihajlović netted early for *Die Roten* before Arben Minga forced home a 30th-minute reply. A further goal by Mihajlović after the break left *Tirona* defeated, yet optimistic ahead of the return.

All hope, however, was extinguished in a two-minute spell either side of the half-time whistle at the Qemal Stafa. After causing Bayern early problems, *Tirona* were suckered by a goal seconds before the break, Thomas Strunz arrowing in an angled drive. Ninety seconds into the second half, substitute Roland Grahammer doubled the West Germans' lead with Jupp Heynckes' side eventually coasting to a 3-0 win – 6-1 on aggregate – Hans Dorfner adding insult to injury in the final minute.

Dinamo were forced to endure a preliminary round double-header against Bulgarian side Chernomorets, and their trip to the Black Sea coastal resort of Burgas seemed to signal another early exit for *Blutë*, a 3-1 defeat – despite an away strike from Sulejman Demollari – putting daylight between them and *Akulite*.

Fewer than 8,000 fans turned out at the Qemal Stafa for the return, a turgid opening 45 minutes seemingly justifying their absence. The paucity of support also pointed to the economic condition of an Albanian state on the brink of collapse. Yet, after the break, the home side roused themselves from their collective torpor, producing a *blitzkrieg* of a second-half performance that floored their opponents. Four times without reply a rampant *Dinamovitet* breached the Bulgarian goal, Agim Canaj, Edmond Abazi, Adrian Jançe and Sulejman Demollari scoring to layer on the embarrassment for their Eastern Bloc rivals. The *Sporti Popullor*'s headline celebrated a '*Gezuar I Shtatorin!*' (Happy September!) for the Blues, their 5-3 aggregate triumph rewarded with a first-round tie that was both intriguing and pertinent to the era.

When the draw was made, Dinamo were paired against Dinamo București; the teams of the Albanian and Romanian secret police – the *Sigurimi* versus the *Securitate*.

A 1-0 *Blutë* win, courtesy of Agim Canaj's 52nd-minute goal at the Qemal Stafa, gave the darlings of the *Sigurimi* a slim lead to defend in Bucharest. It wasn't to be, the team of the *Securitate* triumphing 2-0 on the day and 2-1 on aggregate with Dorin Mateuț and Iulian Mihăescu scoring inside the first quarter of an hour.

By the time Dinamo București faced Partizan Belgrade in the quarter-finals of the 1989/90 edition of the European Cup Winners' Cup in March, just five months later, the *Securitate* were no more – Romanian communism dead along with its secret police and murderously despotic leader, Nicolae Ceaușescu. For Albanian Stalinism and the *Sigurimi*, their demise would take a little longer.

In the UEFA Cup, Apolonia from the south-western city of Fier endured the briefest of dalliances with European football, ruthlessly dismantled in their debut appearance on the continental stage by wily French opponents Auxerre 5-0 at the Stade Abbé-Deschamps, a 3-0 defeat in the home leg at Stadiumi Flamurtari completing an eight-goal Gallic annihilation.

Onwards to 1990/91, the final year that Albania appeared in European competition as a communist entity, and the football teams of the Hermit Kingdom would bring spectacularly terse closure to an unmissed political era.

All three qualifiers – Dinamo (European Cup), Partizani (UEFA Cup) and Flamurtari (European Cup Winners' Cup) – fell at the first-round hurdle without a win between them, Partizani losing 1-0 in both legs to a modest Universitatea Craiova side and Flamurtari ruthlessly dispatched by Greeks Olympiakos 5-1 on aggregate.

But it was Dinamo who produced the moment that, most fittingly, signalled the end of almost five decades of misery. Three months shy of the student protests in the northern Gheg cities of Shkodër and Kavaja, with Albanians privy to an external drip-feed of limited information divulging the happenings on the surrounding continent, Dinamo were drawn against Franz Beckenbauer-led Olympique de Marseille at the Stade Vélodrome on 18 September 1990.

The game itself was a cakewalk for *Les Phocéens*, comfortable 5-1 victors; Jean-Pierre Papin (with a hat-trick) and Eric Cantona among the scorers. As the Albanians assembled at Marseille Airport for their flight home, something was amiss. After a rudimentary head count, it became clear that one of their number was missing. Talented defender and recently capped Albanian international Pjerin Noga, a stalwart of their title-winning side of the previous season, had gone AWOL.

After a frantic search confirmed the unpalatable truth, Dinamo returned to Tirana Noga-less. In an interview with

Albanian periodical *Panorama* in 2022, Noga weaved a romantic tale about the motivations behind his defection. The seeds were sown early in life when Noga, as a young boy, acquired a copy of *The Count of Monte Cristo* by French author Alexandre Dumas. By owning a copy of the book alone, Noga had – in the warped reasonings of Stalinist Albania's Constitution 55, the law punishing 'agitation and political propaganda' – already committed a criminal act. Noga was enamoured by the plight of the imprisoned main character, Edmond Dantès, and the protagonist's subsequent escape from the brutal Château d'If across the straits of Marseille. Forbidden Western literature had offered Noga a portal into an alternate world with different, attainable pathways. It was a figurative journey Noga was keen to make real, and it would prompt others to follow in his footsteps.

When European competition resumed in September 1991 – six months prior to The Party's downfall – the dire extent of national suffering was laid bare to a Feyenoord squad drawn to play Partizani in the European Cup Winners' Cup first round. On arrival in Tirana, the Feyenoord players – privy, first-hand, to the feculent aftermath of 50 years of hellish rule – were appalled by what they saw. Everything was broken, everything leaked, there was hardly anything to eat. Footage of the day depicts infant beggars descending on the Dutch side's hotel in search of some small gratuity. The people of Albania had absolutely nothing.

Eager to erase the past, angry citizens had taken to the streets smashing anything that served as a reminder to the dying regime. Unfortunately, that included just about everything, revolutionary droves reducing Tirana to a state of lawless pandemonium.

The inevitable mass exodus of Albanians to far-flung lands affected all aspects of society with Albania's boldest and brightest sailing the monied stream that filtered out of the Hermit Kingdom. Football was probably worst affected.

All of Albania's best players departed, leaving behind a Kampionati Kombetar that was a husk of the league of old.

From a European club football context, Albania has never recovered from the stigma of Stalinist rule, its teams rarely impacting on UEFA tournaments beyond the primary rounds. It's no wonder that some Albanians who lived through the Stalinist era, the rare subjects unaffected by Enver Hoxha's toxic rule, view it with moist-eyed nostalgia – it seems better by default – forgetting that it was Stalinism that laid the foundations for their country's troubled present.

However, when systems fail, football prevails. Peering beyond the past into a future lit with potential, it is reassuring that Albania – at national team level, at least – has re-found itself as a credible footballing entity offering genuine hope in modern times. Albanian football has survived, retaining the ardour of its *tifozët*, a small victory in the face of overwhelming odds. A paucity of European performances akin to the great shocks created by *Tirona*, Partizani and Flamurtari have negated hopes of glory at club level, but the small Balkan outpost still compete; a dream of future European success remains.

And if any country deserves to dream, Albania does.

Chapter Seventeen

The Final Years: 1985–1991

ON 11 April 1985, Enver Hoxha – the man who'd held Albania in his iron grip for 40 years – died, finally succumbing to a diabetic condition that blighted his health for two decades.

Upon his demise, Albania was the third-poorest nation in the world, the broken by-product of his wasteful and paranoid rule. As forced eulogies were written and recited and a ridiculously protracted period of mourning observed, many citizens were already mutedly anticipating the prospect of a different kind of future devoid of Comrade Enver's omnipresence.

Hoxha's dark charisma had been the glue that affixed his bond with common Albanians. His Machiavellian allure entrenched a distorted loyalty and mock trust in both his ideas and methods. It also implanted in his people a xenophobic, underdog spirit centred on accepted untruths, erroneous national pride and collective societal discipline. But the most potent lubricant in the maintenance of social order was fear. When Hoxha was succeeded by the deeply uncharismatic and weak Ramiz Alia in mid-1985, this essential elixir composed of national allegiance, shared responsibility and innate terror began to err.

In footballing circles, the miasma of subliminal dissent became apparent. The 1985/86 Kampionati Kombetar witnessed a stark increase in cautions and expulsions on the pitch, resulting in three clubs (Dinamo, Flamurtari and 17

Nëntori) receiving three-point deductions, with Apolonia Fier handed a six-point debit at the start of the 1986/87 season – all of the guilty clubs collecting in excess of 20 red and yellow cards. The penalty would hit Flamurtari especially hard, losing out on the league title to Partizani by a three-point margin.

Any optimism derived from *Shqiponjat*'s World Cup 1986 qualifiers was quickly forgotten, the national side in a state of regress during their Euro '88 campaign – six games observing six losses with heavy and undisciplined defeats in Graz, Bucharest and Seville. With the defection of Vllaznia pair Arvid Hoxha and Lulzim Bërshemi – absconding on their return from European club duty in Finland in late 1987 – adding to the wretched malaise, self-pride in Albania was running on empty.

Point deductions administered to Apolonia (-1), Besëlidhja (-3) and Partizani (-2) in 1988/89, again for on-pitch indiscretions, added credence to the notion that collective national discipline was on the wane. The deductions proved fatal to two of the three teams affected during the 1989/90 season, Besëlidhja relegated after finishing bottom of the 12-team division, when the three points docked would've placed them in eighth, two points outside of the relegation zone. Labinoti – champions in 1984 – were the lucky benefactors, surviving the drop by a point.

At the top end of the table, Partizani were the big losers after finishing second, Dinamo taking the title by a single point. *Blutë* compounded *Demat e Kuq* misery by completing the double, beating Flamurtari in the Albanian Cup Final 4-2 on penalties after a 1-1 draw at the Stadiumi Lokomotiva in Durrës.

During the same season, a second-tier promotion face-off between KS Erzeni of Shijak and KS Industriali from the north-western town of Laç descended into pitch violence with Erzeni and Industriali – the top two – docked six and eight points respectively for their equal parts in the carnage. Their misdemeanours would enable KS Kastrioti Krujë to take the sole promotion place available, two points ahead of their rivals.

Opinion attested to a shared train of thought: all of the fighting and insubordination would never have taken place if Comrade Enver were still at the helm. With Albania amid an economic and ideological crisis, it was a point – good or bad – that was impossible to contest.

The political landscape in eastern Europe would undergo unparalleled change in late 1989 with revolution calling time on communism throughout the continent. Yet in Alia's Albania, borders were tightened and media coverage of external news blanketed.

To Albania's north, events were unfurling that could no longer be hidden by the media blackout. In 1990, Yugoslavia was falling apart – communism in its death throes – with calls for independence from its disparate states. Kosovo declared independence in July 1990, an act that drew support from neighbouring Albania. Many Kosovans escaped the violent Serbian backlash their cry for freedom provoked, arriving in Albania via the northern Macedonian border. Their stories of communism's collapse must have made interesting listening for their Albanian cousins. However, in a rapidly shifting world, Albanian Stalinism limped onwards with unabated obstinance.

Qualification for the 1990 World Cup, to be hosted across the Adriatic in Italy, summoned some decent performances – notably in narrow home defeats to Sweden and England – although they were aligned with stats similarly negative to those of the Euro '88 campaign of six games and six defeats, again.

December 1990, the mid-point of the 1990/91 Kampionati Kombetar – a title race won at a canter by Flamurtari – witnessed protestors from the Enver Hoxha University in

Tirana taking to the streets of the capital in a call to end Alia's regime. What began as a strike by 700 students, deriding poor living conditions and power outages, quickly escalated. Their numbers would swell to over 3,000 in a show of public dissension unseen in Albania during the Stalinist era, impassioned cries for democracy resulting in the formation of the Albanian Democratic Party – communist Albania's first opposition party. Albanians were allowed to travel abroad – those who could afford it – with Western embassies swamped by thousands of requests for political asylum. As the regime was forced to soften its approach, criminal laws were amended leading to the release of political prisoners back into society. The government later restored the right to practice religion. Those pesky intellectuals, whom Hoxha had mercilessly culled during his tenure, were back en masse and in the mood for a fight.

Rebellion in Tirana, dovetailed with Pjerin Noga's much-publicised defection in Marseille and anti-communist chanting at a Kampionati match between Besa and Partizani – all in the same month – stoked the coals for an all-encompassing *revolucion*.

In February 1991, protestors returned to the city in their droves, toppling the 30ft gilt statue of Enver Hoxha that occupied a corner of Skanderbeg Square, dragging its shattered remnants through the streets of Tirana to the university grounds amid scenes of wild celebration.

The following month, Albania's first parliamentary election since 1923 neatly coincided with Flamurtari securing their first title win, a victory symbolic of the nation's changing tides. However, with the government still in control of TV and radio programming, the election was won by Alia and The Party; the communists achieving a 56 per cent majority.

The floors of the voting booths had barely been swept and the ballot boxes placed in storage when a national strike – called by the newly empowered unions – sounded the death knell for The Party and five decades of Albanian Stalinism.

Football's lustre had diminished during communism's final years. As living standards dipped, so did attendances at the games. The big three – Partizani, Dinamo and 17 Nëntori – had reasserted themselves, sharing the title between each other in the years immediately after Hoxha's death. Flamurtari broke the triopoly in 1990/91.

With Hoxha, and his uniquely absurd brand of communism, consigned to history's boneyard, the future was wide open for Albania. But after the tears of relief and joy were shed, residual anger that had remained under a lid for half a century was taken to the streets, all vestiges of the previous era broken and burned.

The Albanian people, whipped into silent obedience – submissive children – for so long were finding their voice again. But they were voices devoid of the nuances of reason and restraint, fuelled chiefly by a need to enact revenge for their years of suffering. Even leftovers that may have proven useful in the rebuilding of the nation were trashed: greenhouses, schools, farmland. No thought was given to how these resources would be replaced; anarchy reigned.

In the years that followed, Albania would come to observe the true nature of freedom. All of the gilded, beguiling perks of capitalism (excess unevenly portrayed by tacky Greek and Italian soap operas, illicitly filtered into Albanian homes during the communist years via homemade sardine-tin satellite dishes), akin to Hoxha's promises of a socialist utopia, were merely a new set of lies.

Naive ambition and unsustainable aspiration would provide the fuel that fired the communist after-years, with football entangled in the avaricious milieu. Albania emerged from the black hole of totalitarian rule unprepared for the stark realities of democracy and the responsibilities that came with it.

Peering through the darkness towards the other side of the abyss, Albanians could only envisage greener pastures; the promise of a brighter future. But, as with all evolution, social and sporting, things would get worse before they got better.

Chapter Eighteen

The Other Side of the Abyss

AS COMMUNISM died its death in Europe, the spectre of Stalinist rule still loomed over Albania during 1991. Poverty, corruption and the residual public hatred of authority was endemic; many of the old Stalinists from the Hoxha era retaining hierarchical positions in Ramiz Alia's rebranded Socialist Party. In spite of dark, uncertain times, football trundled on.

With the Socialist Party holding on to an increasingly untenable rule, the lead-up to the 1991/92 league campaign witnessed a mass name change for Albanian clubs with many reverting to their pre-communist monikers, the most notable of the changes being 17 Nëntori who, in August 1991 – to the delight of their *tifozët* – reclaimed the pre-war name of SK Tirana. In an inverse echo to a previous chapter, the Albanian people – on the brink of liberty – seemed to understand the seismic significance of these changes. Liberalism, the green kryptonite to autocracy, had slipped its iron bars and was dispersing itself freely via the shared, unfiltered musings of an emboldened population. Cafe politicians, whom Enver Hoxha had once sneeringly dubbed 'scum', were everywhere.

The final year of communist rule heralded a league title win for Vllaznia, the team from the rebel city – Shkodër, the cradle of Albanian scholarship, culture and religion – an apt conclusion to 1991/92 and the perfect primer to a new era for Albanian football.

As the season unfolded, Astrit Hafizi's compelling team, fired by the considerable goal contribution of Edmir Bilali, were dominant, romping to the championship ahead of a distant Partizani. In the cup final, Dashamir Stringa's KS Elbasani – shedding their communist appellation of Labinoti – defeated Besa 2-1 at the Stadiumi Qemal Stafa.

Vllaznia netted 63 times in their 30 league fixtures, 21 more than the second-highest scorers in the Kampionati. In a cup semi, Besa inflicted a humiliating 3-0 defeat on Partizani to secure their final berth. With Dinamo finishing a distant and inept fifth, the accepted order of communist Albanian football appeared to be under threat from a new roster of worthy challengers.

By October 1991, Albania entered full meltdown, national discontent again spilling on to the streets. Albanian people protested with renewed vehemence against the country's faltering regime and it was a mood of rebellion that quickly transposed itself to the football terraces. For the first time in the history of the Albanian game, crowd violence was manifesting itself inside the stadiums of the country, and not just sporadically, but regularly and throughout the 26 districts.

Petulance on the pitch also bloomed apace, Flamurtari fined 12 points for leaving the field and refusing to return during an away game at Elbasan when a penalty was awarded against them. The deduction was later reduced to six points, ultimately saving the previous season's champions from the ignominy of relegation.

As all hell broke loose in the *stadiumet* of Albania, FSHF and Alia's fragile regime had to be seen to be doing something to address the bedlam. In November – and until the end of the 1991/92 season – all matches, league and cup, were played at neutral venues. Violence subsided (on the terraces, at least), but this was due chiefly to the one-man-and-his-dog paucity of supporters in attendance.

By the season's end, the one-party state was no more, democratic elections observing Sali Berisha's inauguration as Albania's new president. As Albania emerged from years of Stalinist hegemony and tiptoed with unease into a market economy, the transition was evidenced by clubs' first dip into the hitherto unexplored world of corporate sponsorship. The conclusion of the troubled 1991/92 campaign witnessed only one club promoted from the second tier.

Punëtori Patos, from the oil-rich straits of Patos-Marinëz in south-western Albania, were to be that team, Fatmir Dogani's modest outfit finishing one point ahead of Naftëtari Kuçovë at the summit.

Their pedigree at top-flight level was negligible, promotion as champions in 1973/74 resulting in one solitary season in the Kampionati. The 1974/75 campaign wasn't remembered with affection, Punëtori finishing bottom of the table, losing 23 of their 26 games, scoring just seven goals and amassing a meagre five points. Portents for success prior to the forthcoming campaign were not good.

However, during the close season, Punëtori would shed the name given to them upon their founding in 1947 and undergo a rebranding that signposted a new, aspirational future for the club and Albanian football.

They would emerge from the summer break – renamed and generously financed – as Albpetrol Patosi. Albpetrol, an ambitious petroleum company operating from their HQ in Patos, had peered west and observed how corporate sponsorship could enhance the worldly kudos of a business, leading them to invest a notable sum of lek into the club coffers.

The 1992/93 season witnessed Albpetrol comfortably stave off relegation, finishing a competitive ninth, but it was in the cup that they really shone. Apropos of no previous comparable success, Dogani's Patos stormed to the Albanian Cup Final after recovering from a 3-1 first-leg semi-final defeat to Elbasani to win the second leg 4-1, going through 5-4 on aggregate.

Ultimately, the final at the rechristened Stadiumi Niko Dovana – previously the Stadiumi Lokomotiva – in Durrës proved a game too far for Albpetrol, losing narrowly in May 1993 to a Partizani side who'd reasserted some semblance of Stalinist-era dominance by lifting the league title a fortnight earlier. Their 1-0 defeat, courtesy of Afrim Myftari's first-half penalty, was disappointing, but it came with an exciting edict. Partizani's league win meant that Albpetrol, in their debut season back in Albania's top tier, would be competing in European club football the following season for the first time.

Albpetrol's tangible European reward, off the back of a half-decent chunk of financial corporate outlay, not only alerted the attention of investors who saw football as a decent marketing tool for their business, but also owners who used clubs as a plaything to boost their egos and enhance their public status.

One such club owner was Pëllumb Xhaferri. Xhaferri bankrolled KF Lushnja – a small-town club originating from the parched central-west flatlands of the country – to an improbable promotion to top-flight football at the end of the 1995/96 season.

Xhaferri, who amassed his fortune as the enabler of the pyramid scheme, Demokracia Popullore – Popular Democracy – loved money and the influence it garnered. His scheme promised those who invested in it astronomical returns, convincing thousands of Albanians, eager to get rich quick, to sell their homes, land and family heirlooms and plough their life savings into his 'foundation'.

Post-promotion, Xhaferri fired coach Adnan Haxhiu, implanting former Albanian international and Partizani manager Hasan Lika in the hotseat. After a less-than-auspicious start to the 1996/97 campaign, Xhaferri wielded the axe again but this time looked beyond the country's

Ionian and Adriatic borders in his quest to find a suitable replacement.

In December 1996, to the disbelief of Albanian fans and the wider, football community, Xhaferri successfully coordinated a coup that brought one of the biggest names in the history of the beautiful game to the arid midlands of rural Albania.

In 1996, Argentinian forward Mario Kempes was at the very start of a managerial journey that would include spells in Malaysia, Venezuela, Bolivia and Spain. But it was as a player that Kempes had achieved legendary status, winning multiple trophies with Spanish club Valencia and the 1978 World Cup with Argentina in a tournament where *El Matador*'s rangy, aggressive and relentless forward play spearheaded *La Albiceleste* to success and saw him win both the Golden Ball and Golden Boot.

When Xhaferri sanctioned an Italian contact to draw up a shortlist for the vacant Lushnja job, Kempes's name was among the five nominated. Xhaferri knew of the Argentine's ability as a player and welcomed the global attention the appointment would bestow upon his small club.

The promise of a huge salary – $350,000 a year plus bonuses – lured Mario and his brother Hugo, a qualified athletics trainer, to the agric nowhere-town of Lushnja. On their arrival in Albania, Kempes and sibling were driven from Tirana to Lushnja, via puddled, potholed roadways populated by tribesmen, shepherds and gun-wielding bandits, in Xhaferri's top-of-the-range Mercedes-Benz. On 21 December 1996, Kempes was unveiled as Lushnja's new coach, becoming the first foreigner to manage an Albanian club. It was a reign that would last little over a month.

Kempes promised Lushnja's small body of fans attractive, winning football and, after a flurry of transfer activity observed the arrival of Brazilian, Nigerian and Italian talent at the club, he appeared to be keeping his word, a 1-0 win at

Stadiumi Roza Haxhiu against perennial rivals Teuta Durrës securing the club's place in the Albanian Cup semi-finals for the first time in 19 years. This was followed by a landmark 5-0 league win over Dinamo Tirana (using their brief, post-communism pseudonym, Olimpik Tiranë), a victory that earmarked *Delegatët*, briefly, as title contenders and prompted Xhaferri and Kempes to approach Italian giants Fiorentina in an insane attempt to entice fellow Argentinian goal machine Gabriel Batistuta to the club.

However, the roller coaster ride shuddered to an abrupt halt in late January of 1997, when Albania was thrust into economic crisis with 25 firms – Xhaferri's included – declared bankrupt with a loss of depositors' money totalling $1.2bn. Xhaferri's subsequent arrest brought panic and violence to the streets of Lushnja, many of its townspeople wholly invested in his scheme.

Stadiumi Roza Haxhiu became the centre of the revolt with Kempes targeted by angry protestors who implored him to 'give the money back'. Two days after the pyramids collapsed, club officials smuggled Kempes and his brother out of Lushnja to Tirana's Rinas Airport where they were railroaded out of the country on a flight to Rome. Despite the abject state of affairs in Albania, Kempes naively plotted his return, attempting to engage ex-team-mates Daniel Passarella and Diego Maradona in his Lushnja project. It was a plan that would never reach fruition, rebellion in the country quickly escalating into full-scale civil war.

The 1996/97 season was immediately suspended 17 games in, and later completed in August with three groups of six clubs entering play-offs. The top six at the time of the suspension in January entered a round robin to play for the title. However, even the August play-offs descended into chaos when, on the final day of the season, the decider between title-challenging SK Tirana and Flamurtari was abandoned after 80 minutes with *Tirona* leading 1-0. Flamurtari players were ordered off the pitch by their chairman in protest when the referee refused to award them a penalty after Leonard Perloshi was fouled in the box. A draw would have given Flamurtari the title; instead *Tirona* were awarded the game 2-0, handing them the championship. Flamurtari were also fined $1,000 for abandoning the match.

Lushnja never achieved their dream of cup success. Shorn of the financial munificence of Xhaferri and the roster of international stars his money subsidised, *Delegatët* lost 2-1 to Partizani in the semi-final. The following year they would reach the final, where – as favourites – they faced a modest Apolonia Fier at Stadiumi Qemal Stafa. Again, it wasn't to be, a chastening 1-0 defeat serving as a fittingly disappointing end to a crazy, fractious 18 months. Lushnja's 15 minutes of fame was over. At the time of writing they reside in the lower reaches of the Albanian second division.

The late 1990s and early 2000s observed rapid growth in illegal gang activity in Albania. In many cases it was the criminals who were running the show, with prominent Albanian political figures cited for their connections to mafia gangs. Criminality's murky silhouette loomed over all areas of society with football unable to avoid its shadow.

As the 1999/2000 season entered its final fortnight, and with Albanian football still reeling from allegations that *Shqiponjat* coach Medin Zhega had charged players $3,500 to be included in the national team squad, Tomori Berat, a club not readily attuned to domestic success, stood near the summit of Albania's top division. An unbeaten run spanning back to December had taken coach Theodhari Arbi's team from the fringes of relegation to the very brink of title glory.

The driving force behind Tomori's rise was young club president Ardian Çobo, the 26-year-old heavily involved in directing the upward trajectory of his beloved *Mistrecët* – though not necessarily in a good way.

Çobo (a multi-property landlord and owner of Berat's most salubrious bar, Shtepia e Bardhe – the White House – a venue attended by the city's culturally elite and criminally affiliated) was a man routinely implicated in connection to unlawful activity. But in new Albania, as with the rest of the world, influential friends and new money exempted the criminally disposed from the legal penalties of wrongdoing, and it was an immunity that Çobo used in his favour.

Çobo became a regular in the match officials' changing room before, during and after matches, a *modus operandi* evidenced by an article in *Gazeta Shqiptare* – an Albanian broadsheet – documenting the observations of former FSHF referee and delegate Besnik Kaimi.

Kaimi recalled a match at the Stadiumi Tomori during the 1999/2000 season – a home 0-0 draw with Teuta. Çobo, Kaimi alleged, persistently asked to meet with the match officials after the game, demands that Kaimi – in his role as league delegate – refused as they were out of step with league regulations. The Berat chief of police also gave instruction forbidding Çobo access to the referee's room, but the decision changed when three of the officials' associates arrived 'clearly equipped with weapons'.

During an impassioned post-match conversation with the referee and his team, Çobo expressed disappointment at the result and the officials' performance, informing them that he would find out where they lived. Shortly afterwards, the chief of police called for reinforcements and the officials were escorted to safety.

Çobo's attempts to influence officials via fear and intimidation would eventually come home to roost. On the penultimate day of the season, Tomori – second and two points behind *Tirona* in the league – visited Stadiumi Dinamo to face Partizani in a game that could make or break their season. After 90 minutes, Tomori had dug out a priceless 1-0 win courtesy of a goal by the league's top scorer, Klodian Arbëri. The game was notable for two reasons. Firstly, defeat for Partizani ended their 53-year status as a top-tier club, *Demat e Kuq* relegated to the second division for the only time in their history to date. Secondly, *Tirona*'s 1-1 draw against Shqiponja – named Luftëtari, during the communist regime, a moniker they would return to in 2002 – meant that they and Tomori would enter the final day of the season level on points.

After-match witness accounts depict a jubilant Ardian Çobo. Seated in the *Tribuna*, Çobo was a portrait of nervous agitation throughout the 90 minutes, celebrating the final whistle with wild delight, joy doubled by news of *Tirona*'s misfire in the south.

Post-victory, at approximately 5.30pm, Çobo – accompanied by the three match officials, Luan Zylfo, Shpëtim Lamçe and Albano Janku, their FSHF-designated chauffeur, Agim Veshi, and sports journalist Dritan Shakohoxha – arrived at Shelgu, a bar outside the stadium. A club president, match officials and the national press adjoined in mutual celebration? It appeared to be a recklessly dubious group.

Quite why Çobo was revelling with members of the Albanian FA is subject to enquiry. What's certain is that shortly after sitting down for drinks, gunman Alfred Çela – a Partizani fan – entered the bar armed with a Kalashnikov rifle, spraying their party with a hail of bullets. Both Çobo and match referee Zylfo were killed in the shooting. The motives for their murders were never accurately ascertained, although revenge is commonly cited.

Despite the lack of any meaningful closure – or disclosure – regarding the reasons behind the shootings, it revealed an innate illness apparent within new Albania at both a societal and sporting level; a nation where its subjects were willing to gravitate outside of accepted social mores to get their own way. It would be a theme revisited many times over the coming years.

With external forces compromising the game's integrity, an ineffectual and contradictory FA struggled to steer domestic football through sour times. During the 2001/02 season, the annulling and awarding of results reached its nadir, key Kampionati games tarred by FSHF meddling. A 1-1 draw between Tomori and Teuta in October was later awarded by the League Committee as a 2-0 win to Teuta. A month later, Partizani and Vllaznia's 1-1 draw was annulled due to a 'technical error' by the referee; both goals had been scored outside of regulation time in the 91st and 92nd minutes. An added veneer of futility was applied to proceedings when, 11 days later, the game was replayed and ended in another draw.

At the season's end, KS Kastrioti of Krujë occupied top spot in the second division, eight points clear of second-placed Naftëtari, and prepared for life in the Kampionati the following season.

Shockingly, FSHF ordered that an additional play-off round robin be played between the top six clubs due to the high number of 'awarded matches' in the regular season. Kastrioti, incensed by the decision, lodged a complaint to the Albanian Sports Arbitration Committee which was immediately upheld. However, FSHF, in a belated attempt to reassert bureaucratic control, overruled and continued with the play-offs regardless. Kastrioti were beaten 3-1 on penalties after extra time by Besa, *Verdhezinjtë* – third in the final table and well off the pace – unjustly promoted in their place.

In contrast to the chaos, the 2004/05 season was the birthing ground to one of the wonderfully improbable stories of the post-communist era. The Kampionati Kombetar underwent a rebrand in 2003/04, renamed Kategoria Superiore – Superior Category.

At the end of the season, the newly named top tier welcomed KF Laçi – previously KS Industriali – to its fold.

Crowned champions of the newly formatted Division A2, a post-communism creation, and coached by the pragmatic Ritvan Kulli, the team hailed from the north-western town of Laç. During the Hoxha years, Laç was home to the Chinese-built asbestos factory that belched vile pollutants into the air and waterways of the local environs. Its toxic legacy remains; to this day it's still considered bad form to dip your toe into the nearby Mati River estuary.

Aesthetically, Laç is to Albania what Barrow is to Las Vegas, although the perennially optimistic Kulli hoped to harness the ugliness of their location to unsettle the visiting footballing big boys. His plan to unnerve the opposition failed to bear fruit. Due to another odd FSHF directive, Laçi only played five games at Stadiumi Laçi, their remaining home fixtures split between venues in Shkodër, Kavaja, Kamëz, Lezhë and Shijak.

Within two games of their top-flight return, it was evident that Laçi were out of their depth. Consequently, Kulli was also out of a job, a 2-0 away loss in Elbasan and a 3-1 home defeat to Shkumbini Peqin culminating in his dismissal. Comparatively though, the opening two defeats weren't that bad.

The role of coach would change another three times during Laçi's ill-fated season, Hysen Dedja, Luan Metani and Sinan Bardhi all trying – and failing – to stop the rot. In hindsight, Dedja could consider himself unfortunate – his three-game tenure observed narrow 1-0 losses at champions-elect *Tirona* and at home to Teuta plus an encouraging 1-1 draw in Lushnja. But that was about as good as it got. Particular low points of the season included 7-0 and 8-0 away defeats at Vllaznia coupled with a 7-1 home thrashing by the same opponents. Dinamo, Teuta and *Tirona* also knocked them for six.

During 2004/05, Laçi lost 34 of their 36 games while achieving two draws, the second of them an incongruous 5-5 away result against Partizani in Kamëz on the final day of the season. They scored just 13 times, conceding 124 goals and losing 31 consecutive matches in a truly wretched season – the worst in Albanian top-flight history.

In a pertinent aside, on that last day of the season all of the Partizani goals were scored by Dorian Bylykbashi, whose haul elevated him above Teuta's Daniel Xhafa as league top scorer. The questionable nature of the 5-5 draw felt wrong; fingers pointed, but no further punishment meted. It was the only time Bylykbashi would top-score in the Albanian league, his 24 strikes occurring in a season where his club finished one place outside the relegation zone. He would move to the consonant-friendly Ukrainian outfit Kryvbas Kryvyi Rih the following year.

Incongruous results became a feature of the Kategoria Superiore. In 2012, a 30-month study harvested by sports data analysts Sportsradar AG dating back to 2009 was submitted to Albanian football chiefs. The Swiss-based company's integrity services scrutinised a vast number of top-tier games in Albania, reaching a definite and unpalatable conclusion; matches were being deliberately manipulated for financial gain.

Sportsradar revealed that 97 games in a two-and-a-half-year period were classified 'suspicious', placing Albania at the summit of a continental blacklist of countries with the most suspected rigged matches, ahead of Italy (70), Moldova (66), Estonia (46), Greece (45), Russia (42), Macedonia (37) and Bulgaria (35). Despite UEFA posting reports to FSHF detailing games they believed had been fixed, Albanian football's overseers were reluctant to take action, an unwillingness that prompted questions about the motives of the country's football hierarchy. It was only when UEFA's Ethics and Disciplinary Inspectorate came sniffing around that Albania's indolent FA finally cranked into action.

UEFA inspectors filed a 93-page report alleging stark, explicit shenanigans in Albanian football. Kategoria Superiore team Skënderbeu Korçë were implicated in a match-fixing scandal that dated back to 2010 with at least 50 of their fixtures flagged as suspicious. According to the report, Skënderbeu players suddenly stopped playing during key matches, deliberately conceding goals that, subsequently, resulted in big financial wins for high-stakes live gamblers connected to the country's criminal gangs.

A second qualifying round tie in the 2015/16 Champions League against Northern Irish champions Crusaders at Seaview, Belfast, drew particular scrutiny. Leading 2-1 on the night and 6-2 on aggregate with minutes remaining, the Albanian side simply shut down, allowing Crusaders to win the game with two goals in injury time. Minutes prior to this, Crusaders had seen two goals disallowed and had hit the Skënderbeu woodwork twice. From a position of total control, the Albanians had somehow contrived to lose 3-2 on the night. Crusaders keeper Sean O'Neill immediately appealed to social media for an inquiry. He wrote on Twitter, 'If there's not a UEFA investigation into our game tonight there is something wrong. [The] last ten minutes I have never seen football like it.' It was a call for intervention that was being heard in UEFA's gilded offices.

In the wake of the report, UEFA revealed that the inspectors had received anonymous death threats. UEFA finally wielded its axe in March 2018, handing the Korca club a ten-year European ban and a fine of €1m; the heaviest punishment ever administered to a European club.

While it was the worst of times for the national game, it was also the best of times for the national team. Embarking on the qualifying campaign for the 2016 Euros, coach Gianni De Biasi, a man of dual Italian-Albanian citizenship, had compiled a squad based around the dual attributes of Italian technique and Albanian grit. The 2014 World Cup qualifiers offered glimpses of promise featuring a pair of excellent 1-0 victories at the Qemal Stafa against Slovenia and an unexpected triumph against Norway in the Ullevaal, but the events that unfolded between September 2014 and October 2015 were unprecedented and, to date, unrepeated.

The campaign began with the toughest of openers – an away fixture in Aveiro against Portugal. De Biasi opted, unsurprisingly, for containment against a Portuguese side, shorn of an injured Cristiano Ronaldo, that struggled to break down Albania's rugged 4-5-1 setup. As the game ebbed past its halfway point, the visitors restricted their hosts to little in the way of clear-cut chances. With 52 minutes played, Albania plotted a rare but well-constructed foray into Portuguese territory, right-sided midfielder Odise Roshi skipping beyond Fábio Coentrão before whipping a delicious cross into the box. The ball was met, near the penalty spot, by the solitary Albanian in Portugal's area, Belik Balaj, the Sparta Praha forward adjusting his stance before thundering a right-footed volley into the bottom-left corner of Rui Patrício's net; 1-0. Remarkably, *Shqiponjat* held out for the most improbable of wins; a perfect start to their campaign.

The result was consolidated by a creditable 1-1 draw against Denmark at Elbasan Arena in October followed by a trip to Serbia. The game, played in a spiteful, hostile atmosphere at the Stadion Partizan in Belgrade, was abandoned after anti-Albanian terrace chants, crowd violence and the insurgence of a drone carrying an Albanian nationalist banner depicting Greater Albania, culminating in a pitch invasion where match stewards attacked Albanian players.

Initially, UEFA awarded Serbia a 3-0 win after Albania had refused to resume the match. This was later reversed, with Albania awarded the 3-0 win due to 'security lapses' and 'acts of violence exacted on Albanian players' by stewards. Serbia were docked three points and ordered to play their next two games behind closed doors.

Further consolidation of their excellent start was achieved at home to Armenia in March 2015. Armenia took a fourth-minute lead, Köln centre-half Mërgim Mavraj spooning a dangerous cross beyond Etrit Berisha into his own net. Two late bullet headers from Mavraj, atoning for his earlier own goal, and Swiss-born Basel forward Shkëlzen Gashi dug *Shqiponjat* out of a hole and completed a vital 2-1 win.

A gritty 0-0 stalemate against their rivals for second place in Group I, Morten Olsen's Denmark, at the Parken Stadion in Copenhagen, left De Biasi's team on the very tip of qualification for Euro 2016 in France. However, a sobering 1-0 home defeat to Portugal at the Elbasan Arena, secured by a 92nd-minute set-piece header from Miguel Veloso, coupled with another loss, 2-0 to Serbia in the same stadium – again dealt via late goals in the 91st and 94th minutes – delayed national celebrations.

With one game to play, Albania needed a win – by any margin – against a tricky Armenian side in Yerevan to secure second place ahead of the Danes who, having completed their games, lay one point ahead of *Shqiponjat* with a superior goal difference.

In an underpopulated Vazgen Sargsyan Republican Stadium, Albania, loath to allow the opportunity of qualification to slip from their grasp for a third time, were magnificent. An early Kamo Hovhannisyan own goal settled the nerves, and centre-half Berat Djimsiti's fine reflex volley put them in total control on 23 minutes. FC Zürich forward Armando Sadiku's late strike merely added gloss to a 3-0 victory that was greeted with tears of joy throughout the 26 districts back home.

In France, Albania proved stubborn, troublesome opponents, losing narrowly to Switzerland – Vladimir Petković's tough, streetwise *Suisse* containing five (count them) starters born of Albanian heritage; namely Valon Behrami, Granit Xhaka, Xherdan Shaqiri, Blerim Džemaili and Admir Mehmedi – 1-0 in Lens and 2-0 to their French hosts in Marseille, both *Les Bleus'* goals coming beyond the 90 minute-mark. A deserved 1-0 victory in their final match against Romania in Lyon, courtesy of Armando Sadiku's smart headed winner, took *Shqiponjat* to within goal difference of qualification for the second round.

Qualification for the finals in France was, to date, the pinnacle for the team, although the personnel for the tournament reflected the changing face of Albanian football since the demise of Stalinism a decade and a half earlier. The squad featured a roster of players who plied their footballing craft in a disparate plethora of countries; Italy, Greece, France, Azerbaijan, Liechtenstein, the US, Switzerland, Germany, Turkey and Croatia all included. Yet only two players from Albanian clubs made the history-making trip to France: Orges Shehi of Skënderbeu and Partizani's Alban Hoxha.

As the Albanian diaspora spreads across the continents, with natives making a home outside of their host country, they take with them a new generation of ethnic Albanians who find themselves playing for national teams in distant corners of the globe; Switzerland, Denmark, Belgium and the US among them. Former Arsenal midfielder Granit Xhaka candidly concedes that he feels 'completely Albanian' yet chooses to wear the colours of Switzerland. Xherdan Shaqiri, another of a host of players eligible to wear the Albanian shirt, refused to sing the Swiss national anthem prior to a game against Albania. Talented winger Adnan Januzaj – formerly of Manchester United – repeatedly refused call-ups for Belgium, declaring several times that he would prefer to play for Albania before finally yielding to *Les Diables Rouges'* beckoning call in April 2014.

Footballing times have changed in the Hermit Kingdom. In a land where fans once revelled in the sublime abilities of home-reared, home-based talents such as Pano, Boriçi, Jashari, Ali Mema, and the hundreds of others who've been touched on within this book, a return to the sporting quality and honesty of the old days seems unlikely in the domestic game; matches consistently hawked to the profit of crime gangs and Albania's greatest talents shipped to the loftier, monied clubs of continental Europe and beyond.

And within the *stadiumet* too; where packed crowds and public order once reigned, there is a scarcity of fans, many deterred by a diminished product, the regular encumbrance of ultras' violence and extensive access to superior, pay-to-view continental football.

Many yearn for things that existed back then, rose-tintedness conjured by the displeasures and dishonesties of modern Albanian life. But people rarely compare in time, they usually compare in space, and the space that surrounds new Albania is full of countries that Albanians are aware have more money; a resonant paean to an adage that could've been scribed by Hoxha himself: ignorance is bliss.

Many rue the lack of jobs, forgetting that they paid a pittance and were back-breakingly mundane. They muse about the free healthcare, but the hospitals were hovels where people went to die. They speak of the subsidised housing, but the only liveable houses were in Blloku.

The only thing people who lived through Albanian Stalinism still celebrate, or seem to agree on, is the football. Ask a *Tirona* fan who the club greats are and they will list Lushta, Kryeziu, Halili, Frasheri, Ben Minga and the Memas. A Partizani fan would cite Pano, Jashari, Resmja and Boriçi among their number. Dinamo *tifozët* would allude to the troika of Pernaska, Zeri and Ballgjini.

Albania still produces great players and its national team is consistently competitive, regularly punching above its perceived weight. But the new, great Albanian players ply their trade elsewhere and are rewarded with huge remuneration and lavish lifestyles, connected to their native people only by ethnicity, not locality or reality.

In the void of time that's elapsed in the decades since Albanian Stalinism's demise – beyond the abyss – memories of a better type of football remain; a football that unified fans and provided a balm during 50 years of horrific suffering. And within the remembrances and the personal memoirs exist football stories from inside the Hermit Kingdom waiting to be retold.

A Footnote

On 17 October 2023, Albanian – courtesy of a 1-1 in Moldova– qualified for the 2024 edition of the European Championships.

The result spurred frenzied excitement amongst the Albanian community; many whom – during the writing of the book - have become friends.

Irvin was overjoyed, inviting me to join him on a trip to Germany in support of the Albanian national team.

It is a generosity and a trait of sharing that is innate in Albanians, and something I have grown to understand and know during this project.

We await tickets eagerly and I will, at some point, travel with him on the hajj to Germany.

For me, it's an apt conclusion to the story; history evolving to reveal another set of stories waiting to be told. As one chapter ends, another begins, and I hope – with deep sincerity – that this proves a bright and fruitful one for the people of Albania.

Bibliography

Books

Eskelund Rota, Davide, *Football in Europe 1986–87 Vol.1* (Amazon, 2021)

Fevziu, Blendi, *Enver Hoxha – The Iron Fist of Albania* (I.B. Tauris, 2016)

Graham, Alex, *Albania – Football League Tables and Results 1930–2013* (Soccer Books Ltd, 2013)

Hamilton, Bill, *Albania – Who Cares?* (Autumn House, 1992)

Hammond, Mike (ed), *The European Football Yearbook* (Sports Projects Ltd)

Kasmi, Andi (article) – *Goodbye My Love – Gerd Müller's Impossible Albanian Sweetheart* (Beyond the Last Man, 2017)

Maranaku, Erla (essay), *A Social History of Socialist Albania, 1975–1991*

Orwell, George, *1984* (Penguin Modern Classics, 2000 reprint)

Pettifer, James, *Albania – Blue Guide* (Black Norton, 1996)

Pipa, Arshi, *Albanian Stalinism* (East European Monographs, 1990)

Rejmer, Margo, *Mud Sweeter Than Honey – Voices of Communist Albania* (Maclehose/Quercus, 2021)

Websites

academicworks.cuny.edu
BBC Sport
fcdinamo.al
fktirana.al
football-legal.com
FSHF.org
giovanniarmillotta.it
globalhistorydialogues
Ling app
macedonia.kroraina.com
panorama.com.al
Partizani.net
The Guardian
the-shamrock.net
The Telegraph
UEFA
vllaznia.al
Wikipedia
worldsoccer.com
YouTube